Texas Rules of Civil Procedure
2018 Edition

Updated through January 1, 2018

Michigan Legal Publishing Ltd.
QUICK DESK REFERENCE SERIES™

Academic and bulk discounts available at
www.michlp.com

WE WELCOME YOUR FEEDBACK: info@michlp.com

ISBN-13: 978-1-64002-028-3
ISBN-10: 1-64002-028-4

TEXAS RULES OF CIVIL PROCEDURE

TABLE OF CONTENTS

SECTION 4. PLEADING 20

SECTION 4. PLEADING 27

SECTION 4. PLEADING 28

TEXAS RULES OF CIVIL PROCEDURE

PART I - GENERAL RULES

RULE 1. OBJECTIVE OF RULES

The proper objective of rules of civil procedure is to obtain a just, fair, equitable and impartial adjudication of the rights of litigants under established principles of substantive law. To the end that this objective may be attained with as great expedition and dispatch and at the least expense both to the litigants and to the state as may be practicable, these rules shall be given a liberal construction.

RULE 2. SCOPE OF RULES

These rules shall govern the procedure in the justice, county, and district courts of the State of Texas in all actions of a civil nature, with such exceptions as may be hereinafter stated. Where any statute in effect immediately prior to September 1, 1941, prescribed a rule of procedure in lunacy, guardianship, or estates of decedents, or any other probate proceedings in the county court differing from these Rules, and not included in the "List of Repealed Statutes," such statute shall apply; and where any statute in effect immediately prior to September 1, 1941, and not included in the "List of Repealed Statutes," prescribed a rule of procedure in any special statutory proceeding differing from these rules, such statute shall apply. All statutes in effect immediately prior to September 1, 1941, prescribing rules of procedure in bond or recognizance forfeitures in criminal cases are hereby continued in effect as rules of procedure governing such cases, but where such statutes prescribed no rules of procedure in such cases, these rules shall apply. All statutes in effect immediately prior to September 1, 1941, prescribing rules of procedure in tax suits are hereby continued in effect as rules of procedure governing such cases, but where such statutes prescribed no rules of procedure in such cases, these rules shall apply; provided, however, that Rule 117a shall control with respect to citation in tax suits.

RULE 3. CONSTRUCTION OF RULES

Unless otherwise expressly provided, the past, present or future tense shall each include the other; the masculine, feminine, or neuter gender shall each include the other; and the singular and plural number shall each include the other.

RULE 3a. LOCAL RULES

Each administrative judicial region, district court, county court, county court at law, and probate court, may make and amend local rules governing practice before such courts, provided:

(1) that any proposed rule or amendment shall not be inconsistent with these rules or with any rule of the administrative judicial region in which the court is located;

(2) no time period provided by these rules may be altered by local rules;

(3) any proposed local rule or amendment shall not become effective until it is submitted and approved by the Supreme Court of Texas;

(4) any proposed local rule or amendment shall not become effective until at least thirty days after its publication in a manner reasonably calculated to bring it to the attention of attorneys practicing before the court or courts for which it is made;

(5) all local rules or amendments adopted and approved in accordance herewith are made available upon request to members of the bar;

(6) no local rule, order, or practice of any court, other than local rules and amendments which fully comply with all requirements of this Rule 3a, shall ever be applied to determine the merits of any matter.

Notes and Comments

Comment to 1990 change: To make Texas Rules of Civil Procedure timetables mandatory and to preclude use of unpublished local rules or other "standing" orders to local practices to determine issues of substantive merit.

RULE 4. COMPUTATION OF TIME

In computing any period of time prescribed or allowed by these rules, by order of court, or by any applicable statute, the day of the act, event, or default after which the designated period of time begins to run is not to be included. The last day of the period so computed is to be included, unless it is a Saturday, Sunday, or legal holiday, in which event the period runs until the end of the next day which is not a Saturday, Sunday, or legal holiday. Saturdays, Sundays, and legal holidays shall not be counted for any purpose in any time period of five days or less in these rules, except that Saturdays, Sundays, and legal holidays shall be counted for purpose of the three-day periods in Rules 21 and 21a, extending other periods by three days when service is made by mail.

Notes and Comments

Comment to 1990 change: Amended to omit counting Saturdays, Sundays and legal holidays in all periods of less than five days with certain exceptions.

RULE 5. ENLARGEMENT OF TIME

When by these rules or by a notice given thereunder or by order of court an act is required or allowed to be done at or within a specified time, the court for cause shown may, at any time in its discretion (a) with or without motion or notice, order the period enlarged if application therefor is made before the expiration of the period originally prescribed or as extended by a previous order; or (b) upon motion permit the act to be done after the expiration of the specified period where good cause is shown for the failure to act. The court may not enlarge the period for taking any action under the rules relating to new trials except as stated in these rules.

If any document is sent to the proper clerk by first-class United States mail in an envelope or wrapper properly addressed and stamped and is deposited in the mail on or before the last day for filing same, the same, if received by the clerk not more than ten days tardily, shall be filed by the clerk and be deemed filed in time. A legible postmark affixed by the United States Postal Service shall be prima facie evidence of the date of mailing.

Notes and Comments

Comment to 1990 change: To make the last date for mailing under Rule 5 coincide with the last date for filing.

RULE 6. SUITS COMMENCED ON SUNDAY

No civil suit shall be commenced nor process issued or served on Sunday, except in cases of injunction, attachment, garnishment, sequestration, or distress proceedings; provided that citation by publication published on Sunday shall be valid.

RULE 7. MAY APPEAR BY ATTORNEY

Any party to a suit may appear and prosecute or defend his rights therein, either in person or by an attorney of the court.

RULE 8. ATTORNEY IN CHARGE

On the occasion of a party's first appearance through counsel, the attorney whose signature first appears on the initial pleadings for any party shall be the attorney in charge, unless another attorney is specifically designated therein. Thereafter, until such designation is changed by written notice to the court and all other parties in accordance with Rule 21a, said attorney in charge shall be responsible for the suit as to such party.

All communications from the court or other counsel with respect to a suit shall be sent to the attorney in charge.

[RULE 8a. Suspended effective December 30, 2003]

RULE 9. NUMBER OF COUNSEL HEARD

Not more than two counsel on each side shall be heard on any question or on the trial, except in important cases, and upon special leave of the court.

RULE 10. WITHDRAWAL OF ATTORNEY

An attorney may withdraw from representing a party only upon written motion for good cause shown. If another attorney is to be substituted as attorney for the party, the motion shall state: the name, address, telephone number, telecopier number, if any, and State Bar of Texas identification number of the substitute attorney; that the party approves the substitution; and that the withdrawal is not sought for delay only. If another attorney is not to be substituted as attorney for the party, the motion shall state: that a copy of the motion has been delivered to the party; that the party has been notified in writing of his right to object to the motion; whether the party consents to the motion; the party's last known address and all pending settings and deadlines. If the motion is granted, the withdrawing attorney shall immediately notify the party in writing of any additional settings or deadlines of which the attorney has knowledge at the time of the withdrawal and has not already notified the party. The Court may impose further conditions upon granting leave to withdraw. Notice or delivery to a party shall be either made to the party in person or mailed to the party's last known address by both certified and regular first class mail. If the attorney in charge withdraws and another attorney remains or becomes substituted, another attorney in charge must be designated of record with notice to all other parties in accordance with Rule 21a.

Notes and Comments

Comment to 1990 change: The amendment repeals the present rule and clarifies the requirements for withdrawal.

RULE 11. AGREEMENTS TO BE IN WRITING

Unless otherwise provided in these rules, no agreement between attorneys or parties touching any suit pending will be enforced unless it be in writing, signed and filed with the papers as part of the record, or unless it be made in open court and entered of record.

Notes and Comments

Comment to 1988 change: The amendment makes it clear that Rule 11 is subject to modification by any other Rule of Civil Procedure.

RULE 12. ATTORNEY TO SHOW AUTHORITY

A party in a suit or proceeding pending in a court of this state may, by sworn written motion stating that he believes the suit or proceeding is being prosecuted or defended without authority, cause the attorney to be cited to appear before the court and show his authority to act. The notice of the motion shall be served upon the challenged attorney at least ten days before the hearing on the motion. At the hearing on the motion, the burden of proof shall be upon the challenged attorney to show sufficient authority to prosecute or defend the suit on behalf of the other party. Upon his failure to show such authority, the court shall refuse to permit the attorney to appear in the cause, and shall strike the pleadings if no person who is authorized to prosecute or defend appears. The motion may be heard and determined at any time before the parties have announced ready for trial, but the trial shall not be unnecessarily continued or delayed for the hearing.

RULE 13. EFFECT OF SIGNING PLEADINGS, MOTIONS AND OTHER PAPERS; SANCTIONS

The signatures of attorneys or parties constitute a certificate by them that they have read the pleading, motion, or other paper; that to the best of their knowledge, information, and belief formed after reasonable inquiry the instrument is not groundless and brought in bad faith or groundless and brought for the purpose of harassment. Attorneys or parties who shall bring a fictitious suit as an experiment to get an opinion of the court, or who shall file any fictitious pleading in a cause for such a purpose, or shall make statements in pleading which they know to be groundless and false, for the purpose of securing a delay of the trial of the cause, shall be held guilty of a contempt. If a pleading, motion or other paper is signed in violation of this rule, the court, upon motion or upon its own initiative, after notice and hearing, shall impose an appropriate sanction available under Rule 215-2b, upon the person who signed it, a represented party, or both.

Courts shall presume that pleadings, motions, and other papers are filed in good faith. No sanctions under this rule may be imposed except for good cause, the particulars of which must be stated in the sanction order. "Groundless" for purposes of this rule means no basis in law or fact and not warranted by good faith argument for the extension, modification, or reversal of existing law. A general denial does not constitute a violation of this rule. The amount requested for damages does not constitute a violation of this rule.

Notes and Comments

Comment to 1990 change: To require notice and hearing before a court determines to impose sanctions, to specify that any sanction imposed be appropriate, and to eliminate the 90-day "grace" period provided in the former version of the rule.

RULE 14. AFFIDAVIT BY AGENT

Whenever it may be necessary or proper for any party to a civil suit or proceeding to make an affidavit, it may be made by either the party or his agent or his attorney.

[RULE 14a. Repealed effective September 1, 1986]

RULE 14b. RETURN OR OTHER DISPOSITION OF EXHIBITS

The clerk of the court in which the exhibits are filed shall retain and dispose of the same as directed by the Supreme Court.

Supreme Court Order Relating to Retention and Disposition of Exhibits

In compliance with the provisions of Rule 14b, the Supreme Court hereby directs that exhibits offered or admitted into evidence shall be retained and disposed of by the clerk of the court in which the exhibits are filed upon the following basis.

This order shall apply only to: (1) those cases in which judgment has been rendered on service of process by publication and in which no motion for new trial was filed within two years after judgment was signed; and, (2) all other cases in which judgment has been signed for one year and in which no appeal was perfected or in which a perfected appeal was dismissed or concluded by a final judgement as to all parties and the issuance of the appellate court's mandate such that the case is no longer pending on appeal or in the trial court.

The party who offered an exhibit may withdraw it from the clerk's office within thirty days of the later of (1) a case becoming subject to this order, or (2) the effective date of this order. The clerk, unless otherwise directed by the court, may dispose of any exhibits remaining after such time period.

RULE 14c. DEPOSIT IN LIEU OF SURETY BOND

Wherever these rules provide for the filing of a surety bond, the party may in lieu of filing the bond deposit cash or other negotiable obligation of the government of the United States of America or any agency thereof, or with leave of court, deposit a negotiable obligation of any bank or savings and loan association chartered by the government of the United States of America or any state thereof that is insured by the government of the United States of America or any agency thereof, in the amount fixed for the surety bond, conditioned in the same manner as would be a surety bond for the protection of other parties. Any interest thereon shall constitute a part of the deposit.

PART II - RULES OF PRACTICE IN DISTRICT AND COUNTY COURTS

SECTION 1. GENERAL RULES

RULE 15. WRITS AND PROCESS

The style of all writs and process shall be "The State of Texas;" and unless otherwise specially provided by law or these rules every such writ and process shall be directed to any sheriff or any constable within the State of Texas, shall be made returnable on the Monday next after expiration of twenty days from the date of service thereof, and shall be dated and attested by the clerk with the seal of the court impressed thereon; and the date of issuance shall be noted thereon.

RULE 16. SHALL ENDORSE ALL PROCESS

Every officer or authorized person shall endorse on all process and precepts coming to his hand the day and hour on which he received them, the manner in which he executed them, and the time and place the process was served and shall sign the returns officially.

RULE 17. OFFICER TO EXECUTE PROCESS

Except where otherwise expressly provided by law or these rules, the officer receiving any process to be executed shall not be entitled in any case to demand his fee for executing the same in advance of such execution, but his fee shall be taxed and collected as other costs in the case.

RULE 18. WHEN JUDGE DIES DURING TERMS, RESIGNS OR IS DISABLED

If the judge dies, resigns, or becomes unable to hold court during the session of court duly convened for the term, and the time provided by law for the holding of said court has not expired, such death, resignation, or inability on the part of the judge shall not operate to adjourn said court for the term, but such court shall be deemed to continue in session. If a successor to such judge shall qualify and assume office during the term, or if a judge be transferred to said district from some other judicial district, he may continue to hold said court for the term provided, and all motions undisposed of shall be heard and determined by him, and statements of facts and bills of exception shall be approved by him. If the time for holding such court expires before a successor shall qualify, and before a judge can be transferred to said district from some other judicial district, then all motions pending, including those for new trial, shall stand as continued in force until such successor has qualified and assumed office, or a judge has been transferred to said district who can hold said court, and thereupon such judge shall have power to act thereon at the succeeding term, or on an earlier day in vacation, on notice to all parties to the motion, and such orders shall have the same effect as if rendered in term time. The time for allowing statement of facts and bills of exception from such orders shall date from the time the motion was decided.

RULE 18a. RECUSAL AND DISQUALIFICATION OF JUDGES

(a) **Motion; Form and Contents**. A party in a case in any trial court other than a statutory probate court or justice court may seek to recuse or disqualify a judge who is sitting in the case by filing a motion with the clerk of the court in which the case is pending. The motion:

    (1) must be verified;

    (2) must assert one or more of the grounds listed in Rule 18b;

    (3) must not be based solely on the judge's ruling in the case; and

(4) must state with detail and particularity facts that:

(A) are within the affiant's personal knowledge, except that facts may be stated on information and belief if the basis for that belief is specifically stated;

(B) would be admissible in evidence; and

(C) if proven, would be sufficient to justify recusal or disqualification.

(b) **Time for Filing Motion.**

(1) *Motion to Recuse.* A motion to recuse:

(A) must be filed as soon as practicable after the movant knows of the ground stated in the motion; and

(B) must not be filed after the tenth day before the date set for trial or other hearing unless, before that day, the movant neither knew nor reasonably should have known:

(i) that the judge whose recusal is sought would preside at the trial or hearing; or

(ii) that the ground stated in the motion existed.

(2) *Motion to Disqualify.* A motion to disqualify should be filed as soon as practicable after the movant knows of the ground stated in the motion.

(c) **Response to Motion.**

(1) *By Another Party.* Any other party in the case may, but need not, file a response to the motion. Any response must be filed before the motion is heard.

(2) *By the Respondent Judge.* The judge whose recusal or disqualification is sought should not file a response to the motion.

(d) **Service of Motion or Response.** A party who files a motion or response must serve a copy on every other party. The method of service must be the same as the method of filing. If possible.

(e) **Duty of the Clerk.**

(1) *Delivery of a Motion or Response.* When a motion or response is filed, the clerk of the court must immediately deliver a copy to the respondent judge and to the presiding judge of the administrative judicial region in which the court is located ("the regional presiding judge").

(2) *Delivery of Order of Recusal or Referral.* When a respondent judge signs and files an order of recusal or referral, the clerk of the court must immediately deliver a copy to the regional presiding judge.

(f) **Duties of the Respondent Judge; Failure to Comply.**

(1) *Responding to the Motion.* Regardless of whether the motion complies with this rule, the respondent judge, within three business days after the motion is filed, must either:

(A) sign and file with the clerk an order of recusal or disqualification; or

(B) sign and file with the clerk an order referring the motion to the regional presiding judge.

(2) *Restrictions on Further Action.*

(A) Motion Filed Before Evidence Offered at Trial. If a motion is filed before evidence has been offered at trial, the respondent judge must take no further action in the case until the motion has been decided, except for good cause stated in writing or on the record.

(B) Motion Filed After Evidence Offered at Trial. If a motion is filed after evidence has been offered at trial, the respondent judge may proceed, subject to stay by the regional presiding judge.

(3) *Failure to Comply*. If the respondent judge fails to comply with a duty imposed by this rule, the movant may notify the regional presiding judge.

(g) **Duties of Regional Presiding Judge**.

(1) *Motion*. The regional presiding judge must rule on a referred motion or assign a judge to rule. If a party files a motion to recuse or disqualify the regional presiding judge, the regional presiding judge may still assign a judge to rule on the original, referred motion. Alternatively, the regional presiding judge may sign and file with the clerk an order referring the second motion to the Chief Justice for consideration.

(2) *Order*. The ruling must be by written order.

(3) *Summary Denial for Noncompliance*.

(A) Motion to Recuse. A motion to recuse that does not comply with this rule may be denied without an oral hearing. The order must state the nature of the noncompliance. Even if the motion is amended to correct the stated noncompliance, the motion will count for purposes of determining whether a tertiary recusal motion has been filed under the Civil Practice and Remedies Code.

(B) Motion to Disqualify. A motion to disqualify may not be denied on the ground that it was not filed or served in compliance with this rule.

(4) *Interim Orders*. The regional presiding judge or judge assigned to decide the motion may issue interim or ancillary orders in the pending case as justice may require.

(5) *Discovery*. Except by order of the regional presiding judge or the judge assigned to decide the motion, a subpoena or discovery request may not issue to the respondent judge and may be disregarded unless accompanied by the order.

(6) *Hearing*.

(A) Time. The motion must be heard as soon as practicable and may be heard immediately after it is referred to the regional presiding judge or an assigned judge.

(B) Notice. Notice of the hearing must be given to all parties in the case.

(C) By Telephone. The hearing may be conducted by telephone on the record. Documents submitted by facsimile or email, otherwise admissible under the rules of evidence, may be considered.

(7) *Reassignment of Case if Motion Granted*. If the motion is granted, the regional presiding judge must transfer the case to another court or assign another judge to the case.

(h) **Sanctions**. After notice and hearing, the judge who hears the motion may order the party or attorney who filed the motion, or both, to pay the reasonable attorney fees and expenses incurred by other parties if the judge determines that the motion was:

(1) groundless and filed in bad faith or for the purpose of harassment, or

(2) clearly brought for unnecessary delay and without sufficient cause.

(i) **Chief Justice**. The Chief Justice of the Supreme Court of Texas may assign judges and issue any orders permitted by this rule or pursuant to statute.

(j) **Appellate Review**.

(1) *Order on Motion to Recuse*.

(A) Denying Motion. An order denying a motion to recuse may be reviewed only for abuse of discretion on appeal from the final judgment.

(B) Granting Motion. An order granting a motion to recuse is final and cannot be reviewed by appeal, mandamus, or otherwise.

(2) *Order on Motion to Disqualify*. An order granting or denying a motion to disqualify may be reviewed by mandamus and may be appealed in accordance with other law.

RULE 18b. GROUNDS FOR RECUSAL AND DISQUALIFICATION OF JUDGES

(a) **Grounds for Disqualification**. A judge must disqualify in any proceeding in which:

(1) the judge has served as a lawyer in the matter in controversy, or a lawyer with whom the judge previously practiced law served during such association as a lawyer concerning the matter;

(2) the judge knows that, individually or as a fiduciary, the judge has an interest in the subject matter in controversy; or

(3) either of the parties may be related to the judge by affinity or consanguinity within the third degree.

(b) **Grounds for Recusal**. A judge must recuse in any proceeding in which:

(1) the judge's impartiality might reasonably be questioned;

(2) the judge has a personal bias or prejudice concerning the subject matter or a party;

(3) the judge has personal knowledge of disputed evidentiary facts concerning the proceeding;

(4) the judge or a lawyer with whom the judge previously practiced law has been a material witness concerning the proceeding;

(5) the judge participated as counsel, adviser, or material witness in the matter in controversy, or expressed an opinion concerning the merits of it, while acting as an attorney in government service;

(6) the judge knows that the judge, individually or as a fiduciary, or the judge's spouse or minor child residing in the judge's household, has a financial interest in the subject matter in controversy or in a party to the proceeding, or any other interest that could be substantially affected by the outcome of the proceeding;

(7) the judge or the judge's spouse, or a person within the third degree of relationship to either of them, or the spouse of such a person:

(A) is a party to the proceeding or an officer, director, or trustee of a party;

(B) is known by the judge to have an interest that could be substantially affected by the outcome of the proceeding; or

(C) is to the judge's knowledge likely to be a material witness in the proceeding.

(8) the judge or the judge's spouse, or a person within the first degree of relationship to either of them, or the spouse of such a person, is acting as a lawyer in the proceeding.

(c) **Financial Interests**. A judge should inform himself or herself about personal and fiduciary financial interests, and make a reasonable effort to inform himself or herself about the personal financial interests of his or her spouse and minor children residing in the household.

(d) **Terminology and Standards**. In this rule:

(1) "proceeding" includes pretrial, trial, or other stages of litigation;

(2) the degree of relationship is calculated according to the civil law system;

(3) "fiduciary" includes such relationships as executor, administrator, trustee, and guardian;

(4) "financial interest" means ownership of a legal or equitable interest, however small, or a relationship as director, adviser, or other active participant in the affairs of a party, except that:

(A) ownership in a mutual or common investment fund that holds securities is not a "financial interest" in such securities unless the judge participates in the management of the fund;

(B) an office in an educational, religious, charitable, fraternal, or civic organization is not a "financial interest" in securities held by the organization;

(C) the proprietary interest of a policyholder in a mutual insurance company, of a depositor in a mutual savings association, or a similar proprietary interest, is a "financial interest" in the organization only if the outcome of the proceeding could substantially affect the value of the interest;

(D) ownership of government securities is a "financial interest" in the issuer only if the outcome of the proceeding could substantially affect the value of the securities;

(E) an interest as a taxpayer or utility ratepayer, or any similar interest, is not a "financial interest" unless the outcome of the proceeding could substantially affect the liability of the judge or a person related to him within the third degree more than other judges.

(e) **Waiving a Ground for Recusal**. The parties to a proceeding may waive any ground for recusal after it is fully disclosed on the record.

(f) **Discovery and Divestiture**. If a judge does not discover that the judge is recused under subparagraphs (b)(6) or (b)(7)(B) until after the judge has devoted substantial time to the matter, the judge is not required to recuse himself or herself if the judge or the person related to the judge divests himself or herself of the interest that would otherwise require recusal.

Comment to 2011 Change: Rule 18a governs the procedure for recusing or disqualifying a judge sitting in any trial court other than a statutory probate court, justice court, or municipal court. Chapter 25 of the Government Code governs statutory probate courts, Rule 528 governs justice courts, and Chapter 29 of the Government Code governs municipal courts. Under Rule 18a, a judge's rulings may not be the sole basis for a motion to recuse or disqualify the judge. But when one or more sufficient other bases are raised, the judge hearing the motion may consider evidence of rulings when considering whether to grant the motion. For purposes of this rule, the term "rulings" is not meant to encompass a judge's statements or remarks about a case.

The amendments to Rule 18b are not intended to be substantive.

RULE 18c. RECORDING AND BROADCASTING OF COURT PROCEEDINGS

A trial court may permit broadcasting, televising, recording, or photographing of proceedings in the courtroom only in the following circumstances:

(a) in accordance with guidelines promulgated by the Supreme Court for civil cases, or

(b) when broadcasting, televising, recording, or photographing will not unduly distract participants or impair the dignity of the proceedings and the parties have consented, and consent to being depicted or recorded is obtained from each witness whose testimony will be broadcast, televised, or photographed, or

(c) the broadcasting, televising, recording, or photographing of investiture, or ceremonial proceedings.

RULE 19. NON-ADJOURNMENT OF TERM

Every term of court shall commence and convene by operation of law at the time fixed by statute without any act, order, or formal opening by a judge or other official thereof, and shall continue to be open at all times until and including the last day of the term unless sooner adjourned by the judge thereof.

RULE 20. MINUTES READ AND SIGNED

On the last day of the session, the minutes shall be read, corrected and signed in open court by the judge. Each special judge shall sign the minutes of such proceedings as were had by him.

RULE 21. FILING AND SERVING PLEADINGS AND MOTIONS

(a) **Filing and Service Required**. Every pleading, plea, motion, or application to the court for an order, whether in the form of a motion, plea, or other form of request, unless presented during a hearing or trial, must be filed with the clerk of the court in writing, must state the grounds therefor, must set forth the relief or order sought, and at the same time a true copy must be served on all other parties, and must be noted on the docket.

(b) **Service of Notice of Hearing**. An application to the court for an order and notice of any hearing thereon, not presented during a hearing or trial, must be served upon all other parties not less than three days before the time specified for the hearing, unless otherwise provided by these rules or shortened by the court.

(c) **Multiple Parties**. If there is more than one other party represented by different attorneys, one copy of each pleading must be served on each attorney in charge.

(d) **Certificate of Service**. The party or attorney of record, must certify to the court compliance with this rule in writing over signature on the filed pleading, plea, motion, or application.

(e) **Additional Copies**. After one copy is served on a party, that party may obtain another copy of the same pleading upon tendering reasonable payment for copying and delivering.

(f) **Electronic Filing**.

    (1) *Requirement*. Except in juvenile cases under Title 3 of the Family Code and truancy cases under Title 3A of the Family Code, attorneys must electronically file documents in courts where electronic filing has been mandated. Attorneys practicing in courts where electronic filing is available but not mandated and unrepresented parties may electronically file documents, but it is not required.

    (2) *Email Address*. The email address of an attorney or unrepresented party who electronically files a document must be included on the document.

    (3) *Mechanism*. Electronic filing must be done through the electronic filing manager established by the Office of Court Administration and an electronic filing service provider certified by the Office of Court Administration.

    (4) *Exceptions*.

        (A) Wills are not required to be filed electronically.

        (B) The following documents must not be filed electronically:

            (i) documents filed under seal or presented to the court in camera; and

            (ii) documents to which access is otherwise restricted by law or court order.

        (C) For good cause, a court may permit a party to file other documents in paper form in a particular case.

    (5) *Timely Filing*. Unless a document must be filed by a certain time of day, a document is considered timely filed if it is electronically filed at any time before midnight (in the court's time zone) on the filing deadline. An electronically filed document is deemed filed when transmitted to the filing party's electronic filing service provider, except:

        (A) if a document is transmitted on a Saturday, Sunday, or legal holiday, it is deemed filed on the next day that is not a Saturday, Sunday, or legal holiday; and

        (B) if a document requires a motion and an order allowing its filing, the document is deemed filed on the date that the motion is granted.

    (6) *Technical Failure*. If a document is untimely due to a technical failure or a system outage, the filing party may seek appropriate relief from the court. If the missed deadline is one imposed by these rules, the filing party must be given a reasonable extension of time to complete the filing.

(7) *Electronic Signatures*. A document that is electronically served, filed, or issued by a court or clerk is considered signed if the document includes:

(A) a "/s/" and name typed in the space where the signature would otherwise appear, unless the document is notarized or sworn; or

(B) an electronic image or scanned image of the signature.

(8) *Format*. An electronically filed document must:

(A) be in text-searchable portable document format (PDF);

(B) be directly converted to PDF rather than scanned, if possible;

(C) not be locked; and

(D) otherwise comply with the Technology Standards set by the Judicial Committee on Information Technology and approved by the Supreme Court.

(9) *Paper Copies*. Unless required by local rule, a party need not file a paper copy of an electronically filed document.

(10) *Electronic Notices From the Court*. The clerk may send notices, orders, or other communications about the case to the party electronically. A court seal may be electronic.

(11) *Non-Conforming Documents*. The clerk may not refuse to file a document that fails to conform with this rule. But the clerk may identify the error to be corrected and state a deadline for the party to resubmit the document in a conforming format.

(12) *Original Wills*. When a party electronically files an application to probate a document as an original will, the original will must be filed with the clerk within three business days after the application is filed.

(13) *Official Record*. The clerk may designate an electronically filed document or a scanned paper document as the official court record. The clerk is not required to keep both paper and electronic versions of the same document unless otherwise required by local rule. But the clerk must retain an original will filed for probate in a numbered file folder.

Comment to 2013 Change: Rule 21 is revised to incorporate rules for electronic filing, in accordance with the Supreme Court's order - Misc. Docket No. 12-9206, amended by Misc. Docket Nos. 13-9092 and 13-9164 - mandating electronic filing in civil cases beginning on January 1, 2014. The mandate will be implemented according to the schedule in the order and will be completed by July 1, 2016. The revisions reflect the fact that the mandate will only apply to a subset of Texas courts until that date.

RULE 21a. METHODS OF SERVICE

(a) **Methods of Service**. Every notice required by these rules, and every pleading, plea, motion, or other form of request required to be served under Rule 21, other than the citation to be served upon the filing of a cause of action and except as otherwise expressly provided in these rules, may be served by delivering a copy to the party to be served, or the party's duly authorized agent or attorney of record in the manner specified below:

(1) *Documents Filed Electronically*. A document filed electronically under Rule 21 must be served electronically through the electronic filing manager if the email address of the party or attorney to be served is on file with the electronic filing manager. If the email address of the party or attorney to be served is not on file with the electronic filing manager, the document may be served on that party or attorney under subparagraph (2).

(2) *Documents Not Filed Electronically*. A document not filed electronically may be served in person, by mail, by commercial delivery service, by fax, by email, or by such other manner as the court in its discretion may direct.

(b) **When Complete**.

(1) Service by mail or commercial delivery service shall be complete upon deposit of the document, postpaid and properly addressed, in the mail or with a commercial delivery service.

(2) Service by fax is complete on receipt. Service completed after 5:00 p.m. local time of the recipient shall be deemed served on the following day.

(3) Electronic service is complete on transmission of the document to the serving party's electronic filing service provider. The electronic filing manager will send confirmation of service to the serving party.

(c) **Time for Action After Service**. Whenever a party has the right or is required to do some act within a prescribed period after the service of a notice or other paper upon him and the notice or paper is served upon him by mail, three days shall be added to the prescribed period.

(d) **Who May Serve**. Notice may be served by a party to the suit, an attorney of record, a sheriff or constable, or by any other person competent to testify.

(e) **Proof of Service**. The party or attorney of record shall certify to the court compliance with this rule in writing over signature and on the filed instrument. A certificate by a party or an attorney of record, or the return of the officer, or the affidavit of any other person showing service of a notice shall be prima facie evidence of the fact of service. Nothing herein shall preclude any party from offering proof that the document was not received, or, if service was by mail, that the document was not received within three days from the date that it was deposited in the mail, and upon so finding, the court may extend the time for taking the action required of such party or grant such other relief as it deems just.

(f) **Procedures Cumulative**. These provisions are cumulative of all other methods of service prescribed by these rules.

Comment to 2013 Change: Rule 21a is revised to incorporate rules for electronic service in accordance with the Supreme Court's order - Misc. Docket No. 12-9206, amended by Misc. Docket Nos. 13-9092 and 13-9164 - mandating electronic filing in civil cases beginning on January 1, 2014.

RULE 21b. SANCTIONS FOR FAILURE TO SERVE OR DELIVER COPY OF PLEADINGS AND MOTIONS

If any party fails to serve on or deliver to the other parties a copy of any pleading, plea, motion, or other application to the court for an order in accordance with Rules 21 and 21a, the court may in its discretion, after notice and hearing, impose an appropriate sanction available under Rule 215-2b.

[RULE 21c. Repealed effective September 1, 1986]

RULE 21c. PRIVACY PROTECTION FOR FILED DOCUMENTS.

(a) **Sensitive Data Defined**. Sensitive data consists of:

(1) a driver's license number, passport number, social security number, tax identification number, or similar government-issued personal identification number;

(2) a bank account number, credit card number, or other financial account number; and

(3) a birth date, a home address, and the name of any person who was a minor when the underlying suit was filed.

(b) **Filing of Documents Containing Sensitive Data Prohibited**. Unless the inclusion of sensitive data is specifically required by a statute, court rule, or administrative regulation, an electronic or paper document, except for wills and documents filed under seal, containing sensitive data may not be filed with a court unless the sensitive data is redacted.

(c) **Redaction of Sensitive Data; Retention Requirement**. Sensitive data must be redacted by using the letter "X" in place of each omitted digit or character or by removing the sensitive data in a manner indicating that the data has been redacted. The filing party must retain an unredacted version of the filed document during the pendency of the case and any related appellate proceedings filed within six months of the date the judgment is signed.

(d) **Notice to Clerk**. If a document must contain sensitive data, the filing party must notify the clerk by:

(1) designating the document as containing sensitive data when the document is electronically filed; or

(2) if the document is not electronically filed, by including, on the upper left- hand side of the first page, the phrase: "NOTICE: THIS DOCUMENT CONTAINS SENSITIVE DATA."

(e) **Non-Conforming Documents**. The clerk may not refuse to file a document that contains sensitive data in violation of this rule. But the clerk may identify the error to be corrected and state a deadline for the party to resubmit a redacted, substitute document.

(f) **Restriction on Remote Access**. Documents that contain sensitive data in violation of this rule must not be posted on the Internet.

Comment to 2013 Change: Rule 21c is added to provide privacy protection for documents filed in civil cases.

SECTION 2. INSTITUTION OF SUIT

RULE 22. COMMENCED BY PETITION

A civil suit in the district or county court shall be commenced by a petition filed in the office of the clerk.

RULE 23. SUITS TO BE NUMBERED CONSECUTIVELY

It shall be the duty of the clerk to designate the suits by regular consecutive numbers, called file numbers, and he shall mark on each paper in every case the file number of the cause.

RULE 24. DUTY OF CLERK

When a petition is filed with the clerk he shall indorse thereon the file number, the day on which it was filed and the time of filing, and sign his name officially thereto.

RULE 25. CLERK'S FILE DOCKET

Each clerk shall keep a file docket which shall show in convenient form the number of the suit, the names of the attorneys, the names of the parties to the suit, and the nature thereof, and, in brief form, the officer's return on the process, and all subsequent proceedings had in the case with the dates thereof.

RULE 26. CLERK'S COURT DOCKET

Each clerk shall also keep a court docket in a permanent record that shall include the number of the case and the names of the parties, the names of the attorneys, the nature of the action, the pleas, the motions, and the ruling of the court as made.

RULE 27. ORDER OF CASES

The cases shall be placed on the docket as they are filed.

SECTION 3. PARTIES TO SUITS

RULE 28. SUITS IN ASSUMED NAME

Any partnership, unincorporated association, private corporation, or individual doing business under an assumed name may sue or be sued in its partnership, assumed or common name for the purpose of enforcing for or against it a substantive right, but on a motion by any party or on the court's own motion the true name may be substituted.

RULE 29. SUIT ON CLAIM AGAINST DISSOLVED CORPORATION

When no receiver has been appointed for a corporation which has dissolved, suit may be instituted on any claim against said corporation as though the same had not been dissolved, and service of process may be obtained on the president, directors, general manager, trustee, assignee, or other person in charge of the affairs of the corporation at the time it was dissolved, and judgment may be rendered as though the corporation had not been dissolved.

RULE 30. PARTIES TO SUITS

Assignors, endorsers and other parties not primarily liable upon any instruments named in the chapter of the Business and Commerce Code, dealing with commercial paper, may be jointly sued with their principal obligors, or may be sued alone in the cases provided for by statute.

RULE 31. SURETY NOT TO BE SUED ALONE

No surety shall be sued unless his principal is joined with him, or unless a judgment has previously been rendered against his principal, except in cases otherwise provided for in the law and these rules.

RULE 32. MAY HAVE QUESTION OF SURETYSHIP TRIED

When any suit is brought against two or more defendants upon any contract, any one or more of the defendants being surety for the other, the surety may cause the question of suretyship to be tried and determined upon the issue made for the parties defendant at the trial of the cause, or at any time before or after the trial or at a subsequent term. Such proceedings shall not delay the suit of the plaintiff.

RULE 33. SUITS BY OR AGAINST COUNTIES

Suits by or against a county or incorporated city, town or village shall be in its corporate name.

RULE 34. AGAINST SHERIFF, ETC.

Whenever a sheriff, constable, or a deputy or either has been sued for damages for any act done in his official character, and has taken an indemnifying bond for the acts upon which the suit is based, he may make the principal and surety on such bond parties defendant in such suit, and the cause may be continued to obtain service on such parties.

RULE 35. ON OFFICIAL BONDS

In suits brought by the State or any county, city, independent school district, irrigation district, or other political subdivision of the State, against any officer who has held an office for more than one term, or against any depository which has been such depository for more than one term, or has given more than one official bond, the sureties on each and all such bonds may be joined as defendants in the same suit whenever it is difficult to determine when the default sued for occurred and which set of sureties on such bonds is liable therefor.

RULE 36. DIFFERENT OFFICIALS AND BONDSMEN

In suits by the State upon the official bond of a State officer, any subordinate officer who has given bond, payable either to the State or such superior officer, to cover all or part of the default sued for, together with the sureties on his official bond, may be joined as defendants with such superior officer and his bondsmen whenever it is alleged in the petition that both of such officers are liable for the money sued for.

RULE 37. ADDITIONAL PARTIES

Before a case is called for trial, additional parties necessary or proper parties to the suit, may be brought in, either by the plaintiff or the defendant, upon such terms as the court may prescribe; but not at a time nor in a manner to unreasonably delay the trial of the case.

RULE 38. THIRD-PARTY PRACTICE

(a) **When Defendant May Bring in Third Party**. At any time after commencement of the action a defending party, as a third-party plaintiff, may cause a citation and petition to be served upon a person not a party to the action who is or may be liable to him or to the plaintiff for all or part of the plaintiff's claim against him. The third-party plaintiff need not obtain leave to make the service if he files the third- party petition not later than thirty (30) days after he serves his original answer. Otherwise, he must obtain leave on motion upon notice to all parties to the action. The person served, hereinafter called the third-party defendant, shall make his defenses to the third-party plaintiff's claim under the rules applicable to the defendant, and his counterclaims against the third -party plaintiff and cross-claims against other third-party defendants as provided in Rule 97. The third-party defendant may assert against the plaintiff any defenses which the third -party plaintiff has to the plaintiff's claim. The third-party defendant may also assert any claim against the plaintiff arising out of the transaction or occurrence that is the subject matter of the plaintiff's claim against the third-party plaintiff. The plaintiff may assert any claim against the third-party defendant arising out of the transaction or occurrence that is the subject matter of the plaintiff's claim against the third-party plaintiff, and the third-party defendant thereupon shall assert his defenses and his counterclaims and cross-claims. Any party may move to strike the third-party claim, or for its severance or separate trial. A third-party defendant may proceed under this rule against any person not a party to the action who is or who may be liable to him or to the third-party plaintiff for all or part of the claim made in the action against the third-party defendant.

(b) **When Plaintiff May Bring in Third Party**. When a counterclaim is asserted against a plaintiff, he may cause a third party to be brought in under circumstances which under this rule would entitle a defendant to do so.

(c) This rule shall not be applied, in tort cases, so as to permit the joinder of a liability or indemnity insurance company, unless such company is by statute or contract liable to the person injured or damaged.

(d) This rule shall not be applied so as to violate any venue statute, as venue would exist absent this rule.

RULE 39. JOINDER OF PERSONS NEEDED FOR JUST ADJUDICATION

(a) **Persons to Be Joined If Feasible**. A person who is subject to service of process shall be joined as a party in the action if

(1) in his absence complete relief cannot be accorded among those already parties, or

(2) he claims an interest relating to the subject of the action and is so situated that the disposition of the action in his absence may

(i) as a practical matter impair or impede his ability to protect that interest or

(ii) leave any of the persons already parties subject to a substantial risk of incurring double, multiple, or otherwise inconsistent obligations by reason of his claimed interest. If he has not been so joined, the court shall order that he be made a party. If he should join as a plaintiff but refuses to do so, he may be made a defendant, or, in a proper case, an involuntary plaintiff.

(b) **Determination by Court Whenever Joinder Not Feasible**. If a person as described in subdivision (a)(1)-(2) hereof cannot be made a party, the court shall determine whether in equity and good conscience the action should proceed among the parties before it, or should be dismissed, the absent person being thus regarded as indispensable. The factors to be considered by the court include: first, to what extent a judgment rendered in the person's absence might be prejudicial to him or those already parties; second, the extent to which, by protective provisions in the judgment, by the shaping of relief, or other measures, the prejudice can be lessened or avoided; third, whether a judgment rendered in the person's absence will be adequate; fourth, whether the plaintiff will have an adequate remedy if the action is dismissed for non-joinder.

(c) **Pleading Reasons for Nonjoinder**. A pleading asserting a claim for relief shall state the names, if known to the pleader, of any persons as described in subdivision (a)(1)-(2) hereof who are not joined, and the reasons why they are not joined.

(d) **Exception of Class Actions**. This rule is subject to the provisions of Rule 42.

RULE 40. PERMISSIVE JOINDER OF PARTIES

(a) **Permissive Joinder**. All persons may join in one action as plaintiffs if they assert any right to relief jointly, severally, or in the alternative in respect of or arising out of the same transaction, occurrence, or series of transactions or occurrences and if any question of law or fact common to all of them will arise in the action. All persons may be joined in one action as defendants if there is asserted against them jointly, severally, or in the alternative any right to relief in respect of or arising out of the same transaction, occurrence, or series of transactions or occurrences and if any question of law or fact common to all of them will arise in the action. A plaintiff or defendant need not be interested in obtaining or defending against all the relief demanded. Judgment may be given for one or more of the plaintiffs according to their respective rights to relief, and against one or more defendants according to their respective liabilities.

(b) **Separate Trials**. The court may make such orders as will prevent a party from being embarrassed, delayed, or put to expense by the inclusion of a party against whom he asserts no claim and who asserts no claim against him, and may order separate trials or make other orders to prevent delay or prejudice.

RULE 41. MISJOINDER OR NON-JOINDER OF PARTIES

Misjoinder of parties is not ground for dismissal of an action. Parties may be dropped or added, or suits filed separately may be consolidated, or actions which have been improperly joined may be severed and each ground of recovery improperly joined may be docketed as a separate suit between the same parties, by order of the court on motion of any party or on its own initiative at any stage of the action, before the time of submission to the jury or to the court if trial is without a jury, on such terms as are just. Any claim against a party may be severed and proceeded with separately.

RULE 42. CLASS ACTIONS

(a) **Prerequisites to a Class Action**. One or more members of a class may sue or be sued as representative parties on behalf of all only if

(1) the class is so numerous that joinder of all members is impracticable,

(2) there are questions of law or fact common to the class,

(3) the claims or defenses of the representative parties are typical of the claims or defenses of the class, and

(4) the representative parties will fairly and adequately protect the interests of the class.

(b) **Class Actions Maintainable**. An action may be maintained as a class action if the prerequisites of subdivision (a) are satisfied, and in addition:

(1) the prosecution of separate actions by or against individual members of the class would create a risk of

(A) inconsistent or varying adjudications with respect to individual members of the class which would establish incompatible standards of conduct for the party opposing the class, or

(B) adjudications with respect to individual members of the class which would as a practical matter be dispositive of the interests of the other members not parties to the adjudications or substantially impair or impede their ability to protect their interests; or

(2) the party opposing the class has acted or refused to act on grounds generally applicable to the class, thereby making appropriate final injunctive relief or corresponding declaratory relief with respect to the class as a whole; or

(3) the questions of law or fact common to the members of the class predominate over any questions affecting only individual members, and a class action is superior to other available methods for the fair and efficient adjudication of the controversy. The matters pertinent to these issues include:

(A) the interest of members of the class in individually controlling the prosecution or defense of separate actions;

(B) the extent and nature of any litigation concerning the controversy already commenced by or against members of the class;

(C) the desirability or undesirability of concentrating the litigation of the claims in the particular forum;

(D) the difficulties likely to be encountered in the management of a class action

(c) **Determination by Order Whether to Certify a Class Action; Notice and Membership in Class**.

(1)

(A) When a person sues or is sued as a representative of a class, the court must -- at an early practicable time -- determine by order whether to certify the action as a class action.Comment to 2003 amendment: The requirement that certification be decided "at an early practicable time" is a change from the previous Texas rule 42 (c)(1) and federal rule 23 (c)(1), which required the trial court to decide the certification issue "as soon as practicable after the commencement of [the suit]." The amended language is not intended to permit undue delay or permit excessive discovery unrelated to certification, but is designed to encourage good practices in making certification decisions only after receiving the information necessary to decide whether certification should be granted or denied and how to define the class if certification is granted.

(B) An order certifying a class action must define the class and the class claims, issues, or defenses, and must appoint class counsel under Rule 42 (g).

(C) An order under Rule 42 (c)(1) may be altered or amended before final judgment. The court may order the naming of additional parties in order to insure the adequacy of representation.

(D) An order granting or denying certification under Rule 42(b)(3) must state:

(i) the elements of each claim or defense asserted in the pleadings;

(ii) any issues of law or fact common to the class members;

(iii) any issues of law or fact affecting only individual class members;

(iv) the issues that will be the object of most of the efforts of the litigants and the court;

(v) other available methods of adjudication that exist for the controversy;

(vi) why the issues common to the members of the class do or do not predominate over individual issues;

(vii) why a class action is or is not superior to other available methods for the fair and efficient adjudication of the controversy; and

(viii) if a class is certified, how the class claims and any issues affecting only individual members, raised by the claims or defenses asserted in the pleadings, will be tried in a manageable, time efficient manner.

(2)

(A) For any class certified under Rule 42(b)(1) or (2), the court may direct appropriate notice to the class. For any class certified under Rule 42(b)(3), the court must direct to class members the best notice practicable under the circumstances including individual notice to all members who can be identified through reasonable effort. The notice must concisely and clearly state in plain, easily understood language:

(i) the nature of the action;

(ii) the definition of the class certified;

(iii) the class claims, issues, or defenses;

(iv) that a class member may enter an appearance through counsel if the member so desires;

(v) that the court will exclude from the class any member who requests exclusion, stating when and how members may elect to be excluded; and

(vi) the binding effect of a class judgment on class members under Rule 42 (c)(3).

(3) The judgment in an action maintained as a class action under subdivisions (b)(1) or (b)(2), whether or not favorable to the class, shall include and describe those whom the court finds to be members of the class. The judgment in an action maintained as a class action under subdivision (b)(4), whether or not favorable to the class, shall include and specify or describe those to whom the notice provided in subdivision (c)(2) was directed, and who have not requested exclusion, and whom the court finds to be members of the class.

(d) **Actions Conducted Partially as Class Actions; Multiple Classes and Subclasses**. When appropriate

(1) an action may be brought or maintained as a class action with respect to particular issues, or

(2) a class may be divided into subclasses and each subclass treated as a class, and the provisions of this rule shall then be construed and applied accordingly.

(e) **Settlement, Dismissal or Compromise**.

(1)

(A) The court must approve any settlement, dismissal, or compromise of the claims, issues, or defenses of a certified class.

(B) Notice of the material terms of the proposed settlement, dismissal or compromise, together with an explanation of when and how the members may elect to be excluded from the class, shall be given to all members in such manner as the court directs.

(C) The court may approve a settlement, dismissal, or compromise that would bind class members only after a hearing and on finding that the settlement, dismissal, or compromise is fair, reasonable, and adequate.

(2) The parties seeking approval of a settlement, dismissal, or compromise under Rule 42(e)(1) must file a statement identifying any agreement made in connection with the proposed settlement, dismissal, or compromise.

(3) In an action previously certified as a class action under Rule 42(b)(3), the court may not approve a settlement unless it affords a new opportunity to request exclusion to individual class members who had an earlier opportunity to request exclusion but did not do so.

(4)

    (A) Any class member may object to a proposed settlement, dismissal, or compromise that requires court approval under Rule 42(e)(1)(A).

    (B) An objection made under Rule 42(e)(4)(A) may be withdrawn only with the court's approval.

(f) **Discovery**. Unnamed members of a class action are not to be considered as parties for purposes of discovery.

(g) **Class Counsel**.

    (1) *Appointing Class Counsel*.

        (A) Unless a statute provides otherwise, a court that certifies a class must appoint class counsel.

        (B) An attorney appointed to serve as class counsel must fairly and adequately represent the interests of the class.

        (C) In appointing class counsel, the court

            (i) must consider:-- the work counsel has done in identifying or investigating potential claims in the action;-- counsel's experience in handling class actions, other complex litigation, and claims of the type asserted in the action;-- counsel's knowledge of the applicable law; and-- the resources counsel will commit to representing the class;

            (ii) may consider any other matter pertinent to counsel's ability to fairly and adequately represent the interests of the class;

            (iii) may direct potential class counsel to provide information on any subject pertinent to the appointment and to propose terms for attorney fees and nontaxable costs; and

            (iv) may make further orders in connection with the appointment.

    (2) *Appointment Procedure*.

        (A) The court may designate interim counsel to act on behalf of the putative class before determining whether to certify the action as a class action.

        (B) When there is one applicant for appointment as class counsel, the court may appoint that applicant only if the applicant is adequate under Rule 42(g)(1)(B) and (C). If more than one adequate applicant seeks appointment as class counsel, the court must appoint the applicant or applicants best able to represent the interests of the class.

        (C) The order appointing class counsel may include provisions about the award of attorney fees or nontaxable costs under Rule 42(h) and (i).

(h) **Procedure for determining Attorney Fees Award**. In an action certified as a class action, the court may award attorney fees in accordance with subdivision (i) and nontaxable costs authorized by law or by agreement of the parties as follows:

    (1) *Motion for Award of Attorney Fees*. A claim for an award of attorney fees and nontaxable costs must be made by motion, subject to the provisions of this subdivision, at a time set by the court. Notice of the motion must be served on all parties and, for motions by class counsel, directed to class members in a reasonable manner.

    (2) *Objections to Motion*. A class member, or a party from whom payment is sought, may object to the motion.

    (3) *Hearing and Findings*. The court must hold a hearing in open court and must find the facts and state its conclusions of law on the motion. The court must state its findings and conclusions in writing or orally on the record.

(i) **Attorney's Fees Award**.

(1) In awarding attorney fees, the court must first determine a lodestar figure by multiplying the number of hours reasonably worked times a reasonable hourly rate. The attorney fees award must be in the range of 25% to 400% of the lodestar figure. In making these determinations, the court must consider the factors specified in Rule 1.04(b), Tex. Disciplinary R. Prof. Conduct.

(2) If any portion of the benefits recovered for the class are in the form of coupons or other noncash common benefits, the attorney fees awarded in the action must be in cash and noncash amounts in the same proportion as the recovery for the class.

(j) **Effective Date**. Rule 42(i) applies only in actions filed after September 1, 2003.

RULE 43. INTERPLEADER

Persons having claims against the plaintiff may be joined as defendants and required to interplead when their claims are such that the plaintiff is or may be exposed to double or multiple liability. It is not ground for objection to the joinder that the claims of the several claimants or the titles on which their claims depend do not have a common origin or are not identical but are adverse to and independent of one another, or that the plaintiff avers that he is not liable in whole or in part to any or all of the claimants. A defendant exposed to similar liability may obtain such interpleader by way of cross-claim or counterclaim. The provisions of this rule supplement and do not in any way limit the joinder of parties permitted in any other rules.

RULE 44. MAY APPEAR BY NEXT FRIEND

Minors, lunatics, idiots, or persons non compos mentis who have no legal guardian may sue and be represented by "next friend" under the following rules:

(1) Such next friend shall have the same rights concerning such suits as guardians have, but shall give security for costs, or affidavits in lieu thereof, when required.

(2) Such next friend or his attorney of record may with the approval of the court compromise suits and agree to judgments, and such judgments, agreements and compromises, when approved by the court, shall be forever binding and conclusive upon the party plaintiff in such suit.

SECTION 4. PLEADING

A. General

RULE 45. DEFINITION AND SYSTEM

Pleadings in the district and county courts shall

(a) be by petition and answer;

(b) consist of a statement in plain and concise language of the plaintiff's cause of action or the defendant's grounds of defense. That an allegation be evidentiary or be of legal conclusion shall not be grounds for objection when fair notice to the opponent is given by the allegations as a whole; and

(c) contain any other matter which may be required by any law or rule authorizing or regulating any particular action or defense.

Pleadings that are not filed electronically must be in writing, on paper measuring approximately 8 ½ inches by 11 inches, and signed by the party or his attorney. The use of recycled paper is strongly encouraged.

All pleadings shall be construed so as to do substantial justice.

RULE 46. PETITION AND ANSWER; EACH ONE INSTRUMENT OF WRITING

The original petition, first supplemental petition, second supplemental petition, and every other, shall each be contained in one instrument of writing, and so with the original answer and each of the supplemental answers.

RULE 47. CLAIMS FOR RELIEF

An original pleading which sets forth a claim for relief, whether an original petition, counterclaim, cross-claim, or third party claim, shall contain

(a) a short statement of the cause of action sufficient to give fair notice of the claim involved;

(b) a statement that the damages sought are within the jurisdictional limits of the court;

(c) except in suits governed by the Family Code, a statement that the party seeks:

(1) only monetary relief of $100,000 or less, including damages of any kind, penalties, costs, expenses, pre-judgment interest, and attorney fees; or

(2) monetary relief of $100,000 or less and non-monetary relief; or

(3) monetary relief over $100,000 but not more than $200,000; or

(4) monetary relief over $200,000 but not more than $1,000,000; or

(5) monetary relief over $1,000,000; and

(d) a demand for judgment for all the other relief to which the party deems himself entitled.

Relief in the alternative or of several different types may be demanded; provided, further, that upon special exception the court shall require the pleader to amend so as to specify the maximum amount claimed. A party that fails to comply with (c) may not conduct discovery until the party's pleading is amended to comply.

Comment to 2013 change: Rule 47 is amended to require a more specific statement of the relief sought by a party. The amendment requires parties to plead into or out of the expedited actions process governed by Rule 169, added to implement section 22.004(h) of the Texas Government Code. Except in a suit governed by the Family Code, the Property Code, the Tax Code, or Chapter 74 of the Civil Practice & Remedies Code, a suit in which the original petition contains the statement in paragraph (c)(1) is governed by the expedited actions process. The further specificity in paragraphs (c)(2)-(5) is to provide information regarding the nature of cases filed and does not affect a party's substantive rights.

RULE 48. ALTERNATIVE CLAIMS FOR RELIEF

A party may set forth two or more statements of a claim or defense alternatively or hypothetically, either in one count or defense or in separate counts or defenses. When two or more statements are made in the alternative and one of them if made independently would be sufficient, the pleading is not made insufficient by the insufficiency of one or more of the alternative statements. A party may also state as many separate claims or defenses as he has regardless of consistency and whether based upon legal or equitable grounds or both.

RULE 49. WHERE SEVERAL COUNTS

Where there are several counts in the petition, and entire damages are given, the verdict or judgment, as the case may be, shall be good, notwithstanding one or more of such counts may be defective.

RULE 50. PARAGRAPHS, SEPARATE STATEMENTS

All averments of claim or defense shall be made in numbered paragraphs, the contents of each of which shall be limited as far as practicable to a statement of a single set of circumstances; and a paragraph may be referred to by number in all succeeding pleadings, so long as the pleading containing such paragraph has not been superseded by an amendment as provided by Rule 65. Each claim founded upon a separate transaction or occurrence and each defense other than denials shall be stated in a separate count or defense whenever a separation facilitates the clear presentation of the matters set forth.

RULE 51. JOINDER OF CLAIMS AND REMEDIES

(a) **Joinder of Claims**. The plaintiff in his petition or in a reply setting forth a counterclaim and the defendant in an answer setting forth a counterclaim may join either as independent or as alternate claims as many claims either legal or equitable or both as he may have against an opposing party. There may be a like joinder of claims when there are multiple parties if the requirements of Rules 39, 40, and 43 are satisfied. There may be a like joinder of cross claims or third-party claims if the requirements of Rules 38 and 97, respectively, are satisfied.

(b) **Joinder of Remedies**. Whenever a claim is one heretofore cognizable only after another claim has been prosecuted to a conclusion, the two claims may be joined in a single action; but the court shall grant relief in that action only in accordance with the relative substantive rights of the parties. This rule shall not be applied in tort cases so as to permit the joinder of a liability or indemnity insurance company, unless such company is by statute or contract directly liable to the person injured or damaged.

RULE 52. ALLEGING A CORPORATION

An allegation that a corporation is incorporated shall be taken as true, unless denied by the affidavit of the adverse party, his agent or attorney, whether such corporation is a public or private corporation and however created.

RULE 53. SPECIAL ACT OR LAW

A pleading founded wholly or in part on any private or special act or law of this State or of the Republic of Texas need only recite the title thereof, the date of its approval, and set out in substance so much of such act or laws as may be pertinent to the cause of action or defense.

RULE 54. CONDITIONS PRECEDENT

In pleading the performance or occurrence of conditions precedent, it shall be sufficient to aver generally that all conditions precedent have been performed or have occurred. When such performances or occurrences have been so plead, the party so pleading same shall be required to prove only such of them as are specifically denied by the opposite party.

RULE 55. JUDGMENT

In pleading a judgment or decision of a domestic or foreign court, judicial or quasi-judicial tribunal, or of a board or officer, it shall be sufficient to aver the judgment or decision without setting forth matter showing jurisdiction to render it.

RULE 56. SPECIAL DAMAGE

When items of special damage are claimed, they shall be specifically stated.

RULE 57. SIGNING OF PLEADINGS

Every pleading of a party represented by an attorney shall be signed by at least one attorney of record in his individual name, with his State Bar of Texas identification number, address, telephone number, email address, and if available, fax number. A party not represented by an attorney shall sign his pleadings, state his address, telephone number, email address, and, if available, fax number.

RULE 58. ADOPTION BY REFERENCE

Statements in a pleading may be adopted by reference in a different part of the same pleading or in another pleading or in any motion, so long as the pleading containing such statements has not been superseded by an amendment as provided by Rule 65.

RULE 59. EXHIBITS AND PLEADING

Notes, accounts, bonds, mortgages, records, and all other written instruments, constituting, in whole or in part, the claim sued on, or the matter set up in defense, may be made a part of the pleadings by copies thereof, or the originals, being attached or filed and referred to as such, or by copying the same in the body of the pleading in aid and explanation of the allegations in the petition or answer made in reference to said instruments and shall be deemed a part thereof for all purposes. Such pleadings shall not be deemed defective because of the lack of any allegations which can be supplied from said exhibit. No other instrument of writing shall be made an exhibit in the pleading.

RULE 60. INTERVENOR'S PLEADINGS

Any party may intervene by filing a pleading, subject to being stricken out by the court for sufficient cause on the motion of any party.

RULE 61. TRIAL: INTERVENORS: RULES APPLY TO ALL PARTIES

These rules of pleading shall apply equally, so far as it may be practicable to intervenors and to parties, when more than one, who may plead separately.

RULE 62. AMENDMENT DEFINED

The object of an amendment, as contra-distinguished from a supplemental petition or answer, is to add something to, or withdraw something from, that which has been previously pleaded so as to perfect that which is or may be deficient, or to correct that which has been incorrectly stated by the party making the amendment, or to plead new matter, additional to that formerly pleaded by the amending party, which constitutes an additional claim or defense permissible to the suit.

RULE 63. AMENDMENTS AND RESPONSIVE PLEADINGS

Parties may amend their pleadings, respond to pleadings on file of other parties, file suggestions of death and make representative parties, and file such other pleas as they may desire by filing such pleas with the clerk at such time as not to operate as a surprise to the opposite party; provided, that any pleadings, responses or pleas offered for filing within seven days of the date of trial or thereafter, or after such time as may be ordered by the judge under Rule 166, shall be filed only after leave of the judge is obtained, which leave shall be granted by the judge unless there is a showing that such filing will operate as a surprise to the opposite party.

RULE 64. AMENDED INSTRUMENT

The party amending shall point out the instrument amended, as "original petition," or "plaintiff's first supplemental petition," or as "original answer," or "defendant's first supplemental answer" or other instrument file by the party and shall amend by filing a substitute therefor, entire and complete in itself, indorsed "amended original petition," or "amended first supplemental petition," or "amended original answer," or "amended first supplemental answer," accordingly as said instruments of pleading are designated.

RULE 65. SUBSTITUTED INSTRUMENT TAKES PLACE OF ORIGINAL

Unless the substituted instrument shall be set aside on exceptions, the instrument for which it is substituted shall no longer be regarded as a part of the pleading in the record of the cause, unless some error of the court in deciding upon the necessity of the amendment, or otherwise in superseding it, be complained of, and exception be taken to the action of the court, or unless it be necessary to look to the superseded pleading upon a question of limitation.

RULE 66. TRIAL AMENDMENT

If evidence is objected to at the trial on the ground that it is not within the issues made by the pleading, or if during the trial any defect, fault or omission in a pleading, either of form or substance, is called to the attention of the court, the court may allow the pleadings to be amended and shall do so freely when the presentation of the merits of the action will be subserved thereby and the objecting party fails to satisfy the court that the allowance of such amendment would prejudice him in maintaining his action or defense upon the merits. The court may grant a postponement to enable the objecting party to meet such evidence.

RULE 67. AMENDMENTS TO CONFORM TO ISSUES TRIED WITHOUT OBJECTION

When issues not raised by the pleadings are tried by express or implied consent of the parties, they shall be treated in all respects as if they had been raised in the pleadings. In such case such amendment of the pleadings as may be necessary to cause them to conform to the evidence and to raise these issues may be made by leave of court upon motion of any party at any time up to the submission of the case to the Court or jury, but failure so to amend shall not affect the result of the trial of these issues; provided that written pleadings, before the time of submission, shall be necessary to the submission of questions, as is provided in Rules 277 and 279.

RULE 68. COURT MAY ORDER REPLEADER

The court, when deemed necessary in any case, may order a repleader on the part of one or both of the parties, in order to make their pleadings substantially conform to the rules.

RULE 69. SUPPLEMENTAL PETITION OR ANSWER

Each supplemental petition or answer, made by either party, shall be a response to the last preceding pleading by the other party, and shall not repeat allegations formerly pleaded further than is necessary as an introduction to that which is stated in the pleading then being drawn up. These instruments, to wit, the original petition and its several supplements, and the original answer and its several supplements, shall respectively, constitute separate and distinct parts of the pleadings of each party; and the position and identity, by number and name, with the indorsement of each instrument, shall be preserved throughout the pleadings of either party.

RULE 70. PLEADING: SURPRISE: COST

When either a supplemental or amended pleading is of such character and is presented at such time as to take the opposite party by surprise, the court may charge the continuance of the cause, if granted, to the party causing the surprise if the other party satisfactorily shows that he is not ready for trial because of the allowance of the filing of such supplemental or amended pleading, and the court may, in such event, in its discretion require the party filing such pleading to pay to the surprised party the amount of reasonable costs and expenses incurred by the other party as a result of the continuance, including attorney fees, or make such other order with respect thereto as may be just.

RULE 71. MISNOMER OF PLEADING

When a party has mistakenly designated any plea or pleading, the court, if justice so requires, shall treat the plea or pleading as if it had been properly designated. Pleadings shall be docketed as originally designated and shall remain identified as designated, unless the court orders redesignation.

Upon court order filed with the clerk, the clerk shall modify the docket and all other clerk records to reflect redesignation.

[RULE 72. Repealed effective September 1, 1990]

[RULE 73. Repealed effective September 1, 1990]

RULE 74. FILING WITH THE COURT DEFINED

The filing of pleadings, other papers and exhibits as required by these rules shall be made by filing them with the clerk of the court, except that the judge may permit the papers to be filed with him, in which event he shall note thereon the filing date and time and forthwith transmit them to the office of the clerk.

RULE 75. FILED PLEADINGS; WITHDRAWAL

All filed pleadings shall remain at all times in the clerk's office or in the court or in custody of the clerk, except that the court may by order entered on the minutes allow a filed pleading to be withdrawn for a limited time whenever necessary, on leaving a certified copy on file. The party withdrawing such pleading shall pay the costs of such order and certified copy.

RULE 75a. FILING EXHIBITS: COURT REPORTER TO FILE WITH CLERK

The court reporter or stenographer shall file with the clerk of the court all exhibits which were admitted in evidence or tendered on bill of exception during the course of any hearing, proceeding, or trial.

RULE 75b. FILED EXHIBITS: WITHDRAWAL

All filed exhibits admitted in evidence or tendered on bill of exception shall, until returned or otherwise disposed of as authorized by Rule 14b, remain at all times in the clerk's office or in the court or in the custody of the clerk except as follows:

(a) The court may by order entered on the minutes allow a filed exhibit to be withdrawn by any party only upon such party's leaving on file a certified, photo, or other reproduced copy of such exhibit. The party withdrawing such exhibit shall pay the costs of such order and copy.

(b) The court reporter or stenographer of the court conducting the hearing, proceedings, or trial in which exhibits are admitted or offered in evidence, shall have the right to withdraw filed exhibits, upon giving the clerk proper receipt therefor, whenever necessary for the court reporter or stenographer to transmit such original exhibits to an appellate court under the provisions of Rule 379 or to otherwise discharge the duties imposed by law upon said court reporter or stenographer.

RULE 76. MAY INSPECT PAPERS

Each attorney at law practicing in any court shall be allowed at all reasonable times to inspect the papers and records relating to any suit or other matter in which he may be interested.

RULE 76a. SEALING COURT RECORDS

1. **Standard for Sealing Court Records**. Court records may not be removed from court files except as permitted by statute or rule. No court order or opinion issued in the adjudication of a case may be sealed. Other court records, as defined in this rule, are presumed to be open to the general public and may be sealed only upon a showing of all of the following:

(a) a specific, serious and substantial interest which clearly outweighs:

(1) this presumption of openness;

(2) any probable adverse effect that sealing will have upon the general public health or safety;

(b) no less restrictive means than sealing records will adequately and effectively protect the specific interest asserted.

2. **Court Records**. For purposes of this rule, court records means:

(a) all documents of any nature filed in connection with any matter before any civil court, except:

(1) documents filed with a court in camera, solely for the purpose of obtaining a ruling on the discoverability of such documents;

(2) documents in court files to which access is otherwise restricted by law;

(3) documents filed in an action originally arising under the Family Code.

(b) settlement agreements not filed of record, excluding all reference to any monetary consideration, that seek to restrict disclosure of information concerning matters that have a probable adverse effect upon the general public health or safety, or the administration of public office, or the operation of government.

(c) discovery, not filed of record, concerning matters that have a probable adverse effect upon the general public health or safety, or the administration of public office, or the operation of government, except discovery in cases originally initiated to preserve bona fide trade secrets or other intangible property rights.

3. **Notice**. Court records may be sealed only upon a party's written motion, which shall be open to public inspection. The movant shall post a public notice at the place where notices for meetings of county governmental bodies are required to be posted, stating: that a hearing will be held in open court on a motion to seal court records in the specific case; that any person may intervene and be heard concerning the sealing of court records; the specific time and place of the hearing; the style and number of the case; a brief but specific description of both the nature of the case and the records which are sought to be sealed; and the identity of the movant. Immediately after posting such notice, the movant shall file a verified copy of the posted notice with the clerk of the court in which the case is pending and with the Clerk of the Supreme Court of Texas.

4. **Hearing**. A hearing, open to the public, on a motion to seal court records shall be held in open court as soon as practicable, but not less than fourteen days after the motion is filed and notice is posted. Any party may participate in the hearing. Non-parties may intervene as a matter of right for the limited purpose of participating in the proceedings, upon payment of the fee required for filing a plea in intervention. The court may inspect records in camera when necessary. The court may determine a motion relating to sealing or unsealing court records in accordance with the procedures prescribed by Rule 120a.

5. **Temporary Sealing Order**. A temporary sealing order may issue upon motion and notice to any parties who have answered in the case pursuant to Rules 21 and 21a upon a showing of compelling need from specific facts shown by affidavit or by verfied petition that immediate and irreparable injury will result to a specific interest of the applicant before notice can be posted and a hearing held as otherwise provided herein. The temporary order shall set the time for the hearing required by paragraph 4 and shall direct that the movant immediately give the public notice required by paragraph 3. The court may modify or withdraw any temporary order upon motion by any party or intervenor, notice to the parties, and hearing conducted as soon as practicable. Issuance of a temporary order shall not reduce in any way the burden of proof of a party requesting sealing at the hearing required by paragraph 4.

6. **Order on Motion to Seal Court Records**. A motion relating to sealing or unsealing court records shall be decided by written order, open to the public, which shall state: the style and number of the case; the specific reasons for finding and concluding whether the showing required by paragraph 1 has been made; the specific portions of court records which are to be sealed; and the time period for which the sealed portions of the court records are to be sealed. The order shall not be included in any judgment or other order but shall be a separate document in the case; however, the failure to comply with this requirement shall not affect its appealability.

7. **Continuing Jurisdiction**. Any person may intervene as a matter of right at any time before or after judgment to seal or unseal court records. A court that issues a sealing order retains continuing jurisdiction to enforce, alter, or vacate that order. An order sealing or unsealing court records shall not be reconsidered on motion of any party or intervenor who had actual notice of the hearing preceding issuance of the order, without first showing changed circumstances materially affecting the order. Such circumstances need not be related to the case in which the order was issued. However, the burden of making the showing required by paragraph 1 shall always be on the party seeking to seal records.

8. **Appeal**. Any order (or portion of an order or judgment) relating to sealing or unsealing court records shall be deemed to be severed from the case and a final judgment which may be appealed by any party

or intervenor who participated in the hearing preceding issuance of such order. The appellate court may abate the appeal and order the trial court to direct that further public notice be given, or to hold further hearings, or to make additional findings.

9. **Application**. Access to documents in court files not defined as court records by this rule remains governed by existing law. This rule does not apply to any court records sealed in an action in which a final judgment has been entered before its effective date. This rule applies to cases already pending on its effective date only with regard to:

(a) all court records filed or exchanged after the effective date;

(b) any motion to alter or vacate an order restricting access to court records, issued before the effective date.

RULE 77. LOST RECORDS AND PAPERS

When any papers or records are lost or destroyed during the pendency of a suit, the parties may, with the approval of the judge, agree in writing on a brief statement of the matters contained therein; or either party may supply such lost records or papers as follows:

a. After three days' notice to the adverse party or his attorney, make written sworn motion before the court stating the loss or destruction of such record or papers, accompanied by certified copies of the originals if obtainable, or by substantial copies thereof.

b. If, upon hearing, the court be satisfied that they are substantial copies of the original, an order shall be made substituting such copies or brief statement for the originals.

c. Such substituted copies or brief statement shall be filed with the clerk, constitute a part of the cause, and have the force and effect of the originals.

SECTION 4. PLEADING

B. Pleadings of Plaintiff

RULE 78. PETITION: ORIGINAL AND SUPPLEMENTAL; INDORSEMENT

The pleading of plaintiff shall consist of an original petition, and such supplemental petitions as may be necessary in the course of pleading by the parties to the suit. The original petition and the supplemental petitions shall be indorsed, so as to show their respective positions in the process of pleading, as "original petition," "plaintiff's first supplemental petition," "plaintiff's second supplemental petition," and so on, to be successively numbered, named, and indorsed.

RULE 78a. CASE INFORMATION SHEET

(a) **Requirement**. A civil case information sheet, in the form promulgated by the Supreme Court of Texas, must accompany the filing of:

(1) an original petition or application; and

(2) a post-judgment petition for modification or motion for enforcement in a case arising under the Family Code.

(b) **Signature**. The civil case information sheet must be signed by the attorney for the party filing the pleading or by the party.

(c) **Enforcement**. The court and clerk must take appropriate measures to enforce this rule. But the clerk may not reject a pleading because the pleading is not accompanied by a civil case information sheet.

(d) **Limitation on Use**. The civil case information sheet is for data collection for statistical and administrative purposes and does not affect any substantive right.

(e) **Applicability**. The civil case information sheet is not required in cases filed in justice courts or small-claims courts, or in cases arising under Title 3 of the Family Code.

Comment: Rule 78a is added to require the submission of a civil case information sheet to collect data for statistical and administrative purposes, see, e.g., TEX. GOV'T CODE § 71.035. A civil case information sheet is not a pleading. Rule 78a is placed with other rules regarding pleadings because civil case information sheets must accompany pleadings.

RULE 79. THE PETITION

The petition shall state the names of the parties and their residences, if known, together with the contents prescribed in Rule 47 above.

RULE 80. PLAINTIFF'S SUPPLEMENTAL PETITION

The plaintiff's supplemental petitions may contain special exceptions, general denials, and the allegations of new matter not before alleged by him, in reply to those which have been alleged by the defendant.

RULE 81. DEFENSIVE MATTERS

When the defendant sets up a counter claim, the plaintiff may plead thereto under rules prescribed for pleadings of defensive matter by the defendant, so far as applicable. Whenever the defendant is required to plead any matter of defense under oath, the plaintiff shall be required to plead such matters under oath when relied on by him.

RULE 82. SPECIAL DEFENSES

The plaintiff need not deny any special matter of defense pleaded by the defendant, but the same shall be regarded as denied unless expressly admitted.

SECTION 4. PLEADING

C. Pleadings of Defendant

RULE 83. ANSWER; ORIGINAL AND SUPPLEMENTAL; INDORSEMENT

The answer of defendant shall consist of an original answer, and such supplemental answers as may be necessary, in the course of pleading by the parties to the suit. The original answer and the supplemental answers shall be indorsed, so as to show their respective positions in the process of pleading, as "original answer," "defendant's first supplemental answer," "defendant's second supplemental answer," and so on, to be successively numbered, named and indorsed.

RULE 84. ANSWER MAY INCLUDE SEVERAL MATTERS

The defendant in his answer may plead as many several matters, whether of law or fact, as he may think necessary for his defense, and which may be pertinent to the cause, and such matters shall be heard in such order as may be directed by the court, special appearance and motion to transfer venue, and the practice thereunder being excepted herefrom.

RULE 85. ORIGINAL ANSWER; CONTENTS

The original answer may consist of motions to transfer venue, pleas to the jurisdiction, in abatement, or any other dilatory pleas; of special exceptions, of general denial, and any defense by way of avoidance or estoppel, and it may present a cross -action, which to that extent will place defendant in the attitude of a plaintiff. Matters in avoidance and estoppel may be stated together, or in several special pleas, each presenting a distinct defense, and numbered so as to admit of separate issues to be formed on them.

RULE 86. MOTION TO TRANSFER VENUE

1. **Time to File**. An objection to improper venue is waived if not made by written motion filed prior to or concurrently with any other plea, pleading or motion except a special appearance motion provided for in Rule 120a. A written consent of the parties to transfer the case to another county may be filed with the clerk of the court at any time. A motion to transfer venue because an impartial trial cannot be had in the county where the action is pending is governed by the provisions of Rule 257.

2. **How to File**. The motion objecting to improper venue may be contained in a separate instrument filed concurrently with or prior to the filing of the movant's first responsive pleading or the motion may be combined with other objections and defenses and included in the movant's first responsive pleading.

3. **Requisites of Motion**. The motion, and any amendments to it, shall state that the action should be transferred to another specified county of proper venue because:

(a) The county where the action is pending is not a proper county; or

(b) Mandatory venue of the action in another county is prescribed by one or more specific statutory provisions which shall be clearly designated or indicated.

The motion shall state the legal and factual basis for the transfer of the action and request transfer of the action and request transfer of the action to a specific county of mandatory or proper venue. Verification of the motion is not required. The motion may be accompanied by supporting affidavits as provided in Rule 87.

4. **Response and Reply**. Except as provided in paragraph 3(a) of Rule 87, a response to the motion to transfer is not required. Verification of a response is not required.

5. **Service**. A copy of any instrument filed pursuant to Rule 86 shall be served in accordance with Rule 21a.

RULE 87. DETERMINATION OF MOTION TO TRANSFER

1. **Consideration of Motion**. The determination of a motion to transfer venue shall be made promptly by the court and such determination must be made in a reasonable time prior to commencement of the trial on the merits. The movant has the duty to request a setting on the motion to transfer. Except on leave of court each party is entitled to at least 45 days notice of a hearing on the motion to transfer.

Except on leave of court, any response or opposing affidavits shall be filed at least 30 days prior to the hearing of the motion to transfer. The movant is not required to file a reply to the response but any reply and any additional affidavits supporting the motion to transfer must, except on leave of court, be filed not later than 7 days prior to the hearing date.

2. **Burden of Establishing Venue**.

(a) *In General*. A party who seeks to maintain venue of the action in a particular county in reliance upon Section 15.001 (General Rule), Sections 15.011-15.017 (Mandatory Venue), Sections 15.031-15.040 (Permissive Venue), or Sections 15.061 and 15.062 (Multiple Claims), Civil Practice and Remedies Code, has the burden to make proof, as provided in paragraph 3 of this rule, that venue is maintainable in the county of suit. A party who seeks to transfer venue of the action to another specified county under Section 15.001 (General Rule), Sections 15.011-15.017 (Mandatory Venue), Sections 15.031-15.040 (Permissive Venue), or Sections 15.061 and 15.062 (Multiple Claims), Civil Practice and Remedies Code, has the burden to make proof, as provided in paragraph 3 of this rule, that venue is maintainable in the county to which transfer is sought. A party who seeks to transfer venue of the action to another specified county under Sections 15.011-15.017, Civil Practice and Remedies Code on the basis that a mandatory venue provision is applicable and controlling has the burden to make proof, as provided in paragraph 3 of this rule, that venue is maintainable in the county to which transfer is sought by virtue of one or more mandatory venue exceptions.

(b) *Cause of Action*. It shall not be necessary for a claimant to prove the merits of a cause of action, but the existence of a cause of action, when pleaded properly, shall be taken as established as alleged by the pleadings. When the defendant specifically denies the venue allegations, the claimant is required, by prima facie proof as provided in paragraph 3 of this rule, to support such pleading that the cause of action taken as established by the pleadings, or a part of such cause of action, accrued in the county of suit. If a defendant seeks transfer to a county where the cause of action or a part thereof accrued, it shall be sufficient for the defendant to plead that if a cause of action exists, then the cause of action or part thereof accrued in the specific county to which transfer is sought, and such allegation shall not constitute an admission that a cause of action in fact exists. But the defendant shall be required to support his pleading by prima facie proof as provided in paragraph 3 of this rule, that, if a cause of action exists, it or a part thereof accrued in the county to which transfer is sought.

(c) *Other Rules*. A motion to transfer venue based on the written consent of the parties shall be determined in accordance with Rule 255. A motion to transfer venue on the basis that an impartial trial cannot be had in the courts where the action is pending shall be determined in accordance with Rules 258 and 259.

3. **Proof**.

(a) *Affidavits and Attachments*. All venue facts, when properly pleaded, shall be taken as true unless specifically denied by the adverse party. When a venue fact is specifically denied, the party pleading the venue fact must make prima facie proof of that venue fact; provided, however, that no party shall ever be required for venue purposes to support prima facie proof the existence of a cause of action or part thereof, and at the hearing the pleadings of the parties shall be taken as conclusive on the issues of existence of a cause of action. Prima facie proof is made when the venue facts are properly pleaded and an affidavit, and any duly proved attachments to the affidavit, are filed fully and specifically setting forth the facts supporting such pleading. Affidavits shall be made on personal knowledge, shall set forth specific facts as would be admissible in evidence, and shall show affirmatively that the affiant is competent to testify.

(b) *The Hearing*. The court shall determine the motion to transfer venue on the basis of the pleadings, any stipulations made by and between the parties and such affidavits and attachments as may be filed by the parties in accordance with the preceding subdivision of this paragraph 3 or of Rule 88.

(c) If a claimant has adequately pleaded and made prima facie proof that venue is proper in the county of suit as provided in subdivision (a) of paragraph 3, then the cause shall not be transferred but shall be retained in the county of suit, unless the motion to transfer is based on the grounds that an impartial trial cannot be had in the county where the action is pending as provided in Rules 257-259 or on an established ground of mandatory venue. A ground of mandatory venue is established when the party relying upon a mandatory exception to the general rule makes prima facie proof as provided in subdivision (a) of paragraph 3 of this rule.

(d) In the event that the parties shall fail to make prima facie proof that the county of suit or the specific county to which transfer is sought is a county of proper venue, then the court may direct the parties to make further proof.

4. **No Jury**. All venue challenges shall be determined by the court without the aid of a jury.

5. **Motion for Rehearing**. If venue has been sustained as against a motion to transfer, or if an action has been transferred to a proper county in response to a motion to transfer, then no further motions to transfer shall be considered regardless of whether the movant was a party to the prior proceedings or was added as a party subsequent to the venue proceedings, unless the motion to transfer is based on the grounds that an impartial trial cannot be had under Rules 257-259 or on the ground of mandatory venue, provided that such claim was not available to the other movant or movants.

Parties who are added subsequently to an action and are precluded by this Rule from having a motion to transfer considered may raise the propriety of venue on appeal, provided that the party has timely filed a motion to transfer.

6. There shall be no interlocutory appeals from such determination.

RULE 88. DISCOVERY AND VENUE

Discovery shall not be abated or otherwise affected by pendency of a motion to transfer venue. Issuing process for witnesses and taking depositions shall not constitute a waiver of a motion to transfer venue, but depositions taken in such case may be read in evidence in any subsequent suit between the same parties concerning the same subject matter in like manner as if taken in such subsequent suit. Deposition transcripts, responses to requests for admission, answers to interrogatories and other discovery products containing information relevant to a determination of proper venue may be considered by the court in making the venue determination when they are attached to, or incorporated by reference in, an affidavit of a party, a witness or an attorney who has knowledge of such discovery.

RULE 89. TRANSFERRED IF MOTION IS SUSTAINED

If a motion to transfer venue is sustained, the cause shall not be dismissed, but the court shall transfer said cause to the proper court; and the costs incurred prior to the time such suit is filed in the court to which said cause is transferred shall be taxed against the plaintiff. The clerk shall make up a transcript of all the orders made in said cause, certifying thereto officially under the seal of the court, and send it with the original papers in the cause to the clerk of the court to which the venue has been changed. Provided, however, if the cause be severable as to parties defendant and shall be ordered transferred as to one or more defendants but not as to all, the clerk, instead of sending the original papers, shall make certified copies of such filed papers as directed by the court and forward the same to the clerk of the court to which the venue has been changed. After the cause has been transferred, as above provided for the clerk of the court to which the cause has been transferred shall mail notification to the plaintiff or his attorney that transfer of the cause has been completed, that the filing fee in the proper court is due and payable within thirty days from the mailing of such notification, and that the case may be dismissed if the filing fee is not timely paid; and if such filing fee is timely paid, the cause will be subject to trial at the expiration of thirty days after the mailing of notification to the parties or their attorneys by the clerk that the papers have been filed in the court to which the cause has been transferred; and if the filing fee is not timely paid, any court of the transferee county to which the case might have been assigned, upon its own motion or the motion of a party, may dismiss the cause without prejudice to the refiling of same.

RULE 90. WAIVER OF DEFECTS IN PLEADING

General demurrers shall not be used. Every defect, omission or fault in a pleading either of form or of substance, which is not specifically pointed out by exception in writing and brought to the attention of the judge in the trial court before the instruction or charge to the jury or, in a non-jury case, before the judgment is signed, shall be deemed to have been waived by the party seeking reversal on such account; provided that this rule shall not apply as to any party against whom default judgment is rendered.

RULE 91. SPECIAL EXCEPTIONS

A special exception shall not only point out the particular pleading excepted to, but it shall also point out intelligibly and with particularity the defect, omission, obscurity, duplicity, generality, or other insufficiency in the allegations in the pleading excepted to.

RULE 91a. DISMISSAL OF BASELESS CAUSES OF ACTION

91a.1 Motion and Grounds.

Except in a case brought under the Family Code or a case governed by Chapter 14 of the Texas Civil Practice and Remedies Code, a party may move to dismiss a cause of action on the grounds that it has no basis in law or fact. A cause of action has no basis in law if the allegations, taken as true, together with inferences reasonably drawn from them do not entitle the claimant to the relief sought. A cause of action has no basis in fact if no reasonable person could believe the facts pleaded.

91a.2 Contents of Motion.

A motion to dismiss must state that it is made pursuant to this rule, must identify each cause of action to which it is addressed, and must state specifically the reasons the cause of action has no basis in law, no basis in fact, or both.

91a.3 Time for Motion and Ruling.

A motion to dismiss must be:

(a) filed within 60 days after the first pleading containing the challenged cause of action is served on the movant;

(b) filed at least 21 days before the motion is heard; and

(c) granted or denied within 45 days after the motion is filed.

91a.4 Time for Response.

Any response to the motion must be filed no later than 7 days before the date of the hearing.

91a.5 Effect of Nonsuit or Amendment; Withdrawal of Motion.

(a) The court may not rule on a motion to dismiss if, at least 3 days before the date of the hearing, the respondent files a nonsuit of the challenged cause of action, or the movant files a withdrawal of the motion.

(b) If the respondent amends the challenged cause of action at least 3 days before the date of the hearing, the movant may, before the date of the hearing, file a withdrawal of the motion or an amended motion directed to the amended cause of action.

(c) Except by agreement of the parties, the court must rule on a motion unless it has been withdrawn or the cause of action has been nonsuited in accordance with (a) or (b). In ruling on the motion, the court must not consider a nonsuit or amendment not filed as permitted by paragraphs (a) or (b).

(d) An amended motion filed in accordance with (b) restarts the time periods in this rule.

91a.6 Hearing; No Evidence Considered.

Each party is entitled to at least 14 days' notice of the hearing on the motion to dismiss. The court may, but is not required to, conduct an oral hearing on the motion. Except as required by 91a.7, the court may not consider evidence in ruling on the motion and must decide the motion based solely on the pleading of the cause of action, together with any pleading exhibits permitted by Rule 59.

91a.7 Award of Costs and Attorney Fees Required.

Except in an action by or against a governmental entity or a public official acting in his or her official capacity or under color of law, the court must award the prevailing party on the motion all costs and reasonable and necessary attorney fees incurred with respect to the challenged cause of action in the trial court. The court must consider evidence regarding costs and fees in determining the award.

91a.8 Effect on Venue and Personal Jurisdiction.

This rule is not an exception to the pleading requirements of Rules 86 and 120a, but a party does not, by filing a motion to dismiss pursuant to this rule or obtaining a ruling on it, waive a special appearance or a motion to transfer venue. By filing a motion to dismiss, a party submits to the Court's jurisdiction only in proceedings on the motion and is bound by the court's ruling, including an award of attorney fees and costs against the party.

91a.9 Dismissal Procedure Cumulative.

This rule is in addition to, and does not supersede or affect, other procedures that authorize dismissal.

Comment to 2013 change: Rule 91a is a new rule implementing section 22.004(g) of the Texas Government Code, which was added in 2011 and calls for rules to provide for the dismissal of causes of action that have no basis in law or fact on motion and without evidence. A motion to dismiss filed under this rule must be ruled on by the court within 45 days unless the motion, pleading, or cause of action is withdrawn, amended, or nonsuited as specified in 91a.5. If an amended motion is filed in response to an amended cause of action in accordance with 91a.5(b), the court must rule on the motion within 45 days of the filing of the amended motion and the respondent must be given an opportunity to respond to the amended motion. The term "hearing" in the rule includes both submission and an oral hearing. Attorney fees awarded under 91a.7 are limited to those associated with challenged cause of action, including fees for preparing or responding to the motion to dismiss.

RULE 92. GENERAL DENIAL

A general denial of matters pleaded by the adverse party which are not required to be denied under oath, shall be sufficient to put the same in issue. When the defendant has pleaded a general denial, and the plaintiff shall afterward amend his pleading, such original denial shall be presumed to extend to all matters subsequently set up by the plaintiff.

When a counterclaim or cross-claim is served upon a party who has made an appearance in the action, the party so served, in the absence of a responsive pleading, shall be deemed to have pleaded a general denial of the counterclaim or cross-claim, but the party shall not be deemed to have waived any special appearance or motion to transfer venue. In all other respects the rules prescribed for pleadings of defensive matter are applicable to answers to counterclaims and cross-claims.

RULE 93. CERTAIN PLEAS TO BE VERIFIED

A pleading setting up any of the following matters, unless the truth of such matters appear of record, shall be verified by affidavit.

1. That the plaintiff has not legal capacity to sue or that the defendant has not legal capacity to be sued.

2. That the plaintiff is not entitled to recover in the capacity in which he sues, or that the defendant is not liable in the capacity in which he is sued.

3. That there is another suit pending in this State between the same parties involving the same claim.

4. That there is a defect of parties, plaintiff or defendant.

5. A denial of partnership as alleged in any pleading as to any party to the suit.

6. That any party alleged in any pleading to be a corporation is not incorporated as alleged.

7. Denial of the execution by himself or by his authority of any instrument in writing, upon which any pleading is founded, in whole or in part and charged to have been executed by him or by his authority, and not alleged to be lost or destroyed. Where such instrument in writing is charged to have been executed by a person then deceased, the affidavit shall be sufficient if it states that the affiant has reason to believe and does believe that such instrument was not executed by the decedent or by his authority. In the absence of such a sworn plea, the instrument shall be received in evidence as fully proved.

8. A denial of the genuineness of the indorsement or assignment of a written instrument upon which suit is brought by an indorsee or assignee and in the absence of such a sworn plea, the indorsement or assignment thereof shall be held as fully proved. The denial required by this subdivision of the rule may be made upon information and belief.

9. That a written instrument upon which a pleading is founded is without consideration, or that the consideration of the same has failed in whole or in part.

10. A denial of an account which is the foundation of the plaintiff's action, and supported by affidavit.

11. That a contract sued upon is usurious. Unless such plea is filed, no evidence of usurious interest as a defense shall be received.

12. That notice and proof of loss or claim for damage has not been given as alleged. Unless such plea is filed such notice and proof shall be presumed and no evidence to the contrary shall be admitted. A denial of such notice or such proof shall be made specifically and with particularity.

13. In the trial of any case appealed to the court from the Industrial Accident Board the following, if pleaded, shall be presumed to be true as pleaded and have been done and filed in legal time and manner, unless denied by verified pleadings:

(a) Notice of injury.

(b) Claim for Compensation.

(c) Award of the Board.

(d) Notice of intention not to abide by the award of the Board.

(e) Filing of suit to set aside the award.

(f) That the insurance company alleged to have been the carrier of the workers' compensation insurance at the time of the alleged injury was in fact the carrier thereof.

(g) That there was good cause for not filing claim with the Industrial Accident Board within the one year period provided by statute.

(h) Wage rate.

A denial of any of the matters set forth in subdivisions (a) or (g) of paragraph 13 may be made on information and belief.

Any such denial may be made in original or amended pleadings; but if in amended pleadings the same must be filed not less than seven days before the case proceeds to trial. In case of such denial the things so denied shall not be presumed to be true, and if essential to the case of the party alleging them, must be proved.

14. That a party plaintiff or defendant is not doing business under an assumed name or trade name as alleged.

15. In the trial of any case brought against an automobile insurance company by an insured under the provisions of an insurance policy in force providing protection against uninsured motorists, an allegation that the insured has complied with all the terms of the policy as a condition precedent to bringing the suit shall be presumed to be true unless denied by verified pleadings which may be upon information and belief.

16. Any other matter required by statute to be pleaded under oath.

RULE 94. AFFIRMATIVE DEFENSES

In pleading to a preceding pleading, a party shall set forth affirmatively accord and satisfaction, arbitration and award, assumption of risk, contributory negligence, discharge in bankruptcy, duress, estoppel, failure of consideration, fraud, illegality, injury by fellow servant, laches, license, payment, release, res judicata, statute of frauds, statute of limitations, waiver, and any other matter constituting an avoidance or affirmative defense. Where the suit is on an insurance contract which insures against certain general hazards, but contains other provisions limiting such general liability, the party suing on such contract shall never be required to allege that the loss was not due to a risk or cause coming within any of the exceptions specified in the contract, nor shall the insurer be allowed to raise such issue unless it shall specifically allege that the loss was due to a risk or cause coming within a particular exception to the general liability; provided that nothing herein shall be construed to change the burden of proof on such issue as it now exists.

RULE 95. PLEAS OF PAYMENT

When a defendant shall desire to prove payment, he shall file with his plea an account stating distinctly the nature of such payment, and the several items thereof; failing to do so, he shall not be allowed to prove the same, unless it be so plainly and particularly described in the plea as to give the plaintiff full notice of the character thereof.

RULE 96. NO DISCONTINUANCE

Where the defendant has filed a counterclaim seeking affirmative relief, the plaintiff shall not be permitted by a discontinuance of his suit, to prejudice the right of the defendant to be heard on such counterclaim.

RULE 97. COUNTERCLAIM AND CROSS-CLAIM

(a) **Compulsory Counterclaims**. A pleading shall state as a counterclaim any claim within the jurisdiction of the court, not the subject of a pending action, which at the time of filing the pleading the pleader has against any opposing party, if it arises out of the transaction or occurrence that is the subject matter of the opposing party's claim and does not require for its adjudication the presence of third parties of whom the court cannot acquire jurisdiction; provided, however, that a judgment based upon a settlement or compromise of a claim of one party to the transaction or occurrence prior to a disposition on the merits shall not operate as a bar to the continuation or assertion of the claims of any other party to the transaction or occurrence unless the latter has consented in writing that said judgment shall operate as a bar.

(b) **Permissive Counterclaims**. A pleading may state as a counterclaim any claim against an opposing party whether or not arising out of the transaction or occurrence that is the subject matter of the opposing party's claim.

(c) **Counterclaim Exceeding Opposing Claim**. A counterclaim may or may not diminish or defeat the recovery sought by the opposing party. It may claim relief exceeding in amount or different in kind from that sought in the pleading of the opposing party, so long as the subject matter is within the jurisdiction of the court.

(d) **Counterclaim Maturing or Acquired After Pleading**. A claim which either matured or was acquired by the pleader after filing his pleading may be presented as a counterclaim by amended pleading.

(e) **Cross-Claim Against Co-Party**. A pleading may state as a cross-claim any claim by one party against a co-party arising out of the transaction or occurrence that is the subject matter either of the original action or of a counterclaim therein. Such cross-claim may include a claim that the party against whom it is asserted is or may be liable to the cross-claimant for all or part of a claim asserted in the action against the cross-claimant.

(f) **Additional Parties**. Persons other than those made parties to the original action may be made parties to a third party action, counterclaim or cross-claim in accordance with the provisions of Rules 38, 39 and 40.

(g) Tort shall not be the subject of set-off or counterclaim against a contractual demand nor a contractual demand against tort unless it arises out of or is incident to or is connected with same.

(h) **Separate Trials; Separate Judgments**. If the court orders separate trials as provided in Rule 174, judgment on a counterclaim or cross-claim may be rendered when the court has jurisdiction so to do, even if the claims of the opposing party have been dismissed or otherwise disposed of.

RULE 98. SUPPLEMENTAL ANSWERS

The defendant's supplemental answers may contain special exceptions, general denial, and the allegations of new matter not before alleged by him, in reply to that which has been alleged by the plaintiff.

SECTION 5. CITATION

RULE 99. ISSUANCE AND FORM OF CITATION

a. **Issuance**. Upon the filing of the petition, the clerk, when requested, shall forthwith issue a citation and deliver the citation as directed by the requesting party. The party requesting citation shall be responsible for obtaining service of the citation and a copy of the petition. Upon request, separate or additional citations shall be issued by the clerk. The clerk must retain a copy of the citation in the court's file.

b. **Form**. The citation shall (1) be styled "The State of Texas," (2) be signed by the clerk under seal of court, (3) contain name and location of the court, (4) show date of filing of the petition, (5) show date of issuance of citation, (6) show file number, (7) show names of parties, (8) be directed to the defendant, (9) show the name and address of attorney for plaintiff, otherwise the address of plaintiff, (10) contain the time within which these rules require the defendant to file a written answer with the clerk who issued citation, (11) contain address of the clerk, and (12) shall notify the defendant that in case of failure of defendant to file and answer, judgment by default may be rendered for the relief demanded in the petition. The citation shall direct the defendant to file a written answer to the plaintiff's petition on or before 10:00 a.m. on the Monday next after the expiration of twenty days after the date of service thereof. The requirement of subsections 10 and 12 of this section shall be in the form set forth in section c of this rule.

c. **Notice**. The citation shall include the following notice to the defendant: "You have been sued. You may employ an attorney. If you or your attorney do not file a written answer with the clerk who issued this citation by 10:00 a.m. on the Monday next following the expiration of twenty days after you were served this citation and petition, a default judgment may be taken against you."

d. **Copies**. The party filing any pleading upon which citation is to be issued and served shall furnish the clerk with a sufficient number of copies thereof for use in serving the parties to be served, and when copies are so furnished the clerk shall make no charge for the copies.

[RULE 100. Repealed effective January 1, 1988]

[RULE 101. Repealed effective January 1, 1988]

[RULE 102. Repealed effective January 1, 1988]

RULE 103. WHO MAY SERVE

Process—including citation and other notices, writs, orders, and other papers issued by the court—may be served anywhere by (1) any sheriff or constable or other person authorized by law, (2) any person authorized by law or by written order of the court who is not less than eighteen years of age, or (3) any person certified under order of the Supreme Court. Service by registered or certified mail and citation by publication must, if requested, be made by the clerk of the court in which the case is pending. But no person who is a party to or interested in the outcome of a suit may serve any process in that suite, and, unless otherwise authorized by a written court order, only a sheriff or constable may serve a citation in an action of forcible entry and detainer, a writ that requires the actual taking of possession of a person, property or thing, or process requiring that an enforcement action be physically enforced by the person delivery the process. The order authorizing a person to serve process may be made without written motion and no fee may be imposed for issuance of such order.

[RULE 104. Repealed effective January 1, 1988]

RULE 105. DUTY OF OFFICER OR PERSON RECEIVING

The officer or authorized person to whom process is delivered shall endorse thereon the day and hour on which he received it, and shall execute and return the same without delay.

RULE 106. METHOD OF SERVICE

(a) Unless the citation or an order of the court otherwise directs, the citation shall be served by any person authorized by Rule 103 by

(1) delivering to the defendant, in person, a true copy of the citation with the date of delivery endorsed thereon with a copy of the petition attached thereto, or

(2) mailing to the defendant by registered or certified mail, return receipt requested, a true copy of the citation with a copy of the petition attached thereto.

(b) Upon motion supported by affidavit stating the location of the defendant's usual place of business or usual place of abode or other place where the defendant can probably be found and stating specifically the facts showing that service has been attempted under either (a)(1) or (a)(2) at the location named in such affidavit but has not been successful, the court may authorize service

(1) by leaving a true copy of the citation, with a copy of the petition attached, with anyone over sixteen years of age at the location specified in such affidavit, or

(2) in any other manner that the affidavit or other evidence before the court shows will be reasonably effective to give the defendant notice of the suit.

RULE 107. RETURN OF SERVICE

(a) The officer or authorized person executing the citation must complete a return of service. The return may, but need not, be endorsed on or attached to the citation.

(b) The return, together with any documents to which it is attached, must include the following information:

(1) the cause number and case name;

(2) the court in which the case is filed;

(3) a description of what was served;

(4) the date and time the process was received for service;

(5) the person or entity served;

(6) the address served;

(7) the date of service or attempted service;

(8) the manner of delivery of service or attempted service;

(9) the name of the person who served or attempted to serve the process;

(10) if the person named in (9) is a process server certified under order of the Supreme Court, his or her identification number and the expiration date of his or her certification; and

(11) any other information required by rule or law.

(c) When the citation was served by registered or certified mail as authorized by Rule 106, the return by the officer or authorized person must also contain the return receipt with the addressee's signature.

(d) When the officer or authorized person has not served the citation, the return shall show the diligence used by the officer or authorized person to execute the same and the cause of failure to execute it, and where the defendant is to be found, if ascertainable.

(e) The officer or authorized person who serves or attempts to serve a citation must sign the return. If the return is signed by a person other than a sheriff, constable, or the clerk of the court, the return must either be verified or be signed under penalty of perjury. A return signed under penalty of perjury must contain the statement below in substantially the following form:

"My name is _____, my date of birth is _____, and (First) (Middle) (Last)

my address is _____,_____,_____, _____, and (Street) (City) (State) (Zip Code)

_____. I declare under penalty of perjury that the foregoing is true and correct. (Country)

Executed in _____County, State of _____, on the _____ day of _____, (Month)

_____. Year

_____." (Declarant)

(f) Where citation is executed by an alternative method as authorized by Rule 106, proof of service shall be made in the manner ordered by the court.

(g) The return and any document to which it is attached must be filed with the court and may be filed electronically or by facsimile, if those methods of filing are available.

(h) No default judgment shall be granted in any cause until proof of service as provided by this rule or by Rules 108 or 108a, or as ordered by the court in the event citation is executed by an alternative method under Rule 106, shall have been on file with the clerk of the court ten days, exclusive of the day of filing and the day of judgment.

RULE 108. SERVICE IN ANOTHER STATE

Where the defendant is absent from the State, or is a nonresident of the State, the form of notice to such defendant of the institution of the suit shall be the same as prescribed for citation to a resident defendant; and such notice may be served by any disinterested person who is not less than eighteen years of age, in the same manner as provided in Rule 106 hereof. The return of service in such cases shall be completed in accordance with Rule 107. A defendant served with such notice shall be required to appear and answer in the same manner and time and under the same penalties as if he had been personally served with a citation within this State to the full extent that he may be required to appear and answer under the Constitution of the United States in an action either in rem or in personam.

RULE 108a. SERVICE OF PROCESS IN FOREIGN COUNTRIES

(1) **Manner.** Service of process may be effected upon a party in a foreign country if service of the citation and petition is made:

(a) in the manner prescribed by the law of the foreign country for service in that country in an action in any of its courts of general jurisdiction; or

(b) as directed by the foreign authority in response to a letter rogatory or a letter of request; or

(c) in the manner provided by Rule 106; or

(d) pursuant to the terms and provisions of any applicable treaty or convention; or

(e) by diplomatic or consular officials when authorized by the United States Department of State; or

(f) by any other means directed by the court that is not prohibited by the law of the country where service is to be made.

The method for service of process in a foreign country must be reasonably calculated, under all of the circumstances, to give actual notice of the proceedings to the defendant in time to answer and defend. A defendant served with process under this rule shall be required to appear and answer in the same manner and time and under the same penalties as if he had been personally served with citation within this state to the full extent that he may be required to appear and answer under the Constitution of the United States or under any applicable convention or treaty in an action either in rem or in personam.

(2) **Return**. Proof of service may be made as prescribed by the law of the foreign country, by order of the court, by Rule 107, or by a method provided in any applicable treaty or convention.

RULE 109. CITATION BY PUBLICATION

When a party to a suit, his agent or attorney, shall make oath that the residence of any party defendant is unknown to affiant, and to such party when the affidavit is made by his agent or attorney, or that such defendant is a transient person, and that after due diligence such party and the affiant have been unable to locate the whereabouts of such defendant, or that such defendant is absent from or is a nonresident of the State, and that the party applying for the citation has attempted to obtain personal service of nonresident notice as provided for in Rule 108, but has been unable to do so, the clerk shall issue citation for such defendant for service by publication. In such cases it shall be the duty of the court trying the case to inquire into the sufficiency of the diligence exercised in attempting to ascertain the residence or whereabouts of the defendant or to obtain service of nonresident notice, as the case may be, before granting any judgment on such service.

RULE 109a. OTHER SUBSTITUTED SERVICE

Whenever citation by publication is authorized, the court may, on motion, prescribe a different method of substituted service, if the court finds, and so recites in its order, that the method so prescribed would be as likely as publication to give defendant actual notice. When such method of substituted service is authorized, the return of the officer executing the citation shall state particularly the manner in which service is accomplished, and shall attach any return receipt, returned mail, or other evidence showing the result of such service. Failure of defendant to respond to such citation shall not render the service invalid. When such substituted service has been obtained and the defendant has not appeared, the provisions of Rules 244 and 329 shall apply as if citation had been served by publication.

RULE 110. EFFECT OF RULES ON OTHER STATUTES

Where by statute or these rules citation by publication is authorized and the statute or rules do not specify the requisites of such citation or the method of service thereof, or where they direct that such citation be issued or served as in other civil actions, the provisions of these rules shall govern. Where, however, the statute authorizing citation by publication provides expressly for requisites of such citation or service thereof, or both, differing from the provisions of Rules 114, 115, and 116, these rules shall not govern, but the special statutory procedure shall continue in force; provided, however, that Rule 117a shall control with respect to citation in tax suits.

RULE 111. CITATION BY PUBLICATION IN ACTION AGAINST UNKNOWN HEIRS OR STOCKHOLDERS OF DEFUNCT CORPORATIONS

If the plaintiff, his agent, or attorney, shall make oath that the names of the heirs or stockholders against whom an action is authorized by Section 17.004, Civil Practice and Remedies Code, are unknown to the affiant, the clerk shall issue a citation for service by publication. Such citation shall be addressed to the defendants by a concise description of their classification, as "the Unknown Heirs of A.B., deceased," or "Unknown Stockholders of _____ Corporation," as the case may be, and shall contain the other requisites prescribed in Rules 114 and 115 and shall be served as provided by Rule 116.

RULE 112. PARTIES TO ACTIONS AGAINST UNKNOWN OWNERS OR CLAIMANTS OF INTEREST IN LAND

In suits authorized by Section 17.005, Civil Practice and Remedies Code, all persons claiming under such conveyance whose names are known to plaintiff shall be made parties by name and cited to appear, in the manner now provided by law as in other suits; all other persons claiming any interest in such land under such conveyance may be made parties to the suit and cited by publication under the designation "all persons claiming any title or interest in land under deed heretofore given to _____ of _____ as grantee" (inserting in the blanks the name and residence of grantee as given in such conveyance). It shall be permissible to join in one suit all persons claiming under two or more conveyances affecting title to the same tract of land.

RULE 113. CITATION BY PUBLICATION IN ACTIONS AGAINST UNKNOWN OWNERS OR CLAIMANTS OF INTEREST IN LAND

In suits authorized by Section 17.005, Civil Practice and Remedies Code, plaintiff, his agent or attorney shall make and file with the clerk of the court an affidavit, stating

(a) the name of the grantee as set out in the conveyance constituting source of title of defendants, and

(b) stating that affiant does not know the names of any persons claiming title or interest under such conveyance other than as stated in plaintiff's petition and

(c) if the conveyance is to a company or association name as grantee, further stating whether grantee is incorporated or unincorporated, if such fact is known, and if such fact is unknown, so stating.

Said clerk shall thereupon issue a citation for service upon all persons claiming any title or interest in such land under such conveyance. The citation in such cases shall contain the requisites and be served in the manner provided in Rules 114, 115 and 116.

RULE 114. CITATION BY PUBLICATION; REQUISITES

Where citation by publication is authorized by these rules, the citation shall contain the requisites prescribed by Rules 15 and 99, in so far as they are not inconsistent herewith, provided that no copy of the plaintiff's petition shall accompany this citation, and the citation shall be styled "The State of Texas" and shall be directed to the defendant or defendants by name, if their names are known, or to the defendant or defendants as designated in the petition, if unknown, or such other classification as may be fixed by any statute or by these rules. Where there are two or more defendants or classes of defendants to be served by publication, the citation may be directed to all of them by name and classification, so that service may be completed by publication of the one citation for the required number of times. The citation shall contain the names of the parties, a brief statement of the nature of the suit (which need not contain the details and particulars of the claim) a description of any property involved and of the interest of the named or unknown defendant or defendants, and, where the suit involves land, the requisites of Rule 115. If issued from the district or county court, the citation shall command such parties to appear and answer at or before 10 o'clock a.m. of the first Monday after the expiration of 42 days from the date of issuance thereof, specifying the day of the week, the day of the month, and the time of day the defendant is required to answer. If issued from the justice of the peace court, such citation shall command such parties to appear and answer on or before the first day of the first term of court which convenes after the expiration of 42 days from the date of issue thereof, specifying the day of the week, and the day of the month, that such term will meet.

RULE 115. FORM OF PUBLISHED CITATION IN ACTIONS INVOLVING LAND

In citations by publication involving land, it shall be sufficient in making the brief statement of the claim in such citation to state the kind of suit, the number of acres of land involved in the suit, or the number of the lot and block, or any other plat description that may be of record if the land is situated in a city or town, the survey on which and the county in which the land is situated, and any special pleas which are relied upon in such suit.

RULE 116. SERVICE OF CITATION BY PUBLICATION

The citation, when issued, shall be served by the sheriff or any constable of any county of the State of Texas or by the clerk of the court in which the case is pending, by having the same published once each week for four (4) consecutive weeks, the first publication to be at least twenty- eight (28) days before the return day of the citation. In all suits which do not involve the title to land or the partition of real estate, such publication shall be made in the county where the suit is pending, if there be a newspaper published in said county, but if not, then in an adjoining county where a newspaper is published. In all suits which involve the title to land or partition of real estate, such publication shall be made in the county where the land, or a portion thereof, is situated, if there be a newspaper in such county, but if not, then in an adjoining county to the county where the land or a part thereof is situated, where a newspaper is published.

RULE 117. RETURN OF CITATION BY PUBLICATION

The return of the officer executing such citation shall show how and when the citation was executed, specifying the dates of such publication, be signed by him officially and shall be accompanied by a printed copy of such publication.

RULE 117a. CITATION IN SUITS FOR DELINQUENT AD VALOREM TAXES

In all suits for collection of delinquent ad valorem taxes, the rules of civil procedure governing issuance and service of citation shall control the issuance and service of citation therein, except as herein otherwise specially provided.

1. **Personal Service: Owner and Residence Known, Within State**. Where any defendant in a tax suit is a resident of the State of Texas and is not subject to citation by publication under subdivision 3 below, the process shall conform substantially to the form hereinafter set out for personal service and shall contain the essential elements and be served and returned and otherwise regulated by the provisions of Rules 99 to 107, inclusive.

2. **Personal Service: Owner and Residence Known, Out of State**. Where any such defendant is absent from the State or is a nonresident of the State and is not subject to citation by publication under subdivision 3 below, the process shall conform substantially to the form hereinafter set out for personal service and shall contain the essential elements and be served and returned and otherwise regulated by the provisions of Rule 108.

3. **Service by Publication: Nonresident, Absent From State, Transient, Name Unknown, Residence Unknown, Owner Unknown, Heirs Unknown, Corporate Officers, Trustees, Receivers or Stockholders Unknown, Any Other Unknown Persons Owing or Claiming or Having an Interest**. Where any defendant in a tax suit is a nonresident of the State, or is absent from the State, or is a transient person, or the name or the residence of any owner of any interest in any property upon which a tax lien is sought to be foreclosed, is unknown to the attorney requesting the issuance of process or filing the suit for the taxing unit, and such attorney shall make affidavit that such defendant is a nonresident of the State, or is absent from the State, or is a transient person, or that the name or residence of such owner is unknown and cannot be ascertained after diligent inquiry, each such person in every such class above mentioned, together with any and all other persons, including adverse claimants, owning or claiming or having any legal or equitable interest in or lien upon such property, may be cited by publication. All unknown owners of any interest in any property upon which any taxing unit seeks to foreclose a lien for taxes, including stockholders of corporations - defunct or otherwise - their successors, heirs, and assigns, may be joined in such suit under the designation of "unknown owners" and citation be had upon them as such; provided, however, that record owners of such property or of any apparent interest therein, including, without limitation, record lien holders, shall not be included in the designation of "unknown owners"; and provided further that where any record owner has rendered the property involved within five years before the tax suit is filed, citation on such record owner may not be had by publication or posting unless citation for personal service has been issued as to such record owner, with a notation thereon setting forth the same address as is contained on the rendition sheet made within such five years, and the sheriff or other person to whom citation has been delivered makes his return thereon that he is unable to locate the defendant. Where any attorney filing a tax suit for a taxing unit, or requesting the issance of process in such suit, shall make affidavit that a corporation is the record owner of any interest in any property upon which a tax lien is sought to be foreclosed, and that he does not know, and after diligent inquiry has been unable to ascertain, the location of the place of business, if any, of such corporation, or the name or place of residence of any officer of such corporation upon whom

personal service may be had, such corporation may be cited by publication as herein provided. All defendants of the classes enumerated above may be joined in the same citation by publication.

An affidavit which complies with the foregoing requirements therefor shall be sufficient basis for the citation above mentioned in connection with it but shall be held to be made upon the criminal responsibility of affiant.

Such citation by publication shall be directed to the defendants by names or by designation as hereinabove provided, and shall be issued and signed by the clerk of the court in which such tax suit is pending. It shall be sufficient if it states the file number and style of the case, the date of the filing of the petition, the names of all parties by name or by designation as hereinabove provided, and the court in which the suit is pending; shall command such parties to appear and defend such suit at or before 10 o'clock a.m. of the first Monday after the expiration of forty-two days from the date of the issuance thereof, specifying such date when such parties are required to answer; shall state the place of holding the court, the nature of the suit, and the date of the issuance of the citation; and shall be signed and sealed by the clerk.

The citation shall be published in the English language one time a week for two weeks in some newspaper published in the county in which the property is located, which newspaper must have been in general circulation for at least one year immediately prior to the first publication and shall in every respect answer the requirements of the law applicable to newspapers which are employed for such a purpose, the first publication to be not less than twenty-eight days prior to the return day fixed in the citation; and the affidavit of the editor or publisher of the newspaper giving the date of publication, together with a printed copy of the citation as published, shall constitute sufficient proof of due publication when returned and filed in court. If there is no newspaper published in the county, then the publication may be made in a newspaper in an adjoining county, which newspaper shall in every respect answer the requirements of the law applicable to newspapers which are employed for such a purpose. The maximum fee for publishing the citation shall be the lowest published word or line rate of that newspaper for classified advertising. If the publication of the citation cannot be had for this fee, chargeable as costs and payable upon sale of the property, as provided by law, and this fact is supported by the affidavit of the attorney for the plaintiff or the attorney requesting the issuance of the process, then service of the citation may be made by posting a copy at the courthouse door of the county in which the suit is pending, the citation to be posted at least twenty-eight days prior to the return day fixed in the citation. Proof of the posting of the citation shall be made by affidavit of the attorney for the plaintiff, or of the person posting it. When citation is served as here provided it shall be sufficient, and no other form of citation or notice to the named defendants therein shall be necessary.

4. **Citation in Tax Suits: General Provisions**. Any process authorized by this rule may issue jointly in behalf of all taxing units who are plaintiffs or intervenors in any tax suit. The statement of the nature of the suit, to be set out in the citation, shall be sufficient if it contains a brief general description of the property upon which the taxes are due and the amount of such taxes, exclusive of interest, penalties, and costs, and shall state, in substance, that in such suit the plaintiff and all other taxing units who may set up their claims therein seek recovery of the delinquent ad valorem taxes due on said property, and the (establishment and foreclosure) of liens, if any, securing the payment of same, as provided by law; that in addition to the taxes all interest, penalties, and costs allowed by law up to and including the day of judgment are included in the suit; and that all parties to the suit, including plaintiff, defendants, and intervenors, shall take notice that claims for any taxes on said property becoming delinquent subsequent to the filing of the suit and up to the day of judgment, together with all interest, penalties, and costs allowed by law thereon, may, upon request therefore, be recovered therein without further citation or notice to any parties thereto. Such citation need not be accompanied by a copy of plaintiff's petition and no such copy need be served. Such citation shall also show the names of all taxing units which assess and collect taxes on said property not made parties to such suit, and shall contain, in substance, a recitation that each party to such suit shall take notice of, and plead and answer to, all claims and pleadings then on file or thereafter filed in said cause by all other parties therein, or who may intervene therein and set up their respective tax claims against said property. After citation or notice has been given on behalf of any plaintiff or

intervenor taxing unit, the court shall have jurisdiction to hear and determine the tax claims of all taxing units who are parties plaintiff, intervenor or defendant at the time such process is issued and of all taxing units intervening after such process is issued, not only for the taxes, interest, penalties, and costs which may be due on said property at the time the suit is filed, but those becoming delinquent thereon at any time thereafter up to and including the day of judgment, without the necessity of further citation or notice to any party to said suit; and any taxing unit having a tax claim against said property may, by answer or intervention, set up and have determined its tax claim without the necessity of further citation or notice to any parties to such suit.

5. **Form of Citation by Publication or Posting**. The form of citation by publication or posting shall be sufficient if it is in substantially the following form, with proper changes to make the same applicable to personal property, where necessary, and if the suit includes or is for the recovery of taxes assessed on personal property, a general description of such personal property shall be sufficient:

THE STATE OF TEXAS   )

COUNTY OF _____)

In the name and by the authority of the State of Texas

Notice is hereby given as follows:

To _____

_____

and any and all other persons, including adverse claimants, owning or having or claiming any legal or equitable interest in or lien upon the following described property delinquent to Plaintiff herein, for taxes, to-wit:

_____

_____

Which said property is delinquent to Plaintiff for taxes in the following amounts:

$ _____, exclusive of interest, penalties, and costs, and there is included in this suit in addition to the taxes all said interest, penalties, and costs thereon, allowed by law up to and including the day of judgment herein.

You are hereby notified that suit has been brought by _____ as Plaintiffs, against

_____ as Defendants, by petition filed on the _____ day of

_____, 19_____, in a certain suit styled

_____ v.

_____ for collection of the taxes on said property and that said suit is now pending in the District Court of _____ County, Texas,

_____ Judicial District, and the file number of said suit is

_____, that the names of all taxing units which assess and collect taxes on the property hereinabove described, not made parties to this suit, are _____.

Plaintiff and all other taxing units who may set up their tax claims herein seek recovery of delinquent ad valorem taxes on the property hereinabove described, and in addition to the taxes all interest, penalties, and costs allowed by law thereon up to and including the day of judgment herein, and the establishment and foreclosure of liens, if any, securing the payment of same, as provided by law.

All parties to this suit, including plaintiff, defendants, and intervenors, shall take notice that claims not only for any taxes which were delinquent on said property at the time this suit was filed but all taxes becoming delinquent thereon at any time thereafter up to the day of judgment, including all interest, penalties, and costs allowed by law thereon, may, upon request therefor, be recovered herein without further citation or notice to any parties herein, and all said parties shall take notice of and plead and answer to all claims and pleadings now on file and which may hereafter be filed in said cause by all other parties herein, and all of those taxing units above named who may intervene herein and set up their respective tax claims against said property.

You are hereby commanded to appear and defend such suit on the first Monday after the expiration of forty-two (42) days from and after the date of issuance hereof, the same being the

_____ day of _____, A.D., 19_____ (which is the return day of such citation), before the honorable District Court of _____ County, Texas, to be held at the courthouse thereof, then and there to show cause why judgment shall not be rendered for such taxes, penalties, interest, and costs, and condemning said property and ordering foreclosure of the constitutional and statutory tax liens thereon for taxes due the plaintiff and the taxing units parties hereto, and those who may intervene herein, together with all interest, penalties, and costs allowed by law up to and including the day of judgment herein, and all costs of this suit.

Issued and given under my hand and seal of said court in the City of _____,

_____ County, Texas, this _____ day of _____, A.D., 19_____.

_____

Clerk of the District Court.

_____ County, Texas,

_____ Judicial District.

6. **Form of Citation by Personal Service in or out of State**. The form of citation for personal service shall be sufficient if it is in substantially the following form, with proper changes to make the same applicable to personal property, where necessary, and if the suit includes or is for the recovery of taxes assessed on personal property, a general description of such personal property shall be sufficient:

THE STATE OF TEXAS

To _____, Defendant,

GREETING:

YOU ARE HEREBY COMMANDED to appear and answer before the Honorable District Court,

_____ Judicial District, _____ County, Texas, at the Courthouse of said county in _____, Texas, at or before 10 o'clock a.m. of the Monday next after the expiration of 20 days from the date of service of this citation, then and there to answer the petition of _____, Plaintiff, filed in said Court on the _____ day of

_____, A.D., 19_____, against _____, Defendant, said

suit being number _____ on the docket of said Court, the nature of which demand is a suit to collect delinquent ad valorem taxes on the property hereinafter described.

The amount of taxes due Plaintiff, exclusive of interest, penalties, and costs, is the sum of $_____, said property being described as follows, to-wit:

_____

_____

The names of all taxing units which assess and collect taxes on said property, not made parties to this suit, are: _____

Plaintiff and all other taxing units who may set up their tax claims herein seek recovery of delinquent ad valorem taxes on the property hereinabove described, and in addition to the taxes all interest, penalties, and costs allowed by law thereon up to and including the day of judgment herein, and the establishment and foreclosure of liens securing the payment of same, as provided by law.

All parties to this suit, including plaintiff, defendants, and intervenors, shall take notice that claims not only for any taxes which were delinquent on said property at the time this suit was filed but all taxes becoming delinquent thereon at any time thereafter up to the day of judgment, including all interest, penalties, and costs allowed by law thereon, may, upon request therefor, be recovered herein without further citation or notice to any parties herein, and all said parties shall take notice of and plead and answer to all claims and pleadings now on file and which may hereafter be filed in this cause by all other parties hereto, and by all of those taxing units above named, who may intervene herein and set up their respective tax claims against said property.

If this citation is not served within 90 days after the date of its issuance, it shall be returned unserved.

The officer executing this return shall promptly serve the same according to the requirements of law and the mandates hereof and make due return as the law directs.

Issued and given under my hand and seal of said Court at _____, Texas, this the

_____ day of _____, A.D., 19_____.

_____

Clerk of the District Court of

_____ County, Texas. By _____, Deputy.

_____

RULE 118. AMENDMENT

At any time in its discretion and upon such notice and on such terms as it deems just, the court may allow any process or proof of service thereof to be amended, unless it clearly appears that material prejudice would result to the substantial rights of the party against whom the process issued.

RULE 119. ACCEPTANCE OF SERVICE

The defendant may accept service of process, or waive the issuance or service thereof by a written memorandum signed by him, or by his duly authorized agent or attorney, after suit is brought, sworn to before a proper officer other than an attorney in the case, and filed among the papers of the cause, and such waiver or acceptance shall have the same force and effect as if the citation had been issued and served as provided by law. The party signing such memorandum shall be delivered a copy of plaintiff's petition, and the receipt of the same shall be acknowledged in such memorandum. In every divorce action such memorandum shall also include the defendant's mailing address.

RULE 119a. COPY OF DECREE

The district clerk shall forthwith mail a certified copy of the final divorce decree or order of dismissal to the party signing a memorandum waiving issuance or service of process. Such divorce decree or order of dismissal shall be mailed to the signer of the memorandum at the address stated in such memorandum or to the office of his attorney of record.

RULE 120. ENTERING APPEARANCE

The defendant may, in person, or by attorney, or by his duly authorized agent, enter an appearance in open court. Such appearance shall be noted by the judge upon his docket and entered in the minutes, and shall have the same force and effect as if the citation had been duly issued and served as provided by law.

RULE 120a. SPECIAL APPEARANCE

1. Notwithstanding the provisions of Rules 121, 122 and 123, a special appearance may be made by any party either in person or by attorney for the purpose of objecting to the jurisdiction of the court over the person or property of the defendant on the ground that such party or property is not amenable to process issued by the courts of this State. A special appearance may be made as to an entire proceeding or as to any severable claim involved therein. Such special appearance shall be made by sworn motion filed prior to motion to transfer venue or any other plea, pleading or motion; provided however, that a motion to transfer venue and any other plea, pleading, or motion may be contained in the same instrument or filed subsequent thereto without waiver of such special appearance; and may be amended to cure defects. The issuance of process for witnesses, the taking of depositions, the serving of requests for admissions, and the use of discovery processes, shall not constitute a waiver of such special appearance. Every appearance, prior to judgment, not in compliance with this rule is a general appearance.

2. Any motion to challenge the jurisdiction provided for herein shall be heard and determined before a motion to transfer venue or any other plea or pleading may be heard. No determination of any issue of fact in connection with the objection to jurisdiction is a determination of the merits of the case or any aspect thereof.

3. The court shall determine the special appearance on the basis of the pleadings, any stipulations made by and between the parties, such affidavits and attachments as may be filed by the parties, the results of discovery processes, and any oral testimony. The affidavits, if any, shall be served at least seven days before the hearing, shall be made on personal knowledge, shall set forth specific facts as would be admissible in evidence, and shall show affirmatively that the affiant is competent to testify.

Should it appear from the affidavits of a party opposing the motion that he cannot for reasons stated present by affidavit facts essential to justify his opposition, the court may order a continuance to permit affidavits to be obtained or depositions to be taken or discovery to be had or may make such other order as is just.

Should it appear to the satisfaction of the court at any time that any of such affidavits are presented in violation of Rule 13, the court shall impose sanctions in accordance with that rule.

4. If the court sustains the objection to jurisdiction, an appropriate order shall be entered. If the objection to jurisdiction is overruled, the objecting party may thereafter appear generally for any purpose. Any such special appearance or such general appearance shall not be deemed a waiver of the objection to jurisdiction when the objecting party or subject matter is not amenable to process issued by the courts of this State.

RULE 121. ANSWER IS APPEARANCE

An answer shall constitute an appearance of the defendant so as to dispense with the necessity for the issuance or service of citation upon him.

RULE 122. CONSTRUCTIVE APPEARANCE

If the citation or service thereof is quashed on motion of the defendant, such defendant shall be deemed to have entered his appearance at ten o'clock a.m. on the Monday next after the expiration of twenty (20) days after the day on which the citation or service is quashed, and such defendant shall be deemed to have been duly served so as to require him to appear and answer at that time, and if he fails to do so, judgment by default may be rendered against him.

RULE 123. REVERSAL OF JUDGMENT

Where the judgment is reversed on appeal or writ of error for the want of service, or because of defective service of process, no new citation shall be issued or served, but the defendant shall be presumed to have entered his appearance to the term of the court at which the mandate shall be filed.

RULE 124. NO JUDGMENT WITHOUT SERVICE

In no case shall judgment be rendered against any defendant unless upon service, or acceptance or waiver of process, or upon an appearance by the defendant, as prescribed in these rules, except where otherwise expressly provided by law or these rules.

When a party asserts a counterclaim or a cross-claim against another party who has entered an appearance, the claim may be served in any manner prescribed for service of citation or as provided in Rule 21(a).

SECTION 6. COSTS AND SECURITY THEREFOR

RULE 125. PARTIES RESPONSIBLE

Each party to a suit shall be liable to the officers of the court for all costs incurred by himself.

RULE 126. FEE FOR SERVICE OF PROCESS IN A COUNTY OTHER THAN THE COUNTY OF SUIT

(a) **General Rule: Fee Due Before Service**. A sheriff or constable may require payment before serving process in a case pending in a county other than the county in which the sheriff or constable is an officer.

(b) **Exception: Statement of Inability to Afford Payment of Court Costs Filed**. If a Statement of Inability to Afford Payment of Court Costs has been filed in a case in which the declarant requests service of process in a county other than in the county of suit, the clerk must indicate on the document to be served that a Statement of Inability to Afford Payment of Court Costs has been filed. The sheriff or constable must execute the service without demanding payment.

RULE 127. PARTIES LIABLE FOR OTHER COSTS

Each party to a suit shall be liable for all costs incurred by him. If the costs cannot be collected from the party against whom they have been judged, execution may issue against any party in such suit for the amount of costs incurred by such party, but no more.

[RULE 128. Repealed effective April 1, 1984]

RULE 129. HOW COSTS COLLECTED

If any party responsible for costs fails or refuses to pay the same within ten days after demand for payment, the clerk or justice of the peace may make certified copy of the bill of costs then due, and place the same in the hands of the sheriff or constable for collection. All taxes imposed on law proceedings shall be included in the bill of costs. Such certified bill of costs shall have the force and effect of an execution. The removal of a case by appeal shall not prevent the issuance of an execution for costs.

RULE 130. OFFICER TO LEVY

The sheriff or constable upon demand and failure to pay said bill of costs, may levy upon a sufficient amount of property of the person from whom said costs are due to satisfy the same, and sell such property as under execution. Where such party is not a resident of the county where such suit is pending, the payment of such costs may be demanded of his attorney of record; and neither the clerk nor justice of the peace shall be allowed to charge any fee for making out such certified bill of costs, unless he is compelled to make a levy.

RULE 131. SUCCESSFUL PARTY TO RECOVER

The successful party to a suit shall recover of his adversary all costs incurred therein, except where otherwise provided.

[RULE 132. Repealed effective April 1, 1984]

RULE 133. COSTS OF MOTION

The court may give or refuse costs on motions at its discretion, except where otherwise provided by law or these rules.

[RULE 134. Repealed effective April 1, 1984]

[RULE 135. Repealed effective April 1, 1984]

RULE 136. DEMAND REDUCED BY PAYMENTS

Where the plaintiff's demand is reduced by payment to an amount which would not have been within the jurisdiction of the court, the defendant shall recover his costs.

RULE 137. IN ASSAULT AND BATTERY, ETC.

In civil actions for assault and battery, slander and defamation of character, if the verdict or judgment shall be for the plaintiff, but for less than twenty dollars, the plaintiff shall not recover his costs, but each party shall be taxed with the costs incurred by him in such suit.

RULE 138. COST OF NEW TRIALS

The costs of new trials may either abide the result of the suit or may be taxed against the party to whom the new trial is granted, as the court may adjudge when he grants such new trial.

RULE 139. ON APPEAL AND CERTIORARI

When a case is appealed, if the judgment of the higher court be against the appellant, but for less amount than the original judgment, such party shall recover the costs of the higher court but shall be adjudged to pay the costs of the court below; if the judgment be against him for the same or a greater amount than in the court below, the adverse party shall recover the costs of both courts. If the judgment of the court above be in favor of the party appealing and for more than the original judgment, such party shall recover the costs of both courts; if the judgment be in his favor, but for the same or a less amount than in the court below, he shall recover the costs of the court below, and pay the costs of the court above.

RULE 140. NO FEE FOR COPY

No fee for a copy of a paper not required by law or these rules to be copied shall be taxed in the bill of costs.

RULE 141. COURT MAY OTHERWISE ADJUDGE COSTS

The court may, for good cause, to be stated on the record, adjudge the costs otherwise than as provided by law or these rules.

RULE 142. SECURITY FOR COSTS

The clerk shall require from the plaintiff fees for services rendered before issuing any process unless filing is requested pursuant to Rule 145 of these rules.

RULE 143. RULE FOR COSTS

A party seeking affirmative relief may be ruled to give security for costs at any time before final judgment, upon motion of any party, or any officer of the court interested in the costs accruing in such suit, or by the court upon its own motion. If such rule be entered against any party and he failed to comply therewith on or before twenty (20) days after notice that such rule has been entered, the claim for affirmative relief of such party shall be dismissed.

RULE 143a. COSTS ON APPEAL TO COUNTY COURT

If the appellant fails to pay the costs on appeal from a judgment of a justice of the peace or small claims court within twenty (20) days after being notified to do so by the county clerk, the appeal shall be deemed not perfected and the county clerk shall return all papers in said cause to the justice of the peace having original jurisdiction and the justice of the peace shall proceed as though no appeal had been attempted.

RULE 144. JUDGMENT ON COST BOND

All bonds given as security for costs shall authorize judgment against all the obligors in such bond for the said costs, to be entered in the final judgment of the cause.

RULE 145. PAYMENT OF COSTS NOT REQUIRED

(a) **General Rule**. A party who files a Statement of Inability to Afford Payment of Court Costs cannot be required to pay costs except by order of the court as provided by this rule. After the Statement is filed, the clerk must docket the case, issue citation, and provide any other service that is ordinarily provided to a party. The Statement must either be sworn to before a notary or made under penalty of perjury. In this rule, "declarant" means the party filing the Statement.

(b) **Supreme Court Form; Clerk to Provide**. The declarant must use the form Statement approved by the Supreme Court, or the Statement must include the information required by the Court-approved form. The clerk must make the form available to all persons without charge or request.

(c) **Costs Defined**. "Costs" mean any fee charged by the court or an officer of the court that could be taxed in a bill of costs, including, but not limited to, filing fees, fees for issuance and service of process, fees for a court-appointed professional, and fees charged by the clerk or court reporter for preparation of the appellate record.

(d) **Defects**. The clerk may refuse to file a Statement that is not sworn to before a notary or made under penalty of perjury. No other defect is a ground for refusing to file a Statement or requiring the party to pay costs. If a defect or omission in a Statement is material, the court--on its own motion or on motion of the clerk or any party--may direct the declarant to correct or clarify the Statement.

(e) **Evidence of Inability to Afford Costs Required**. The Statement must say that the declarant cannot afford to pay costs. The declarant must provide in the Statement, and, if available, in attachments to the Statement, evidence of the declarant's inability to afford costs, such as evidence that the declarant:

(1) receives benefits from a government entitlement program, eligibility for which is dependent on the recipient's means;

(2) is being represented in the case by an attorney who is providing free legal services to the declarant, without contingency, through:

    (A) a provider funded by the Texas Access to Justice Foundation;

    (B) a provider funded by the Legal Services Corporation; or

    (C) a nonprofit that provides civil legal services to persons living at or below 200% of the federal poverty guidelines published annually by the United States Department of Health and Human Services;

(3) has applied for free legal services for the case through a provider listed in (e)(2) and was determined to be financially eligible but was declined representation; or

(4) does not have funds to afford payment of costs.

(f) **Requirement to Pay Costs Notwithstanding Statement**. The court may order the declarant to pay costs only as follows:

(1) *On Motion by the Clerk or a Party*. The clerk or any party may move to require the declarant to pay costs only if the motion contains sworn evidence, not merely on information or belief:

    (A) that the Statement was materially false when it was made; or

    (B) that because of changed circumstances, the Statement is no longer true in material respects.

(2) *On Motion by the Attorney Ad Litem for a Parent in Certain Cases*. An attorney ad litem appointed to represent a parent under Section 107.013, Family Code, may move to require the parent to pay costs only if the motion complies with (f)(1).

(3) *On Motion by the Court Reporter*. When the declarant requests the preparation of a reporter's record but cannot make arrangements to pay for it, the court reporter may move to require the declarant to prove the inability to afford costs.

(4) *On the Court's Own Motion*. Whenever evidence comes before the court that the declarant may be able to afford costs, or when an officer or professional must be appointed in the case, the court may require the declarant to prove the inability to afford costs.

(5) *Notice and Hearing*. The declarant may not be required to pay costs without an oral evidentiary hearing. The declarant must be given 10 days' notice of the hearing. Notice must either be in writing and served in accordance with Rule 21a or given in open court. At the hearing, the burden is on the declarant to prove the inability to afford costs.

(6) *Findings Required*. An order requiring the declarant to pay costs must be supported by detailed findings that the declarant can afford to pay costs.

(7) *Partial and Delayed Payment*. The court may order that the declarant pay the part of the costs the declarant can afford or that payment be made in installments. But the court must not delay the case if payment is made in installments.

(g) **Review of Trial Court Order**.

(1) *Only Declarant May Challenge; Motion*. Only the declarant may challenge an order issued by the trial court under this rule. The declarant may challenge the order by motion filed in the court of appeals with jurisdiction over an appeal from the judgment in the case. The declarant is not required to pay any filing fees related to the motion in the court of appeals.

(2) *Time for Filing; Extension*. The motion must be filed within 10 days after the trial court's order is signed. The court of appeals may extend the deadline by 15 days if the declarant demonstrates good cause for the extension in writing.

(3) *Record*. After a motion is filed, the court of appeals must promptly send notice to the trial court clerk and the court reporter requesting preparation of the record of all trial court proceedings on the declarant's claim of indigence. The court may set a deadline for filing the record. The record must be provided without charge.

(4) *Court of Appeals to Rule Promptly*. The court of appeals must rule on the motion at the earliest practicable time.

(h) *Judgment*. The judgment must not require the declarant to pay costs, and a provision in the judgment purporting to do so is void, unless the court has issued an order under (f), or the declarant has obtained a monetary recovery, and the court orders the recovery to be applied toward payment of costs.

Comment to 2016 Change: The rule has been rewritten. Access to the civil justice system cannot be denied because a person cannot afford to pay court costs. Whether a particular fee is a court cost is governed by this rule, Civil Practice and Remedies Code Section 31.007, and case law.

The issue is not merely whether a person can pay costs, but whether the person can afford to pay costs. A person may have sufficient cash on hand to pay filing fees, but the person cannot afford the fees if paying them would preclude the person from paying for basic essentials, like housing or food. Experience indicates that almost all filers described in (e)(1)-(3), and most filers described in (e)(4), cannot in fact afford to pay costs.

Because costs to access the system--filing fees, fees for issuance of process and notices, and fees for service and return--are kept relatively small, the expense involved in challenging a claim of inability to afford costs often exceeds the costs themselves. Thus, the rule does not allow the clerk or a party to challenge a litigant's claim of inability to afford costs without sworn evidence that the claim is false. The filing of a Statement of Inability to Afford Payment of Court Costs--which may either be sworn to before a notary or made under penalty of perjury, as permitted by Civil Practice and Remedies Code Section 132.001--is all that is needed to require the clerk to provide ordinary services without payment of fees and costs. But evidence may come to light that the claim was false when made. And the declarant's circumstances may change, so that the claim is no longer true. Importantly, costs may increase with the appointment of officers or professionals in the case, or when a reporter's record must be prepared. The reporter is always allowed to challenge a claim of inability to afford costs before incurring the substantial expense of record preparation. The trial court always retains discretion to require evidence of an inability to afford costs.

RULE 146. DEPOSIT FOR COSTS

In lieu of a bond for costs, the party required to give the same may deposit with the clerk of court or the justice of the peace such sum as the court or justice from time to time may designate as sufficient to pay the accrued costs.

RULE 147. APPLIES TO ANY PARTY

The foregoing rules as to security and rule for costs shall apply to any party who seeks a judgment against any other party.

RULE 148. SECURED BY OTHER BOND

No further security shall be required if the costs are secured by the provisions of an attachment or other bond filed by the party required to give security for costs.

RULE 149. EXECUTION FOR COSTS

When costs have been adjudged against a party and are not paid, the clerk or justice of the court in which the suit was determined may issue execution, accompanied by an itemized bill of costs, against such party to be levied and collected as in other cases; and said officer, on demand of any party to whom any such costs are due, shall issue execution for costs at once. This rule shall not apply to executors, administrators or guardians in cases where costs are adjudged against the estate of a deceased person or of a ward. No execution shall issue in any case for costs until after judgment rendered therefor by the court.

SECTION 7. ABATEMENT AND DISCONTINUANCE OF SUIT

RULE 150. DEATH OF PARTY

Where the cause of action is one which survives, no suit shall abate because of the death of any party thereto before the verdict or decision of the court is rendered, but such suit may proceed to judgment as hereinafter provided.

RULE 151. DEATH OF PLAINTIFF

If the plaintiff dies, the heirs, or the administrator or executor of such decedent may appear and upon suggestion of such death being entered of record in open court, may be made plaintiff, and the suit shall proceed in his or their name. If no such appearance and suggestion be made within a reasonable time after the death of the plaintiff, the clerk upon the application of defendant, his agent or attorney, shall issue a scire facias for the heirs or the administrator or executor of such decedent, requiring him to appear and prosecute such suit. After service of such scire facias, should such heir or administrator or executor fail to enter appearance within the time provided, the defendant may have the suit dismissed.

RULE 152. DEATH OF DEFENDANT

Where the defendant shall die, upon the suggestion of death being entered of record in open court, or upon petition of the plaintiff, the clerk shall issue a scire facias for the administrator or executor or heir requiring him to appear and defend the suit and upon the return of such service, the suit shall proceed against such administrator or executor or heir.

RULE 153. WHEN EXECUTOR, ETC. DIES

When an executor or administrator shall be a party to any suit, whether as plaintiff or as defendant, and shall die or cease to be such executor or administrator, the suit may be continued by or against the person succeeding him in the administration, or by or against the heirs, upon like proceedings being had as provided in the two preceding rules, or the suit may be dismissed, as provided in Rule 151.

RULE 154. REQUISITES OF SCIRE FACIAS

The scire facias and returns thereon, provided for in this section, shall conform to the requisites of citations and the returns thereon, under the provisions of these rules.

RULE 155. SURVIVING PARTIES

Where there are two or more plaintiffs or defendants, and one or more of them die, upon suggestion of such death being entered upon the record, the suit shall at the instance of either party proceed in the name of the surviving plaintiffs or against the surviving defendants, as the case may be.

RULE 156. DEATH AFTER VERDICT OR CLOSE OF EVIDENCE

When a party in a jury case dies between verdict and judgment, or a party in a non- jury case dies after the evidence is closed and before judgment is pronounced, judgment shall be rendered and entered as if all parties were living.

[RULE 157. Repealed effective January 1, 1988]

RULE 158. SUIT FOR THE USE OF ANOTHER

When a plaintiff suing for the use of another shall die before verdict, the person for whose use such suit was brought, upon such death being suggested on the record in open court, may prosecute the suit in his own name, and shall be as responsible for costs as if he brought the suit

RULE 159. SUIT FOR INJURIES RESULTING IN DEATH

In cases arising under the provisions of the title relating to injuries resulting in death, the suit shall not abate by the death of either party pending the suit, but in such case, if the plaintiff dies, where there is only one plaintiff, some one or more of the parties entitled to the money recovered may be substituted and the suit prosecuted to judgment in the name of such party or parties, for the benefit of the person entitled; if the defendant dies, his executor, administrator or heir may be made a party, and the suit prosecuted to judgment.

RULE 160. DISSOLUTION OF CORPORATION

The dissolution of a corporation shall not operate to abate any pending suit in which such corporation is a defendant, but such suit shall continue against such corporation and judgment shall be rendered as though the same were not dissolved.

RULE 161. WHERE SOME DEFENDANTS NOT SERVED

When some of the several defendants in a suit are served with process in due time and others are not so served, the plaintiff may either dismiss as to those not so served and proceed against those who are, or he may take new process against those not served, or may obtain severance of the case as between those served and those not served, but no dismissal shall be allowed as to a principal obligor without also dismissing the parties secondarily liable except in cases provided by statute. No defendant against whom any suit may be so dismissed shall be thereby exonerated from any liability, but may at any time be proceeded against as if no such suit had been brought and no such dismissal ordered.

RULE 162. DISMISSAL OR NON-SUIT

At any time before the plaintiff has introduced all of his evidence other than rebuttal evidence, the plaintiff may dismiss a case, or take a non-suit, which shall be entered in the minutes. Notice of the dismissal or non-suit shall be served in accordance with Rule 21a on any party who has answered or has been served with process without necessity of court order.

Any dismissal pursuant to this rule shall not prejudice the right of an adverse party to be heard on a pending claim for affirmative relief or excuse the payment of all costs taxed by the clerk. A dismissal under this rule shall have no effect on any motion for sanctions, attorney's fees or other costs, pending at the time of dismissal, as determined by the court. Any dismissal pursuant to this rule which terminates the case shall authorize the clerk to tax court costs against dismissing party unless otherwise ordered by the court.

RULE 163. DISMISSAL AS TO PARTIES SERVED, ETC.

When it will not prejudice another party, the plaintiff may dismiss his suit as to one or more of several parties who were served with process, or who have answered, but no such dismissal shall in any case, be allowed as to a principal obligor, except in the cases provided for by statute.

[RULE 164. Repealed effective January 1, 1988]

RULE 165. ABANDONMENT

A party who abandons any part of his claim or defense, as contained in the pleadings, may have that fact entered of record, so as to show that the matters therein were not tried.

RULE 165a. DISMISSAL FOR WANT OF PROSECUTION

1. **Failure to Appear**. A case may be dismissed for want of prosecution on failure of any party seeking affirmative relief to appear for any hearing or trial of which the party had notice. Notice of the court's intention to dismiss and the date and place of the dismissal hearing shall be sent by the clerk to each attorney of record, and to each party not represented by an attorney and whose address is shown on the docket or in the papers on file, by posting same in the United States Postal Service. At the dismissal

hearing, the court shall dismiss for want of prosecution unless there is good cause for the case to be maintained on the docket. If the court determines to maintain the case on the docket, it shall render a pretrial order assigning a trial date for the case and setting deadlines for the joining of new parties, all discovery, filing of all pleadings, the making of a response or supplemental responses to discovery and other pretrial matters. The case may be continued thereafter only for valid and compelling reasons specifically determined by court order. Notice of the signing of the order of dismissal shall be given as provided in Rule 306a. Failure to mail notices as required by this rule shall not affect any of the periods mentioned in Rule 306a except as provided in that rule.

2. **Non-Compliance With Time Standards**. Any case not disposed of within time standards promulgated by the Supreme Court under its Administrative Rules may be placed on a dismissal docket.

3. **Reinstatement**. A motion to reinstate shall set forth the grounds therefor and be verified by the movant or his attorney. It shall be filed with the clerk within 30 days after the order of dismissal is signed or within the period provided by Rule 306a. A copy of the motion to reinstate shall be served on each attorney of record and each party not represented by an attorney whose address is shown on the docket or in the papers on file. The clerk shall deliver a copy of the motion to the judge, who shall set a hearing on the motion as soon as practicable. The court shall notify all parties or their attorneys of record of the date, time and place of the hearing.

The court shall reinstate the case upon finding after a hearing that the failure of the party or his attorney was not intentional or the result of conscious indifference but was due to an accident or mistake or that the failure has been otherwise reasonably explained.

In the event for any reason a motion for reinstatement is not decided by signed written order within seventy-five days after the judgment is signed, or, within such other time as may be allowed by Rule 306a, the motion shall be deemed overruled by operation of law. If a motion to reinstate is timely filed by any party, the trial court, regardless of whether an appeal has been perfected, has plenary power to reinstate the case until 30 days after all such timely filed motions are overruled, either by a written and signed order or by operation of law, whichever occurs first.

4. **Cumulative Remedies**. This dismissal and reinstatement procedure shall be cumulative of the rules and laws governing any other procedures available to the parties in such cases. The same reinstatement procedures and timetable are applicable to all dismissals for want of prosecution including cases which are dismissed pursuant to the court's inherent power, whether or not a motion to dismiss has been filed.

SECTION 8. PRE-TRIAL PROCEDURE

RULE 166. PRE-TRIAL CONFERENCE

In an appropriate action, to assist in the disposition of the case without undue expense or burden to the parties, the court may in its discretion direct the attorneys for the parties and the parties or their duly authorized agents to appear before it for a conference to consider:

(a) All pending dilatory pleas, motions and exceptions;

(b) The necessity or desirability of amendments to the pleadings;

(c) A discovery schedule;

(d) Requiring written statements of the parties' contentions;

(e) Contested issues of fact and the simplification of the issues;

(f) The possibility of obtaining stipulations of fact;

(g) The identification of legal matters to be ruled on or decided by the court;

(h) The exchange of a list of direct fact witnesses, other than rebuttal or impeaching witnesses the necessity of whose testimony cannot reasonably be anticipated before the time of trial, who will be called to testify at trial, stating their address and telephone number, and the subject of the testimony of each such witness;

(i) The exchange of a list of expert witnesses who will be called to testify at trial, stating their address and telephone number, and the subject of the testimony and opinions that will be proffered by each expert witness;

(j) Agreed applicable propositions of law and contested issues of law;

(k) Proposed jury charge questions, instructions, and definitions for a jury case or proposed findings of fact and conclusions of law for a nonjury case;

(l) The marking and exchanging of all exhibits that any party may use at trial and stipulation to the authenticity and admissibility of exhibits to be used at trial;

(m) Written trial objections to the opposite party's exhibits, stating the basis for each objection;

(n) The advisability of a preliminary reference of issues to a master or auditor for findings to be used as evidence when the trial is to be by jury;

(o) The settlement of the case, and to aid such consideration, the court may encourage settlement;

(p) Such other matters as may aid in the disposition of the action.

The court shall make an order which recites the action taken at the pretrial conference, the amendments allowed to the pleadings, the time within which same may be filed, and the agreements made by the parties as to any of the matters considered, and which limits the issues for trial to those not disposed of by admissions, agreements of counsel, or rulings of the court; and such order when issued shall control the subsequent course of the action, unless modified at the trial to prevent manifest injustice. The court in its discretion may establish by rule a pretrial calendar on which actions may be placed for consideration as above provided and may either confine the calendar to jury actions or extend it to all actions.

Pretrial proceedings in multidistrict litigation may also be governed by Rules 11 and 13 of the Rules of Judicial Administration.

RULE 166a. SUMMARY JUDGMENT

(a) **For Claimant**. A party seeking to recover upon a claim, counterclaim, or cross-claim or to obtain a declaratory judgment may, at any time after the adverse party has appeared or answered, move with or without supporting affidavits for a summary judgment in his favor upon all or any part thereof. A summary judgment, interlocutory in character, may be rendered on the issue of liability alone although there is a genuine issue as to amount of damages.

(b) **For Defending Party**. A party against whom a claim, counterclaim, or cross-claim is asserted or a declaratory judgment is sought may, at any time, move with or without supporting affidavits for a summary judgment in his favor as to all or any part thereof.

(c) **Motion and Proceedings Thereon**. The motion for summary judgment shall state the specific grounds therefor. Except on leave of court, with notice to opposing counsel, the motion and any supporting affidavits shall be filed and served at least twenty-one days before the time specified for hearing. Except on leave of court, the adverse party, not later than seven days prior to the day of hearing may file and serve opposing affidavits or other written response. No oral testimony shall be received at the hearing. The judgment sought shall be rendered forthwith if (i) the deposition transcripts, interrogatory answers, and other discovery responses referenced or set forth in the motion or response, and (ii) the pleadings, admissions, affidavits, stipulations of the parties, and authenticated or certified public records, if any, on file at the time of the hearing, or filed thereafter and before judgment with permission of the court, show that, except as to the amount of damages, there is no genuine issue as to any material fact and the moving party is entitled to judgment as a matter of law on the issues expressly set out in the motion or in an answer or any other response. Issues not expressly presented to the trial court by written motion, answer or other response shall not be considered on appeal as grounds for reversal. A summary judgment may be based on uncontroverted testimonial evidence of an interested witness, or of an expert witness as to subject matter concerning which the trier of fact must be guided solely by the opinion testimony of experts, if the evidence is clear, positive and direct, otherwise credible and free from contradictions and inconsistencies, and could have been readily controverted.

(d) **Appendices, References and Other Use of Discovery Not Otherwise on File**. Discovery products not on file with the clerk may be used as summary judgment evidence if copies of the material, appendices containing the evidence, or a notice containing specific references to the discovery or specific references to other instruments, are filed and served on all parties together with a statement of intent to use the specified discovery as summary judgment proofs: (i) at least twenty-one days before the hearing if such proofs are to be used to support the summary judgment; or (ii) at least seven days before the hearing if such proofs are to be used to oppose the summary judgment.

(e) **Case Not Fully Adjudicated on Motion**. If summary judgment is not rendered upon the whole case or for all the relief asked and a trial is necessary, the judge may at the hearing examine the pleadings and the evidence on file, interrogate counsel, ascertain what material fact issues exist and make an order specifying the facts that are established as a matter of law, and directing such further proceedings in the action as are just.

(f) **Form of Affidavits; Further Testimony**. Supporting and opposing affidavits shall be made on personal knowledge, shall set forth such facts as would be admissible in evidence, and shall show affirmatively that the affiant is competent to testify to the matters stated therein. Sworn or certified copies of all papers or parts thereof referred to in an affidavit shall be attached thereto or served therewith. The court may permit affidavits to be supplemented or opposed by depositions or by further affidavits. Defects in the form of affidavits or attachments will not be grounds for reversal unless specifically pointed out by objection by an opposing party with opportunity, but refusal, to amend.

(g) **When Affidavits Are Unavailable**. Should it appear from the affidavits of a party opposing the motion that he cannot for reasons stated present by affidavit facts essential to justify his opposition, the court may refuse the application for judgment or may order a continuance to permit affidavits to be obtained or depositions to be taken or discovery to be had or may make such other order as is just.

(h) **Affidavits Made in Bad Faith**. Should it appear to the satisfaction of the court at any time that any of the affidavits presented pursuant to this rule are presented in bad faith or solely for the purpose of delay, the court shall forthwith order the party employing them to pay to the other party the amount of the reasonable expenses which the filing of the affidavits caused him to incur, including reasonable attorney's fees, and any offending party or attorney may be adjudged guilty of contempt.

(i) **No-Evidence Motion**. After adequate time for discovery, a party without presenting summary judgment evidence may move for summary judgment on the ground that there is no evidence of one or more essential elements of a claim or defense on which an adverse party would have the burden of proof at trial. The motion must state the elements as to which there is no evidence. The court must grant the motion unless the respondent produces summary judgment evidence raising a genuine issue of material fact.

[RULE 166b. Repealed effective January 1, 1999]

[RULE 166c. Repealed effective January 1, 1999]

RULE 167. OFFER OF SETTLEMENT; AWARD OF LITIGATION COSTS

167.1. Generally.

Certain litigation costs may be awarded against a party who rejects an offer made substantially in accordance with this rule to settle a claim for monetary damages - including a counterclaim, crossclaim, or third-party claim - except in:

(a) a class action;

(b) a shareholder's derivative action;

(c) an action by or against the State, a unit of state government, or a political subdivision of the State;

(d) an action brought under the Family Code;

(e) an action to collect workers' compensation benefits under title 5, subtitle A of the Labor Code; or

(f) an action filed in a justice of the peace court or small claims court.

167.2. Settlement Offer

(a) **Defendant's declaration a prerequisite; deadline**. A settlement offer under this rule may not be made until a defendant -- a party against whom a claim for monetary damages is made -- files a declaration invoking this rule. When a defendant files such a declaration, an offer or offers may be made under this rule to settle only those claims by and against that defendant. The declaration must be filed no later than 45 days before the case is set for conventional trial on the merits.

(b) **Requirements of an offer**. A settlement offer must:

(1) be in writing;

(2) state that it is made under Rule 167 and Chapter 42 of the Texas Civil Practice and Remedies Code;

(3) identify the party or parties making the offer and the party or parties to whom the offer is made;

(4) state the terms by which all monetary claims - including any attorney fees, interest, and costs that would be recoverable up to the time of the offer - between the offeror or offerors on the one hand and the offeree or offerees on the other may be settled;

(5) state a deadline - no sooner than 14 days after the offer is served - by which the offer must be accepted;

(6) be served on all parties to whom the offer is made.

(c) **Conditions of offer**. An offer may be made subject to reasonable conditions, including the execution of appropriate releases, indemnities, and other documents. An offeree may object to a condition by written notice served on the offeror before the deadline stated in the offer. A condition to which no such objection is made is presumed to have been reasonable. Rejection of an offer made subject to a condition determined by the trial court to have been unreasonable cannot be the basis for an award of litigation costs under this rule.

(d) **Non-monetary and excepted claims not included**. An offer must not include non-monetary claims and other claims to which this rule does not apply.

(e) **Time limitations**. An offer may not be made:

(1) before a defendant's declaration is filed;

(2) within 60 days after the appearance in the case of the offeror or offeree, whichever is later;

(3) within 14 days before the date the case is set for a conventional trial on the merits, except that an offer may be made within that period if it is in response to, and within seven days of, a prior offer.

(f) **Successive offers**. A party may make an offer after having made or rejected a prior offer. A rejection of an offer is subject to imposition of litigation costs under this rule only if the offer is more favorable to the offeree than any prior offer.

167.3. Withdrawal, Acceptance, and Rejection of Offer

(a) **Withdrawal of offer**. An offer can be withdrawn before it is accepted. Withdrawal is effective when written notice of the withdrawal is served on the offeree. Once an unaccepted offer has been withdrawn, it cannot be accepted or be the basis for awarding litigation costs under this rule.

(b) **Acceptance of offer**. An offer that has not been withdrawn can be accepted only by written notice served on the offeror by the deadline stated in the offer. When an offer is accepted, the offeror or offeree may file the offer and acceptance and may move the court to enforce the settlement.

(c) **Rejection of offer**. An offer that is not withdrawn or accepted is rejected. An offer may also be rejected by written notice served on the offeror by the deadline stated in the offer.

(d) **Objection to offer made before an offeror's joinder or designation of responsible third party**. An offer made before an offeror joins another party or designates a responsible third party may not be the basis for awarding litigation costs under this rule against an offeree who files an objection to the offer within 15 days after service of the offeror's pleading or designation.

167.4. Awarding Litigation Costs

(a) **Generally**. If a settlement offer made under this rule is rejected, and the judgment to be awarded on the monetary claims covered by the offer is significantly less favorable to the offeree than was the offer, the court must award the offeror litigation costs against the offeree from the time the offer was rejected to the time of judgment.

(b) **"Significantly less favorable" defined**. A judgment award on monetary claims is significantly less favorable than an offer to settle those claims if:

(1) the offeree is a claimant and the judgment would be less than 80 percent of the offer; or

(2) the offeree is a defendant and the judgment would be more than 120 percent of the offer.

(c) **Litigation costs**. Litigation costs are the expenditures actually made and the obligations actually incurred - directly in relation to the claims covered by a settlement offer under this rule - for the following:

(1) court costs;

(2) reasonable deposition costs, in cases filed on or after September 1, 2011;

(3) reasonable fees for not more than two testifying expert witnesses; and

(4) reasonable attorney fees.

(d) **Limits on litigation costs**. The litigation costs that may be awarded under this rule must not exceed the following amount:

(1) In cases filed before September 1, 2011, litigation costs that may be awarded under this rule must not exceed the following amount:

(A) the sum of the noneconomic damages, the exemplary or additional damages, and one-half of the economic damages to be awarded to the claimant in the judgment; minus

(B) the amount of any statutory or contractual liens in connection with the occurrences or incidents giving rise to the claim.

(2) In cases files on or after September 1, 2011, the litigation costs that may be awarded to any party under this rule must not exceed the total amount that the claimant recovers or would recover before adding an award of litigation costs under this rule in favor of the claimant or subtracting as an offset an award of litigation costs under this rule in favor of the defendant.

(e) **No double recovery permitted**. A party who is entitled to recover attorney fees and costs under another lawmay not recover those same attorney fees and costs as litigation costs under this rule.

(f) **Limitation on attorney fees and costs recovered by a party against whom litigation costs are awarded**. A party against whom litigation costs are awarded may not recover attorney fees and costs under another law incurred after the date the party rejected the settlement offer made the basis of the award.

(g) **Litigation costs to be awarded to defendant as a setoff**. Litigation costs awarded to a defendant must be made a setoff to the claimant's judgment against the defendant.

167.5. Procedures

(a) **Modification of time limits**. On motion, and for good cause shown, the court may -- by written order made before commencement of trial on the merits -- modify the time limits for filing a declaration under Rule 167.2(a) or for making an offer.

(b) **Discovery permitted**. On motion, and for good cause shown, a party against whom litigation costs are to be awarded may conduct discovery to ascertain the reasonableness of the costs requested. If the court determines the costs to be reasonable, it must order the party requesting discovery to pay all attorney fees and expenses incurred by other parties in responding to such discovery.

(c) **Hearing required**. The court must, upon request, conduct a hearing on a request for an award of litigation costs, at which the affected parties may present evidence.

167.6. Evidence Not Admissible

Evidence relating to an offer made under this rule is not admissible except for purposes of enforcing a settlement agreement or obtaining litigation costs. The provisions of this rule may not be made known to the jury by any means.

167.7. Other Settlement Offers Not Affected

This rule does not apply to any offer made in a mediation or arbitration proceeding. A settlement offer not made in compliance with this rule, or a settlement offer not made under this rule, or made in an action to which this rule does not apply, cannot be the basis for awarding litigation costs under this rule as to any party. This rule does not limit or affect a party's right to make a settlement offer that does not comply with this rule, or in an action to which this rule does not apply.

[RULE 167a. Repealed effective January 1, 1999]

RULE 168. PERMISSION TO APPEAL

On a party's motion or on its own initiative, a trial court may permit an appeal from an interlocutory order that is not otherwise appealable, as provided by statute. Permission must be stated in the order to be appealed. An order previously issued may be amended to include such permission. The permission must identify the controlling question of law as to which there is a substantial ground for difference of opinion, and must state why an immediate appeal may materially advance the ultimate termination of the litigation.

Comment to 2011 change: Rule 168 is a new rule, added to implement amendments to section 51.014(d)- (f) of the Texas Civil Practice and Remedies Code. Rule 168 applies only to cases filed on or after September 1, 2011. Rule 168 clarifies that the trial court's permission to appeal should be included in the order to be appealed rather than in a separate order. Rule of Appellate Procedure 28.3 sets out the corollary requirements for permissive appeals in the courts of appeals.

RULE 169. EXPEDITED ACTIONS

(a) **Application**.

(1) The expedited actions process in this rule applies to a suit in which all claimants, other than counter-claimants, affirmatively plead that they seek only monetary relief aggregating $100,000 or less, including damages of any kind, penalties, costs, expenses, pre-judgment interest, and attorney fees.

(2) The expedited actions process does not apply to a suit in which a party has filed a claim governed by the Family Code, the Property Code, the Tax Code, or Chapter 74 of the Civil Practice & Remedies Code.

(b) **Recovery**. In no event may a party who prosecutes a suit under this rule recover a judgment in excess of $100,000, excluding post-judgment interest.

(c) **Removal from Process**.

(1) A court must remove a suit from the expedited actions process:

(A) on motion and a showing of good cause by any party; or

(B) if any claimant, other than a counter-claimant, files a pleading or an amended or supplemental pleading that seeks any relief other than the monetary relief allowed by (a)(1).

(2) A pleading, amended pleading, or supplemental pleading that removes a suit from the expedited actions process may not be filed without leave of court unless it is filed before the earlier of 30 days after the discovery period is closed or 30 days before the date set for trial. Leave to amend may be granted only if good cause for filing the pleading outweighs any prejudice to an opposing party.

(3) If a suit is removed from the expedited actions process, the court must reopen discovery under Rule 190.2(c).

(d) **Expedited Actions Process**.

(1) *Discovery*. Discovery is governed by Rule 190.2.

(2) *Trial Setting; Continuances*. On any party's request, the court must set the case for a trial date that is within 90 days after the discovery period in Rule 190.2(b)(1) ends. The court may continue the case twice, not to exceed a total of 60 days.

(3) *Time Limits for Trial*. Each side is allowed no more than eight hours to complete jury selection, opening statements, presentation of evidence, examination and cross-examination of witnesses, and closing arguments. On motion and a showing of good cause by any party, the court may extend the time limit to no more than twelve hours per side.

(A) The term "side" has the same definition set out in Rule 233.

(B) Time spent on objections, bench conferences, bills of exception, and challenges for cause to a juror under Rule 228 are not included in the time limit.

(4) *Alternative Dispute Resolution*.

(A) Unless the parties have agreed not to engage in alternative dispute resolution, the court may refer the case to an alternative dispute resolution procedure once, and the procedure must:

(i) not exceed a half-day in duration, excluding scheduling time;

(ii) not exceed a total cost of twice the amount of applicable civil filing fees; and

(iii) be completed no later than 60 days before the initial trial setting.

(B) The court must consider objections to the referral unless prohibited by statute.

(C) The parties may agree to engage in alternative dispute resolution other than that provided for in (A).

(5) *Expert Testimony*. Unless requested by the party sponsoring the expert, a party may only challenge the admissibility of expert testimony as an objection to summary judgment evidence under Rule 166a or during the trial on the merits. This paragraph does not apply to a motion to strike for late designation.

Comments to 2013 change:

1. Rule 169 is a new rule implementing section 22.004(h) of the Texas Government Code, which was added in 2011 and calls for rules to promote the prompt, efficient, and cost-effective resolution of civil actions when the amount in controversy does not exceed $100,000.

2. The expedited actions process created by Rule 169 is mandatory; any suit that falls within the definition of 169(a)(1) is subject to the provisions of the rule.

3. In determining whether there is good cause to remove the case from the process or extend the time limit for trial, the court should consider factors such as whether the damages sought by multiple claimants against the same defendant exceed in the aggregate the relief allowed under 169(a)(1), whether a defendant has filed a compulsory counterclaim in good faith that seeks relief other than that allowed under 169(a)(1), the number of parties and witnesses, the complexity of the legal and factual issues, and whether an interpreter is necessary.

4. Rule 169(b) specifies that a party who prosecutes a suit under this rule cannot recover a judgment in excess of $100,000. Thus, the rule in Greenhalgh v. Service Lloyds Ins. Co., 787 S.W.2d 938 (Tex. 1990), does not apply if a jury awards damages in excess of $100,000 to the party. The limitation of 169(b) does not apply to a counter-claimant that seeks relief other than that allowed under 169(a)(1).

5. The discovery limitations for expedited actions are set out in Rule 190.2, which is also amended to implement section 22.004(h) of the Texas Government Code.

[RULE 170. Repealed effective April 1, 1984]

RULE 171. MASTER IN CHANCERY

The court may, in exceptional cases, for good cause appoint a master in chancery, who shall be a citizen of this State, and not an attorney for either party to the action, nor related to either party, who shall perform all of the duties required of him by the court, and shall be under orders of the court, and have such power as the master of chancery has in a court of equity.

The order of references to the master may specify or limit his powers, and may direct him to report only upon particular issues, or to do or perform particular acts, or to receive and report evidence only and may fix the time and place for beginning and closing the hearings, and for the filing of the master's report. Subject to the limitations and specifications stated in the order, the master has and shall exercise the power to regulate all proceedings in every hearing before him and to do all acts and take all measures necessary or proper for the efficient performance of his duties under the order. He may require the production before him of evidence upon all matters embraced in the reference, including the production of books, papers, vouchers, documents and other writings applicable thereto. He may rule upon the admissibility of evidence, unless otherwise directed by the order of reference and has the authority to put witnesses on oath, and may, himself, examine them, and may call the parties to the action and examine them upon oath. When a party so requests, the master shall make a record of the evidence offered and excluded in the same manner as provided for a court sitting in the trial of a case.

The clerk of the court shall forthwith furnish the master with a copy of the order of reference.

The parties may procure the attendance of witnesses before the master by the issuance and service of process as provided by law and these rules.

The court may confirm, modify, correct, reject, reverse or recommit the report, after it is filed, as the court may deem proper and necessary in the particular circumstances of the case. The court shall award reasonable compensation to such master to be taxed as costs of suit.

RULE 172. AUDIT

When an investigation of accounts or examination of vouchers appears necessary for the purpose of justice between the parties to any suit, the court shall appoint an auditor or auditors to state the accounts between the parties and to make report thereof to the court as soon as possible. The auditor shall verify his report by his affidavit stating that he has carefully examined the state of the account between the parties, and that his report contains a true statement thereof, so far as the same has come within his knowledge. Exceptions to such report or of any item thereof must be filed within 30 days of the filing of such report. The court shall award reasonable compensation to such auditor to be taxed as costs of suit.

RULE 173. GUARDIAN AD LITEM

173.1. Appointment Governed by Statute or Other Rules

This rule does not apply to an appointment of a guardian ad litem governed by statute or other rules.

173.2. Appointment of Guardian ad Litem

(a) **When Appointment Required or Prohibited**. The court must appoint a guardian ad litem for a party represented by a next friend or guardian only if:

(1) the next friend or guardian appears to the court to have an interest adverse to the party; or

(2) the parties agree.

(b) **Appointment of the Same Person for Different Parties**. The court must appoint the same guardian ad litem for similarly situated parties unless the court finds that the appointment of different guardians ad litem is necessary.

173.3. Procedure

(a) **Motion Permitted But Not Required**. The court may appoint a guardian ad litem on the motion of any party or on its own initiative.

(b) **Written Order Required**. An appointment must be made by written order.

(c) **Objections**. Any party may object to the appointment of a guardian ad litem.

173.4. Role of Guardian ad Litem

(a) **Court Officer and Advisor**. A guardian ad litem acts as an officer and advisor to the court.

(b) **Determination of Adverse Interest**. A guardian ad litem must determine and advise the court whether a party's next friend or guardian has an interest adverse to the party.

(c) **When Settlement Proposed**. When an offer has been made to settle the claim of a party represented by a next friend or guardian, a guardian ad litem has the limited duty to determine and advise the court whether the settlement is in the party's best interest.

(d) **Participation in Litigation Limited**. A guardian ad litem:

(1) may participate in mediation or a similar proceeding to attempt to reach a settlement;

(2) must participate in any proceeding before the court whose purpose is to determine whether a party's next friend or guardian has an interest adverse to the party, or whether a settlement of the party's claim is in the party's best interest;

(3) must not participate in discovery, trial, or any other part of the litigation unless:

(A) further participation is necessary to protect the party's interest that is adverse to the next friend's or guardian's, and

(B) the participation is directed by the court in a written order stating sufficient reasons.

173.5. Communications Privileged

Communications between the guardian ad litem and the party, the next friend or guardian, or their attorney are privileged as if the guardian ad litem were the attorney for the party.

173.6. Compensation

(a) **Amount**. If a guardian ad litem requests compensation, he or she may be reimbursed for reasonable and necessary expenses incurred and may be paid a reasonable hourly fee for necessary services performed.

(b) **Procedure**. At the conclusion of the appointment, a guardian ad litem may file an application for compensation. The application must be verified and must detail the basis for the compensation requested. Unless all parties agree to the application, the court must conduct an evidentiary hearing to determine the total amount of fees and expenses that are reasonable and necessary. In making this determination, the court must not consider compensation as a percentage of any judgment or settlement.

(c) **Taxation as Costs**. The court may tax a guardian ad litem's compensation as costs of court.

(d) **Other Benefit Prohibited**. A guardian ad litem may not receive, directly or indirectly, anything of value in consideration of the appointment other than as provided by this rule.

173.7. Review

(a) **Right of Appeal**. Any party may seek mandamus review of an order appointing a guardian ad litem or directing a guardian ad litem's participation in the litigation. Any party and a guardian ad litem may appeal an order awarding the guardian ad litem compensation.

(b) **Severance**. On motion of the guardian ad litem or any party, the court must sever any order awarding a guardian ad litem compensation to create a final, appealable order.

(c) **No Effect on Finality of Settlement or Judgment**. Appellate proceedings to review an order pertaining to a guardian ad litem do not affect the finality of a settlement or judgment.

RULE 174. CONSOLIDATION; SEPARATE TRIALS

(a) **Consolidation**. When actions involving a common question of law or fact are pending before the court, it may order a joint hearing or trial of any or all the matters in issue in the actions; it may order all the actions consolidated; and it may make such orders concerning proceedings therein as may tend to avoid unnecessary costs or delay.

(b) **Separate Trials**. The court in furtherance of convenience or to avoid prejudice may order a separate trial of any claim, cross-claim, counterclaim, or third-party claim, or of any separate issue or of any number of claims, cross-claims, counterclaims, third-party claims, or issues.

RULE 175. ISSUE OF LAW AND DILATORY PLEAS

When a case is called for trial in which there has been no pretrial hearing as provided by Rule 166, the issues of law arising on the pleadings, all pleas in abatement and other dilatory pleas remaining undisposed of shall be determined; and it shall be no cause for postponement of a trial of the issues of law that a party is not prepared to try the issues of fact.

SECTION 9. EVIDENCE AND DISCOVERY

A. EVIDENCE

[RULE 176. Repealed effective January 1, 1999; see, Rule 176.3]

RULE 176. SUBPOENAS

176.1 Form.

Every subpoena must be issued in the name of "The State of Texas" and must:

    (a) state the style of the suit and its cause number;

    (b) state the court in which the suit is pending;

    (c) state the date on which the subpoena is issued;

    (d) identify the person to whom the subpoena is directed;

(e) state the time, place, and nature of the action required by the person to whom the subpoena is directed, as provided in Rule 176.2;

(f) identify the party at whose instance the subpoena is issued, and the party's attorney of record, if any;

(g) state the text of Rule 176.8(a); and

(h) be signed by the person issuing the subpoena.

176.2 Required Actions.

A subpoena must command the person to whom it is directed to do either or both of the following:

(a) attend and give testimony at a deposition, hearing, or trial;

(b) produce and permit inspection and copying of designated documents or tangible things in the possession, custody, or control of that person.

176.3 Limitations.

(a) **Range**. A person may not be required by subpoena to appear or produce documents or other things in a county that is more than 150 miles from where the person resides or is served. However, a person whose appearance or production at a deposition may be compelled by notice alone under Rules 199.3 or 200.2 may be required to appear and produce documents or other things at any location permitted under Rules 199.2(b)(2).

(b) **Use for discovery**. A subpoena may not be used for discovery to an extent, in a manner, or at a time other than as provided by the rules governing discovery.

176.4 Who May Issue.

A subpoena may be issued by:

(a) the clerk of the appropriate district, county, or justice court, who must provide the party requesting the subpoena with an original and a copy for each witness to be completed by the party;

(b) an attorney authorized to practice in the State of Texas, as an officer of the court; or

(c) an officer authorized to take depositions in this State, who must issue the subpoena immediately on a request accompanied by a notice to take a deposition under Rules 199 or 200, or a notice under Rule 205.3, and who may also serve the notice with the subpoena.

176.5 Service.

(a) **Manner of service**. A subpoena may be served at any place within the State of Texas by any sheriff or constable of the State of Texas, or any person who is not a party and is 18 years of age or older. A subpoena must be served by delivering a copy to the witness and tendering to that person any fees required by law. If the witness is a party and is represented by an attorney of record in the proceeding, the subpoena may be served on the witness's attorney of record.

(b) **Proof of service**. Proof of service must be made by filing either:

(1) the witness's signed written memorandum attached to the subpoena showing that the witness accepted the subpoena; or

(2) a statement by the person who made the service stating the date, time, and manner of service, and the name of the person served.

176.6 Response.

(a) **Compliance required**. Except as provided in this subdivision, a person served with a subpoena must comply with the command stated therein unless discharged by the court or by the party summoning such witness. A person commanded to appear and give testimony must remain at the place of deposition, hearing, or trial from day to day until discharged by the court or by the party summoning the witness.

(b) **Organizations**. If a subpoena commanding testimony is directed to a corporation, partnership, association, governmental agency, or other organization, and the matters on which examination is requested are described with reasonable particularity, the organization must designate one or more persons to testify on its behalf as to matters known or reasonably available to the organization.

(c) **Production of documents or tangible things**. A person commanded to produce documents or tangible things need not appear in person at the time and place of production unless the person is also commanded to attend and give testimony, either in the same subpoena or a separate one. A person must produce documents as they are kept in the usual course of business or must organize and label them to correspond with the categories in the demand. A person may withhold material or information claimed to be privileged but must comply with Rule 193.3. A nonparty's production of a document authenticates the document for use against the nonparty to the same extent as a party's production of a document is authenticated for use against the party under Rule 193.7.

(d) **Objections**. A person commanded to produce and permit inspection or copying of designated documents and things may serve on the party requesting issuance of the subpoena - before the time specified for compliance - written objections to producing any or all of the designated materials. A person need not comply with the part of a subpoena to which objection is made as provided in this paragraph unless ordered to do so by the court. The party requesting the subpoena may move for such an order at any time after an objection is made.

(e) **Protective orders**. A person commanded to appear at a deposition, hearing, or trial, or to produce and permit inspection and copying of designated documents and things, and any other person affected by the subpoena, may move for a protective order under Rule 192.6(b)--before the time specified for compliance--either in the court in which the action is pending or in a district court in the county where the subpoena was served. The person must serve the motion on all parties in accordance with Rule 21a. A person need not comply with the part of a subpoena from which protection is sought under this paragraph unless ordered to do so by the court. The party requesting the subpoena may seek such an order at any time after the motion for protection is filed.

(f) **Trial subpoenas**. A person commanded to attend and give testimony, or to produce documents or things, at a hearing or trial, may object or move for protective order before the court at the time and place specified for compliance, rather than under paragraphs (d) and (e).

176.7 Protection of Person from Undue Burden and Expense.

A party causing a subpoena to issue must take reasonable steps to avoid imposing undue burden or expense on the person served. In ruling on objections or motions for protection, the court must provide a person served with a subpoena an adequate time for compliance, protection from disclosure of privileged material or information, and protection from undue burden or expense. The court may impose reasonable conditions on compliance with a subpoena, including compensating the witness for undue hardship.

176.8 Enforcement of Subpoena.

(a) **Contempt**. Failure by any person without adequate excuse to obey a subpoena served upon that person may be deemed a contempt of the court from which the subpoena is issued or a district court in the county in which the subpoena is served, and may be punished by fine or confinement, or both.

(b) **Proof of payment of fees required for fine or attachment**. A fine may not be imposed, nor a person served with a subpoena attached, for failure to comply with a subpoena without proof by affidavit of the party requesting the subpoena or the party's attorney of record that all fees due the witness by law were paid or tendered.

[RULE 177. Repealed effective January 1, 1999]

[RULE 177a. Repealed effective January 1, 1999]

[RULE 178. Repealed effective January 1, 1999]

[RULE 179. Repealed effective January 1, 1999]

RULE 180. REFUSAL TO TESTIFY

Any witness refusing to give evidence may be committed to jail, there to remain without bail until such witness shall consent to give evidence.

RULE 181. PARTY AS WITNESS

Either party to a suit may examine the opposing party as a witness, and shall have the same process to compel his attendance as in the case of any other witness.

[RULE 182. Repealed effective January 1, 1988]

[RULE 182a. Repealed effective January 1, 1988]

RULE 183. INTERPRETERS

The court may appoint an interpreter of its own selection and may fix the interpreter's reasonable compensation. The compensation shall be paid out of funds provided by law or by one or more of the parties as the court may direct, and may be taxed ultimately as costs, in the discretion of the court.

[RULE 184. Repealed effective September 1, 1990]

[RULE 184A. Repealed effective September 1, 1990]

RULE 185. SUIT ON ACCOUNT

When any action or defense is founded upon an open account or other claim for goods, wares and merchandise, including any claim for a liquidated money demand based upon written contract or founded on business dealings between the parties, or is for personal service rendered, or labor done or labor or materials furnished, on which a systematic record has been kept, and is supported by the affidavit of the party, his agent or attorney taken before some officer authorized to administer oaths, to the effect that such claim is, within the knowledge of affiant, just and true, that it is due, and that all just and lawful offsets, payments and credits have been allowed, the same shall be taken as prima facie evidence thereof, unless the party resisting such claim shall file a written denial, under oath. A party resisting such a sworn claim shall comply with the rules of pleading as are required in any other kind of suit, provided, however, that if he does not timely file a written denial, under oath, he shall not be permitted to deny the claim, or any item therein, as the case may be. No particularization or description of the nature of the component parts of the account or claim is necessary unless the trial court sustains special exceptions to the pleadings.

SECTION 9. EVIDENCE AND DISCOVERY

B. Discovery

[RULES 186 to 186b. Repealed effective April 1, 1984]

[RULE 187. Repealed effective January 1, 1999]

[RULE 188. Repealed effective January 1, 1999]

[RULE 189. Repealed effective April 1, 1984]

RULE 190. DISCOVERY LIMITATIONS

190.1 Discovery Control Plan Required.

Every case must be governed by a discovery control plan as provided in this Rule. A plaintiff must allege in the first numbered paragraph of the original petition whether discovery is intended to be conducted under Level 1, 2, or 3 of this Rule.

190.2 Discovery Control Plan - Expedited Actions and Divorces Involving $50,000 or Less (Level 1)

(a) **Application**. This subdivision applies to:

(1) any suit that is governed by the expedited actions process in Rule 169; and

(2) unless the parties agree that rule 190.3 should apply or the court orders a discovery control plan under Rule 190.4, any suit for divorce not involving children in which a party pleads that the value of the marital estate is more than zero but not more than $ 50,000.

(b) **Limitations**. Discovery is subject to the limitations provided elsewhere in these rules and to the following additional limitations:

(1) *Discovery period*. All discovery must be conducted during the discovery period, which begins when the suit is filed and continues until 180 days after the date the first request for discovery of any kind is served on a party.

(2) *Total time for oral depositions*. Each party may have no more than six hours in total to examine and cross-examine all witnesses in oral depositions. The parties may agree to expand this limit up to ten hours in total, but not more except by court order. The court may modify the deposition hours so that no party is given unfair advantage.

(3) *Interrogatories.* Any party may serve on any other party no more than 15 written interrogatories, excluding interrogatories asking a party only to identify or authenticate specific documents. Each discrete subpart of an interrogatory is considered a separate interrogatory.

(4) *Requests for Production*. Any party may serve on any other party no more than 15 written requests for production. Each discrete subpart of a request for production is considered a separate request for production.

(5) *Requests for Admissions*. Any party may serve on any other party no more than 15 written requests for admissions. Each discrete subpart of a request for admission is considered a separate request for admission.

(6) *Requests for Disclosure*. In addition to the content subject to disclosure under Rule 194.2, a party may request disclosure of all documents, electronic information, and tangible items that the disclosing party has in its possession, custody, or control and may use to support its claims or defenses. A request for disclosure made pursuant to this paragraph is not considered a request for production.

(c) **Reopening Discovery**. If a suit is removed from the expedited actions process in Rule 169 or, in a divorce, the filing of a pleading renders this subdivision no longer applicable, the discovery period reopens, and discovery must be completed within the limitations provided in Rules 190.3 or 190.4, whichever is applicable. Any person previously deposed may be redeposed. On motion of any party, the court should continue the trial date if necessary to permit completion of discovery.

190.3 Discovery Control Plan - By Rule (Level 2)

(a) **Application**. Unless a suit is governed by a discovery control plan under Rules 190.2 or 190.4, discovery must be conducted in accordance with this subdivision.

(b) **Limitations**. Discovery is subject to the limitations provided elsewhere in these rules and to the following additional limitations:

(1) *Discovery period.* All discovery must be conducted during the discovery period, which begins when suit is filed and continues until:

(A) 30 days before the date set for trial, in cases under the Family Code; or

(B) in other cases, the earlier of

(i) 30 days before the date set for trial, or

(ii) nine months after the earlier of the date of the first oral deposition or the due date of the first response to written discovery.

(2) *Total time for oral depositions.* Each side may have no more than 50 hours in oral depositions to examine and cross-examine parties on the opposing side, experts designated by those parties, and persons who are subject to those parties' control. "Side" refers to all the litigants with generally common interests in the litigation. If one side designates more than two experts, the opposing side may have an additional six hours of total deposition time for each additional expert designated. The court may modify the deposition hours and must do so when a side or party would be given unfair advantage.

(3) *Interrogatories.* Any party may serve on any other party no more than 25 written interrogatories, excluding interrogatories asking a party only to identify or authenticate specific documents. Each discrete subpart of an interrogatory is considered a separate interrogatory.

190.4 Discovery Control Plan - By Order (Level 3)

(a) **Application.** The court must, on a party's motion, and may, on its own initiative, order that discovery be conducted in accordance with a discovery control plan tailored to the circumstances of the specific suit. The parties may submit an agreed order to the court for its consideration. The court should act on a party's motion or agreed order under this subdivision as promptly as reasonably possible.

(b) **Limitations.** The discovery control plan ordered by the court may address any issue concerning discovery or the matters listed in Rule 166, and may change any limitation on the time for or amount of discovery set forth in these rules. The discovery limitations of Rule 190.2, if applicable, or otherwise of Rule 190.3 apply unless specifically changed in the discovery control plan ordered by the court. The plan must include:

(1) a date for trial or for a conference to determine a trial setting;

(2) a discovery period during which either all discovery must be conducted or all discovery requests must be sent, for the entire case or an appropriate phase of it;

(3) appropriate limits on the amount of discovery; and

(4) deadlines for joining additional parties, amending or supplementing pleadings, and designating expert witnesses.

190.5 Modification of Discovery Control Plan

The court may modify a discovery control plan at any time and must do so when the interest of justice requires. Unless a suit is governed by the expedited actions process in Rule 169, the court must allow additional discovery:

(a) related to new, amended or supplemental pleadings, or new information disclosed in a discovery response or in an amended or supplemental response, if:

(1) the pleadings or responses were made after the deadline for completion of discovery or so nearly before that deadline that an adverse party does not have an adequate opportunity to conduct discovery related to the new matters, and

(2) the adverse party would be unfairly prejudiced without such additional discovery;

(b) regarding matters that have changed materially after the discovery cutoff if trial is set or postponed so that the trial date is more than three months after the discovery period ends.

Comment to 2013 change: Rule 190 is amended to implement section 22.004(h) of the Texas Government Code, which calls for rules to promote the prompt, efficient, and cost-effective resolution of civil actions when the amount in controversy does not exceed $100,000. Rule 190.2 now applies to expedited actions, as defined by Rule 169. Rule 190.2 continues to apply to divorces not involving children in which the value of the marital estate is not more than $50,000, which are otherwise exempt from the expedited actions process. Amended Rule 190.2(b) ends the discovery period 180 days after the date the first discovery request is served; imposes a fifteen limit maximum on interrogatories, requests for production, and requests for admission; and allows for additional disclosures. Although expedited actions are not subject to mandatory additional discovery under amended Rule 190.5, the court may still allow additional discovery if the conditions of Rule 190(a) are met.

190.6 Certain Types of Discovery Excepted

This rule's limitations on discovery do not apply to or include discovery conducted under Rule 202 ("Depositions Before Suit or to Investigate Claims"), or Rule 621a ("Discovery and Enforcement of Judgment"). But Rule 202 cannot be used to circumvent the limitations of this rule.

RULE 191. MODIFYING DISCOVERY PROCEDURES AND LIMITATIONS; CONFERENCE REQUIREMENT; SIGNING DISCLOSURES; DISCOVERY REQUESTS, RESPONSES, AND OBJECTIONS; FILING REQUIREMENTS

191.1 Modification of Procedures

Except where specifically prohibited, the procedures and limitations set forth in the rules pertaining to discovery may be modified in any suit by the agreement of the parties or by court order for good cause. An agreement of the parties is enforceable if it complies with Rule 11 or, as it affects an oral deposition, if it is made a part of the record of the deposition.

191.2 Conference.

Parties and their attorneys are expected to cooperate in discovery and to make any agreements reasonably necessary for the efficient disposition of the case. All discovery motions or requests for hearings relating to discovery must contain a certificate by the party filing the motion or request that a reasonable effort has been made to resolve the dispute without the necessity of court intervention and the effort failed.

191.3 Signing of Disclosures, Discovery Requests, Notices, Responses, and Objections

(a) **Signature required**. Every disclosure, discovery request, notice, response, and objection must be signed:

(1) by an attorney, if the party is represented by an attorney, and must show the attorney's State Bar of Texas identification number, address, telephone number, and fax number, if any; or

(2) by the party, if the party is not represented by an attorney, and must show the party's address, telephone number, and fax number, if any.

(b) **Effect of signature on disclosure**. The signature of an attorney or party on a disclosure constitutes a certification that to the best of the signer's knowledge, information, and belief, formed after a reasonable inquiry, the disclosure is complete and correct as of the time it is made.

(c) **Effect of signature on discovery request, notice, response, or objection**. The signature of an attorney or party on a discovery request, notice, response, or objection constitutes a certification that to the best of the signer's knowledge, information, and belief, formed after a reasonable inquiry, the request, notice, response, or objection:

(1) is consistent with the rules of civil procedure and these discovery rules and warranted by existing law or a good faith argument for the extension, modification, or reversal of existing law;

(2) has a good faith factual basis;

(3) is not interposed for any improper purpose, such as to harass or to cause unnecessary delay or needless increase in the cost of litigation; and

(4) is not unreasonable or unduly burdensome or expensive, given the needs of the case, the discovery already had in the case, the amount in controversy, and the importance of the issues at stake in the litigation.

(d) **Effect of failure to sign**. If a request, notice, response, or objection is not signed, it must be stricken unless it is signed promptly after the omission is called to the attention of the party making the request, notice, response, or objection. A party is not required to take any action with respect to a request or notice that is not signed.

(e) **Sanctions**. If the certification is false without substantial justification, the court may, upon motion or its own initiative, impose on the person who made the certification, or the party on whose behalf the request, notice, response, or objection was made, or both, an appropriate sanction as for a frivolous pleading or motion under Chapter 10 of the Civil Practice and Remedies Code.

191.4 Filing of Discovery Materials.

(a) **Discovery materials not to be filed**. The following discovery materials must not be filed:

(1) discovery requests, deposition notices, and subpoenas required to be served only on parties;

(2) responses and objections to discovery requests and deposition notices, regardless on whom the requests or notices were served;

(3) documents and tangible things produced in discovery; and

(4) statements prepared in compliance with Rule 193.3(b) or (d).

(b) **Discovery materials to be filed**. The following discovery materials must be filed:

(1) discovery requests, deposition notices, and subpoenas required to be served on nonparties;

(2) motions and responses to motions pertaining to discovery matters; and

(3) agreements concerning discovery matters, to the extent necessary to comply with Rule 11.

(c) **Exceptions**. Notwithstanding paragraph (a):

(1) the court may order discovery materials to be filed;

(2) a person may file discovery materials in support of or in opposition to a motion or for other use in a court proceeding; and

(3) a person may file discovery materials necessary for a proceeding in an appellate court.

(d) **Retention requirement for persons**. Any person required to serve discovery materials not required to be filed must retain the original or exact copy of the materials during the pendency of the case and any related appellate proceedings begun within six months after judgment is signed, unless otherwise provided by the trial court.

(e) **Retention requirement for courts**. The clerk of the court shall retain and dispose of deposition transcripts and depositions upon written questions as directed by the Supreme Court.

191.5 Service of Discovery Materials.

Every disclosure, discovery request, notice, response, and objection required to be served on a party or person must be served on all parties of record.

RULE 192. PERMISSIBLE DISCOVERY: FORMS AND SCOPE; WORK PRODUCT; PROTECTIVE ORDERS; DEFINITIONS

192.1 Forms of Discovery.

Permissible forms of discovery are:

(a) requests for disclosure;

(b) requests for production and inspection of documents and tangible things;

(c) requests and motions for entry upon and examination of real property;

(d) interrogatories to a party;

(e) requests for admission;

(f) oral or written depositions; and

(g) motions for mental or physical examinations.

192.2 Sequence of Discovery.

The permissible forms of discovery may be combined in the same document and may be taken in any order or sequence.

192.3 Scope of Discovery.

(a) **Generally**. In general, a party may obtain discovery regarding any matter that is not privileged and is relevant to the subject matter of the pending action, whether it relates to the claim or defense of the party seeking discovery or the claim or defense of any other party. It is not a ground for objection that the information sought will be inadmissible at trial if the information sought appears reasonably calculated to lead to the discovery of admissible evidence.

(b) **Documents and tangible things**. A party may obtain discovery of the existence, description, nature, custody, condition, location, and contents of documents and tangible things (including papers, books, accounts, drawings, graphs, charts, photographs, electronic or videotape recordings, data, and data compilations) that constitute or contain matters relevant to the subject matter of the action. A person is required to produce a document or tangible thing that is within the person's possession, custody, or control.

(c) **Persons with knowledge of relevant facts**. A party may obtain discovery of the name, address, and telephone number of persons having knowledge of relevant facts, and a brief statement of each identified person's connection with the case. A person has knowledge of relevant facts when that person has or may have knowledge of any discoverable matter. The person need not have admissible information or personal knowledge of the facts. An expert is "a person with knowledge of relevant facts" only if that knowledge was obtained first-hand or if it was not obtained in preparation for trial or in anticipation of litigation.

(d) **Trial witnesses**. A party may obtain discovery of the name, address, and telephone number of any person who is expected to be called to testify at trial. This paragraph does not apply to rebuttal or impeaching witnesses the necessity of whose testimony cannot reasonably be anticipated before trial.

(e) **Testifying and consulting experts**. The identity, mental impressions, and opinions of a consulting expert whose mental impressions and opinions have not been reviewed by a testifying expert are not discoverable. A party may discover the following information regarding a testifying expert or regarding a consulting expert whose mental impressions or opinions have been reviewed by a testifying expert:

(1) the expert's name, address, and telephone number;

(2) the subject matter on which a testifying expert will testify;

(3) the facts known by the expert that relate to or form the basis of the expert's mental impressions and opinions formed or made in connection with the case in which the discovery is sought, regardless of when and how the factual information was acquired;

(4) the expert's mental impressions and opinions formed or made in connection with the case in which discovery is sought, and any methods used to derive them;

(5) any bias of the witness;

(6) all documents, tangible things, reports, models, or data compilations that have been provided to, reviewed by, or prepared by or for the expert in anticipation of a testifying expert's testimony;

(7) the expert's current resume and bibliography.

(f) **Indemnity and insuring agreements**. Except as otherwise provided by law, a party may obtain discovery of the existence and contents of any indemnity or insurance agreement under which any person may be liable to satisfy part or all of a judgment rendered in the action or to indemnify or reimburse for payments made to satisfy the judgment. Information concerning the indemnity or insurance agreement is not by reason of disclosure admissible in evidence at trial.

(g) **Settlement agreements**. A party may obtain discovery of the existence and contents of any relevant portions of a settlement agreement. Information concerning a settlement agreement is not by reason of disclosure admissible in evidence at trial.

(h) **Statements of persons with knowledge of relevant facts**. A party may obtain discovery of the statement of any person with knowledge of relevant facts--a "witness statement"-- regardless of when the statement was made. A witness statement is (1) a written statement signed or otherwise adopted or approved in writing by the person making it, or (2) a stenographic, mechanical, electrical, or other type of recording of a witness's oral statement, or any substantially verbatim transcription of such a recording. Notes taken during a conversation or interview with a witness are not a witness statement. Any person may obtain, upon written request, his or her own statement concerning the lawsuit, which is in the possession, custody or control of any party.

(i) **Potential parties**. A party may obtain discovery of the name, address, and telephone number of any potential party.

(j) **Contentions**. A party may obtain discovery of any other party's legal contentions and the factual bases for those contentions.

192.4 Limitations on Scope of Discovery.

The discovery methods permitted by these rules should be limited by the court if it determines, on motion or on its own initiative and on reasonable notice, that:

(a) the discovery sought is unreasonably cumulative or duplicative, or is obtainable from some other source that is more convenient, less burdensome, or less expensive; or

(b) the burden or expense of the proposed discovery outweighs its likely benefit, taking into account the needs of the case, the amount in controversy, the parties' resources, the importance of the issues at stake in the litigation, and the importance of the proposed discovery in resolving the issues.

192.5 Work Product.

(a) **Work product defined**. Work product comprises:

(1) material prepared or mental impressions developed in anticipation of litigation or for trial by or for a party or a party's representatives, including the party's attorneys, consultants, sureties, indemnitors, insurers, employees, or agents; or

(2) a communication made in anticipation of litigation or for trial between a party and the party's representatives or among a party's representatives, including the party's attorneys, consultants, sureties, indemnitors, insurers, employees, or agents.

(b) **Protection of work product**.

(1) Protection of core work product--attorney mental processes. Core work product - the work product of an attorney or an attorney's representative that contains the attorney's or the attorney's representative's mental impressions, opinions, conclusions, or legal theories - is not discoverable.

(2) Protection of other work product. Any other work product is discoverable only upon a showing that the party seeking discovery has substantial need of the materials in the preparation of the party's case and that the party is unable without undue hardship to obtain the substantial equivalent of the material by other means.

(3) Incidental disclosure of attorney mental processes. It is not a violation of subparagraph (1) if disclosure ordered pursuant to subparagraph (2) incidentally discloses by inference attorney mental processes otherwise protected under subparagraph (1).

(4) Limiting disclosure of mental processes. If a court orders discovery of work product pursuant to subparagraph (2), the court must--insofar as possible--protect against disclosure of the mental impressions, opinions, conclusions, or legal theories not otherwise discoverable.

(c) **Exceptions**. Even if made or prepared in anticipation of litigation or for trial, the following is not work product protected from discovery:

(1) information discoverable under Rule 192.3 concerning experts, trial witnesses, witness statements, and contentions;

(2) trial exhibits ordered disclosed under Rule 166 or Rule 190.4;

(3) the name, address, and telephone number of any potential party or any person with knowledge of relevant facts;

(4) any photograph or electronic image of underlying facts (e.g., a photograph of the accident scene) or a photograph or electronic image of any sort that a party intends to offer into evidence; and

(5) any work product created under circumstances within an exception to the attorney-client privilege in Rule 503(d) of the Rules of Evidence.

(d) **Privilege**. For purposes of these rules, an assertion that material or information is work product is an assertion of privilege.

192.6 Protective Order.

(a) **Motion**. A person from whom discovery is sought, and any other person affected by the discovery request, may move within the time permitted for response to the discovery request for an order protecting that person from the discovery sought. A person should not move for protection when an objection to written discovery or an assertion of privilege is appropriate, but a motion does not waive the objection or assertion of privilege. If a person seeks protection regarding the time or place of discovery, the person must state a reasonable time and place for discovery with which the person will comply. A person must comply with a request to the extent protection is not sought unless it is unreasonable under the circumstances to do so before obtaining a ruling on the motion.

(b) **Order**. To protect the movant from undue burden, unnecessary expense, harassment, annoyance, or invasion of personal, constitutional, or property rights, the court may make any order in the interest of justice and may - among other things - order that:

(1) the requested discovery not be sought in whole or in part;

(2) the extent or subject matter of discovery be limited;

(3) the discovery not be undertaken at the time or place specified;

(4) the discovery be undertaken only by such method or upon such terms and conditions or at the time and place directed by the court;

(5) the results of discovery be sealed or otherwise protected, subject to the provisions of Rule 76a.

192.7 Definitions.

As used in these rules

(a) Written discovery means requests for disclosure, requests for production and inspection of documents and tangible things, requests for entry onto property, interrogatories, and requests for admission.

(b) Possession, custody, or control of an item means that the person either has physical possession of the item or has a right to possession of the item that is equal or superior to the person who has physical possession of the item.

(c) A testifying expert is an expert who may be called to testify as an expert witness at trial.

(d) A consulting expert is an expert who has been consulted, retained, or specially employed by a party in anticipation of litigation or in preparation for trial, but who is not a testifying expert.

RULE 193. WRITTEN DISCOVERY: RESPONSE; OBJECTION; ASSERTION OF PRIVILEGE; SUPPLEMENTATION AND AMENDMENT; FAILURE TO TIMELY RESPOND; PRESUMPTION OF AUTHENTICITY

193.1 Responding to Written Discovery; Duty to Make Complete Response.

A party must respond to written discovery in writing within the time provided by court order or these rules. When responding to written discovery, a party must make a complete response, based on all information reasonably available to the responding party or its attorney at the time the response is made. The responding party's answers, objections, and other responses must be preceded by the request to which they apply.

193.2 Objecting to Written Discovery

(a) **Form and time for objections**. A party must make any objection to written discovery in writing - either in the response or in a separate document - within the time for response. The party must state specifically the legal or factual basis for the objection and the extent to which the party is refusing to comply with the request.

(b) **Duty to respond when partially objecting; objection to time or place of production**. A party must comply with as much of the request to which the party has made no objection unless it is unreasonable under the circumstances to do so before obtaining a ruling on the objection. If the responding party objects to the requested time or place of production, the responding party must state a reasonable time and place for complying with the request and must comply at that time and place without further request or order.

(c) **Good faith basis for objection**. A party may object to written discovery only if a good faith factual and legal basis for the objection exists at the time the objection is made.

(d) **Amendment**. An objection or response to written discovery may be amended or supplemented to state an objection or basis that, at the time the objection or response initially was made, either was inapplicable or was unknown after reasonable inquiry.

(e) **Waiver of objection**. An objection that is not made within the time required, or that is obscured by numerous unfounded objections, is waived unless the court excuses the waiver for good cause shown.

(f) **No objection to preserve privilege**. A party should not object to a request for written discovery on the grounds that it calls for production of material or information that is privileged but should instead comply with Rule 193.3. A party who objects to production of privileged material or information does not waive the privilege but must comply with Rule 193.3 when the error is pointed out.

193.3 Asserting a Privilege

A party may preserve a privilege from written discovery in accordance with this subdivision.

(a) **Withholding privileged material or information**. A party who claims that material or information responsive to written discovery is privileged may withhold the privileged material or information from the response. The party must state--in the response (or an amended or supplemental response) or in a separate document--that:

(1) information or material responsive to the request has been withheld,

(2) the request to which the information or material relates, and

(3) the privilege or privileges asserted.

(b) **Description of withheld material or information**. After receiving a response indicating that material or information has been withheld from production, the party seeking discovery may serve a written request that the withholding party identify the information and material withheld. Within 15 days of service of that request, the withholding party must serve a response that:

(1) describes the information or materials withheld that, without revealing the privileged information itself or otherwise waiving the privilege, enables other parties to assess the applicability of the privilege, and

(2) asserts a specific privilege for each item or group of items withheld.

(c) **Exemption**. Without complying with paragraphs (a) and (b), a party may withhold a privileged communication to or from a lawyer or lawyer's representative or a privileged document of a lawyer or lawyer's representative

(1) created or made from the point at which a party consults a lawyer with a view to obtaining professional legal services from the lawyer in the prosecution or defense of a specific claim in the litigation in which discovery is requested, and

(2) concerning the litigation in which the discovery is requested.

(d) **Privilege not waived by production**. A party who produces material or information without intending to waive a claim of privilege does not waive that claim under these rules or the Rules of Evidence if - within ten days or a shorter time ordered by the court, after the producing party actually discovers that such production was made - the producing party amends the response, identifying the material or information produced and stating the privilege asserted. If the producing party thus amends the response to assert a privilege, the requesting party must promptly return the specified material or information and any copies pending any ruling by the court denying the privilege.

193.4 Hearing and Ruling on Objections and Assertions of Privilege.

(a) **Hearing**. Any party may at any reasonable time request a hearing on an objection or claim of privilege asserted under this rule. The party making the objection or asserting the privilege must present any evidence necessary to support the objection or privilege. The evidence may be testimony presented at the hearing or affidavits served at least seven days before the hearing or at such other reasonable time as the court permits. If the court determines that an in camera review of some or all of the requested discovery is necessary, that material or information must be segregated and produced to the court in a sealed wrapper within a reasonable time following the hearing.

(b) **Ruling**. To the extent the court sustains the objection or claim of privilege, the responding party has no further duty to respond to that request. To the extent the court overrules the objection or claim of privilege, the responding party must produce the requested material or information within 30 days after the court's ruling or at such time as the court orders. A party need not request a ruling on that party's own objection or assertion of privilege to preserve the objection or privilege.

(c) **Use of material or information withheld under claim of privilege**. A party may not use-- at any hearing or trial--material or information withheld from discovery under a claim of privilege, including a claim sustained by the court, without timely amending or supplementing the party's response to that discovery.

193.5 Amending or Supplementing Responses to Written Discovery.

(a) **Duty to amend or supplement**. If a party learns that the party's response to written discovery was incomplete or incorrect when made, or, although complete and correct when made, is no longer complete and correct, the party must amend or supplement the response:

(1) to the extent that the written discovery sought the identification of persons with knowledge of relevant facts, trial witnesses, or expert witnesses, and

(2) to the extent that the written discovery sought other information, unless the additional or corrective information has been made known to the other parties in writing, on the record at a deposition, or through other discovery responses.

(b) **Time and form of amended or supplemental response**. An amended or supplemental response must be made reasonably promptly after the party discovers the necessity for such a response. Except as otherwise provided by these rules, it is presumed that an amended or supplemental response made less than 30 days before trial was not made reasonably promptly. An amended or supplemental response must be in the same form as the initial response and must be verified by the party if the original response was required to be verified by the party, but the failure to comply with this requirement does not make the amended or supplemental response untimely unless the party making the response refuses to correct the defect within a reasonable time after it is pointed out.

193.6 Failing to Timely Respond - Effect on Trial

(a) **Exclusion of evidence and exceptions**. A party who fails to make, amend, or supplement a discovery response in a timely manner may not introduce in evidence the material or information that was not timely disclosed, or offer the testimony of a witness (other than a named party) who was not timely identified, unless the court finds that:

(1) there was good cause for the failure to timely make, amend, or supplement the discovery response; or

(2) the failure to timely make, amend, or supplement the discovery response will not unfairly surprise or unfairly prejudice the other parties.

(b) **Burden of establishing exception**. The burden of establishing good cause or the lack of unfair surprise or unfair prejudice is on the party seeking to introduce the evidence or call the witness. A finding of good cause or of the lack of unfair surprise or unfair prejudice must be supported by the record.

(c) **Continuance**. Even if the party seeking to introduce the evidence or call the witness fails to carry the burden under paragraph (b), the court may grant a continuance or temporarily postpone the trial to allow a response to be made, amended, or supplemented, and to allow opposing parties to conduct discovery regarding any new information presented by that response.

193.7 Production of Documents Self-Authenticating

A party's production of a document in response to written discovery authenticates the document for use against that party in any pretrial proceeding or at trial unless - within ten days or a longer or shorter time ordered by the court, after the producing party has actual notice that the document will be used -

the party objects to the authenticity of the document, or any part of it, stating the specific basis for objection. An objection must be either on the record or in writing and must have a good faith factual and legal basis. An objection made to the authenticity of only part of a document does not affect the authenticity of the remainder. If objection is made, the party attempting to use the document should be given a reasonable opportunity to establish its authenticity.

RULE 194. REQUESTS FOR DISCLOSURE

194.1 Request.

A party may obtain disclosure from another party of the information or material listed in Rule 194.2 by serving the other party - no later than 30 days before the end of any applicable discovery period - the following request: "Pursuant to Rule 194, you are requested to disclose, within 30 days of service of this request, the information or material described in Rule [state rule, e.g., 194.2, or 194.2(a), (c), and (f), or 194.2(d)-(g)]."

194.2 Content.

A party may request disclosure of any or all of the following:

(a) the correct names of the parties to the lawsuit;

(b) the name, address, and telephone number of any potential parties;

(c) the legal theories and, in general, the factual bases of the responding party's claims or defenses (the responding party need not marshal all evidence that may be offered at trial);

(d) the amount and any method of calculating economic damages;

(e) the name, address, and telephone number of persons having knowledge of relevant facts, and a brief statement of each identified person's connection with the case;

(f) for any testifying expert:

    (1) the expert's name, address, and telephone number;

    (2) the subject matter on which the expert will testify;

    (3) the general substance of the expert's mental impressions and opinions and a brief summary of the basis for them, or if the expert is not retained by, employed by, or otherwise subject to the control of the responding party, documents reflecting such information;

    (4) if the expert is retained by, employed by, or otherwise subject to the control of the responding party:

        (A) all documents, tangible things, reports, models, or data compilations that have been provided to, reviewed by, or prepared by or for the expert in anticipation of the expert's testimony; and

        (B) the expert's current resume and bibliography;

(g) any indemnity and insuring agreements described in Rule 192.3(f);

(h) any settlement agreements described in Rule 192.3(g);

(i) any witness statements described in Rule 192.3(h);

(j) in a suit alleging physical or mental injury and damages from the occurrence that is the subject of the case, all medical records and bills that are reasonably related to the injuries or damages asserted or, in lieu thereof, an authorization permitting the disclosure of such medical records and bills;

(k) in a suit alleging physical or mental injury and damages from the occurrence that is the subject of the case, all medical records and bills obtained by the responding party by virtue of an authorization furnished by the requesting party;

(l) the name, address, and telephone number of any person who may be designated as a responsible third party.

194.3 Response.

The responding party must serve a written response on the requesting party within 30 days after service of the request, except that:

(a) a defendant served with a request before the defendant's answer is due need not respond until 50 days after service of the request, and

(b) a response to a request under Rule 194.2(f) is governed by Rule 195.

194.4 Production.

Copies of documents and other tangible items ordinarily must be served with the response. But if the responsive documents are voluminous, the response must state a reasonable time and place for the production of documents. The responding party must produce the documents at the time and place stated, unless otherwise agreed by the parties or ordered by the court, and must provide the requesting party a reasonable opportunity to inspect them.

194.5 No Objection or Assertion of Work Product.

No objection or assertion of work product is permitted to a request under this rule.

194.6 Certain Responses Not Admissible.

A response to requests under Rule 194.2(c) and (d) that has been changed by an amended or supplemental response is not admissible and may not be used for impeachment.

RULE 195. DISCOVERY REGARDING TESTIFYING EXPERT WITNESSES

195.1 Permissible Discovery Tools.

A party may request another party to designate and disclose information concerning testifying expert witnesses only through a request for disclosure under Rule 194 and through depositions and reports as permitted by this rule.

195.2 Schedule for Designating Experts.

Unless otherwise ordered by the court, a party must designate experts - that is, furnish information requested under Rule 194.2(f) - by the later of the following two dates: 30 days after the request is served, or

(a) with regard to all experts testifying for a party seeking affirmative relief, 90 days before the end of the discovery period;

(b) with regard to all other experts, 60 days before the end of the discovery period.

195.3 Scheduling Depositions.

(a) **Experts for party seeking affirmative relief**. A party seeking affirmative relief must make an expert retained by, employed by, or otherwise in the control of the party available for deposition as follows:

(1) *If no report furnished*. If a report of the expert's factual observations, tests, supporting data, calculations, photographs, and opinions is not produced when the expert is designated, then the party must make the expert available for deposition reasonably promptly after the expert is designated. If the deposition cannot--due to the actions of the tendering party--reasonably be

concluded more than 15 days before the deadline for designating other experts, that deadline must be extended for other experts testifying on the same subject.

(2) *If report furnished.* If a report of the expert's factual observations, tests, supporting data, calculations, photographs, and opinions is produced when the expert is designated, then the party need not make the expert available for deposition until reasonably promptly after all other experts have been designated.

(b) **Other experts.** A party not seeking affirmative relief must make an expert retained by, employed by, or otherwise in the control of the party available for deposition reasonably promptly after the expert is designated and the experts testifying on the same subject for the party seeking affirmative relief have been deposed.

195.4 Oral Deposition.

In addition to disclosure under Rule 194, a party may obtain discovery concerning the subject matter on which the expert is expected to testify, the expert's mental impressions and opinions, the facts known to the expert (regardless of when the factual information was acquired) that relate to or form the basis of the testifying expert's mental impressions and opinions, and other discoverable matters, including documents not produced in disclosure, only by oral deposition of the expert and by a report prepared by the expert under this rule.

195.5 Court-Ordered Reports.

If the discoverable factual observations, tests, supporting data, calculations, photographs, or opinions of an expert have not been recorded and reduced to tangible form, the court may order these matters reduced to tangible form and produced in addition to the deposition.

195.6 Amendment and Supplementation.

A party's duty to amend and supplement written discovery regarding a testifying expert is governed by Rule 193.5. If an expert witness is retained by, employed by, or otherwise under the control of a party, that party must also amend or supplement any deposition testimony or written report by the expert, but only with regard to the expert's mental impressions or opinions and the basis for them.

195.7 Cost of Expert Witnesses.

When a party takes the oral deposition of an expert witness retained by the opposing party, all reasonable fees charged by the expert for time spent in preparing for, giving, reviewing, and correcting the deposition must be paid by the party that retained the expert.

RULE 196. REQUESTS FOR PRODUCTION AND INSPECTION TO PARTIES; REQUESTS AND MOTIONS FOR ENTRY UPON PROPERTY

196.1 Request for Production and Inspection to Parties.

(a) **Request.** A party may serve on another party--no later than 30 days before the end of the discovery period--a request for production or for inspection, to inspect, sample, test, photograph and copy documents or tangible things within the scope of discovery.

(b) **Contents of request.** The request must specify the items to be produced or inspected, either by individual item or by category, and describe with reasonable particularity each item and category. The request must specify a reasonable time (on or after the date on which the response is due) and place for production. If the requesting party will sample or test the requested items, the means, manner and procedure for testing or sampling must be described with sufficient specificity to inform the producing party of the means, manner, and procedure for testing or sampling.

(c) **Requests for production of medical or mental health records regarding nonparties**.

(1) *Service of request on nonparty*. If a party requests another party to produce medical or mental health records regarding a nonparty, the requesting party must serve the nonparty with the request for production under Rule 21a.

(2) *Exceptions*. A party is not required to serve the request for production on a nonparty whose medical records are sought if:

    (A) the nonparty signs a release of the records that is effective as to the requesting party;

    (B) the identity of the nonparty whose records are sought will not directly or indirectly be disclosed by production of the records; or

    (C) the court, upon a showing of good cause by the party seeking the records, orders that service is not required.

(3) *Confidentiality*. Nothing in this rule excuses compliance with laws concerning the confidentiality of medical or mental health records.

196.2 Response to Request for Production and Inspection.

(a) **Time for response**. The responding party must serve a written response on the requesting party within 30 days after service of the request, except that a defendant served with a request before the defendant's answer is due need not respond until 50 days after service of the request.

(b) **Content of response**. With respect to each item or category of items, the responding party must state objections and assert privileges as required by these rules, and state, as appropriate, that:

    (1) production, inspection, or other requested action will be permitted as requested;

    (2) the requested items are being served on the requesting party with the response;

    (3) production, inspection, or other requested action will take place at a specified time and place, if the responding party is objecting to the time and place of production; or

    (4) no items have been identified - after a diligent search - that are responsive to the request.

196.3 Production.

(a) **Time and place of production**. Subject to any objections stated in the response, the responding party must produce the requested documents or tangible things within the person's possession, custody or control at either the time and place requested or the time and place stated in the response, unless otherwise agreed by the parties or ordered by the court, and must provide the requesting party a reasonable opportunity to inspect them.

(b) **Copies**. The responding party may produce copies in lieu of originals unless a question is raised as to the authenticity of the original or in the circumstances it would be unfair to produce copies in lieu of originals. If originals are produced, the responding party is entitled to retain the originals while the requesting party inspects and copies them.

(c) **Organization**. The responding party must either produce documents and tangible things as they are kept in the usual course of business or organize and label them to correspond with the categories in the request.

196.4 Electronic or Magnetic Data.

To obtain discovery of data or information that exists in electronic or magnetic form, the requesting party must specifically request production of electronic or magnetic data and specify the form in which the requesting party wants it produced. The responding party must produce the electronic or magnetic data that is responsive to the request and is reasonably available to the responding party in its ordinary course of business. If the responding party cannot - through reasonable efforts - retrieve the data or information requested or produce it in the form requested, the responding party must state an objection complying with these rules. If the court orders the responding party to comply with the request, the court must also order that the requesting party pay the reasonable expenses of any extraordinary steps required to retrieve and produce the information.

196.5 Destruction or Alteration.

Testing, sampling or examination of an item may not destroy or materially alter an item unless previously authorized by the court.

196.6 Expenses of Production.

Unless otherwise ordered by the court for good cause, the expense of producing items will be borne by the responding party and the expense of inspecting, sampling, testing, photographing, and copying items produced will be borne by the requesting party.

196.7 Request of Motion for Entry Upon Property.

(a) **Request or motion**. A party may gain entry on designated land or other property to inspect, measure, survey, photograph, test, or sample the property or any designated object or operation thereon by serving - no later than 30 days before the end of any applicable discovery period -

(1) a request on all parties if the land or property belongs to a party, or

(2) a motion and notice of hearing on all parties and the nonparty if the land or property belongs to a nonparty. If the identity or address of the nonparty is unknown and cannot be obtained through reasonable diligence, the court must permit service by means other than those specified in Rule 21a that are reasonably calculated to give the nonparty notice of the motion and hearing.

(b) **Time, place, and other conditions**. The request for entry upon a party's property, or the order for entry upon a nonparty's property, must state the time, place, manner, conditions, and scope of the inspection, and must specifically describe any desired means, manner, and procedure for testing or sampling, and the person or persons by whom the inspection, testing, or sampling is to be made.

(c) **Response to request for entry**.

(1) Time to respond. The responding party must serve a written response on the requesting party within 30 days after service of the request, except that a defendant served with a request before the defendant's answer is due need not respond until 50 days after service of the request.

(2) Content of response. The responding party must state objections and assert privileges as required by these rules, and state, as appropriate, that:

(A) entry or other requested action will be permitted as requested;

(B) entry or other requested action will take place at a specified time and place, if the responding party is objecting to the time and place of production; or

(C) entry or other requested action cannot be permitted for reasons stated in the response.

(d) **Requirements for order for entry on nonparty's property**. An order for entry on a nonparty's property may issue only for good cause shown and only if the land, property, or object thereon as to which discovery is sought is relevant to the subject matter of the action.

RULE 197. INTERROGATORIES TO PARTIES

197.1 Interrogatories.

A party may serve on another party - no later than 30 days before the end of the discovery period - written interrogatories to inquire about any matter within the scope of discovery except matters covered by Rule 195. An interrogatory may inquire whether a party makes a specific legal or factual contention and may ask the responding party to state the legal theories and to describe in general the factual bases for the party's claims or defenses, but interrogatories may not be used to require the responding party to marshal all of its available proof or the proof the party intends to offer at trial.

197.2 Response to Interrogatories.

(a) **Time for response**. The responding party must serve a written response on the requesting party within 30 days after service of the interrogatories, except that a defendant served with interrogatories before the defendant's answer is due need not respond until 50 days after service of the interrogatories.

(b) **Content of response**. A response must include the party's answers to the interrogatories and may include objections and assertions of privilege as required under these rules.

(c) **Option to produce records**. If the answer to an interrogatory may be derived or ascertained from public records, from the responding party's business records, or from a compilation, abstract or summary of the responding party's business records, and the burden of deriving or ascertaining the answer is substantially the same for the requesting party as for the responding party, the responding party may answer the interrogatory by specifying and, if applicable, producing the records or compilation, abstract or summary of the records. The records from which the answer may be derived or ascertained must be specified in sufficient detail to permit the requesting party to locate and identify them as readily as can the responding party. If the responding party has specified business records, the responding party must state a reasonable time and place for examination of the documents. The responding party must produce the documents at the time and place stated, unless otherwise agreed by the parties or ordered by the court, and must provide the requesting party a reasonable opportunity to inspect them.

(d) **Verification required; exceptions**. A responding party - not an agent or attorney as otherwise permitted by Rule 14 - must sign the answers under oath except that:

(1) when answers are based on information obtained from other persons, the party may so state, and

(2) a party need not sign answers to interrogatories about persons with knowledge of relevant facts, trial witnesses, and legal contentions.

197.3 Use.

Answers to interrogatories may be used only against the responding party. An answer to an interrogatory inquiring about matters described in Rule 194.2(c) and (d) that has been amended or supplemented is not admissible and may not be used for impeachment.

RULE 198. REQUESTS FOR ADMISSIONS

198.1 Request for Admissions.

A party may serve on another party - no later than 30 days before the end of the discovery period - written requests that the other party admit the truth of any matter within the scope of discovery, including statements of opinion or of fact or of the application of law to fact, or the genuineness of any documents served with the request or otherwise made available for inspection and copying. Each matter for which an admission is requested must be stated separately.

198.2 Response to Requests for Admissions.

(a) **Time for response**. The responding party must serve a written response on the requesting party within 30 days after service of the request, except that a defendant served with a request before the defendant's answer is due need not respond until 50 days after service of the request.

(b) **Content of response**. Unless the responding party states an objection or asserts a privilege, the responding party must specifically admit or deny the request or explain in detail the reasons that the responding party cannot admit or deny the request. A response must fairly meet the substance of the request. The responding party may qualify an answer, or deny a request in part, only when good faith requires. Lack of information or knowledge is not a proper response unless the responding party states that a reasonable inquiry was made but that the information known or easily obtainable is insufficient to enable the responding party to admit or deny. An assertion that the request presents an issue for trial is not a proper response.

(c) **Effect of failure to respond**. If a response is not timely served, the request is considered admitted without the necessity of a court order.

198.3 Effect of Admissions; Withdrawal or Amendment.

Any admission made by a party under this rule may be used solely in the pending action and not in any other proceeding. A matter admitted under this rule is conclusively established as to the party making the admission unless the court permits the party to withdraw or amend the admission. The court may permit the party to withdraw or amend the admission if:

(a) the party shows good cause for the withdrawal or amendment; and

(b) the court finds that the parties relying upon the responses and deemed admissions will not be unduly prejudiced and that the presentation of the merits of the action will be subserved by permitting the party to amend or withdraw the admission.

RULE 199. DEPOSITIONS UPON ORAL EXAMINATION

199.1 Oral Examination; Alternative Methods of Conducting or Recording.

(a) **Generally**. A party may take the testimony of any person or entity by deposition on oral examination before any officer authorized by law to take depositions. The testimony, objections, and any other statements during the deposition must be recorded at the time they are given or made.

(b) **Depositions by telephone or other remote electronic means**. A party may take an oral deposition by telephone or other remote electronic means if the party gives reasonable prior written notice of intent to do so. For the purposes of these rules, an oral deposition taken by telephone or other remote electronic means is considered as having been taken in the district and at the place where the witness is located when answering the questions. The officer taking the deposition may be located with the party noticing the deposition instead of with the witness if the witness is placed under oath by a person who is present with the witness and authorized to administer oaths in that jurisdiction.

(c) **Non-stenographic recording**. Any party may cause a deposition upon oral examination to be recorded by other than stenographic means, including videotape recording. The party requesting the non-stenographic recording will be responsible for obtaining a person authorized by law to administer the oath and for assuring that the recording will be intelligible, accurate, and trustworthy. At least five days prior to the deposition, the party must serve on the witness and all parties a notice, either in the notice of deposition or separately, that the deposition will be recorded by other than stenographic means. This notice must state the method of non-stenographic recording to be used and whether the deposition will also be recorded stenographically. Any other party may then serve written notice designating another method of recording in addition to the method specified, at the expense of such other party unless the court orders otherwise.

199.2 Procedure for Noticing Oral Depositions.

(a) **Time to notice deposition**. A notice of intent to take an oral deposition must be served on the witness and all parties a reasonable time before the deposition is taken. An oral deposition may be taken outside the discovery period only by agreement of the parties or with leave of court.

(b) **Content of notice**.

(1) *Identity of witness; organizations*. The notice must state the name of the witness, which may be either an individual or a public or private corporation, partnership, association, governmental agency, or other organization. If an organization is named as the witness, the notice must describe with reasonable particularity the matters on which examination is requested. In response, the organization named in the notice must - a reasonable time before the deposition - designate one or

more individuals to testify on its behalf and set forth, for each individual designated, the matters on which the individual will testify. Each individual designated must testify as to matters that are known or reasonably available to the organization. This subdivision does not preclude taking a deposition by any other procedure authorized by these rules.

(2) *Time and place.* The notice must state a reasonable time and place for the oral deposition. The place may be in:

> (A) the county of the witness's residence;
>
> (B) the county where the witness is employed or regularly transacts business in person;
>
> (C) the county of suit, if the witness is a party or a person designated by a party under Rule 199.2(b)(1);
>
> (D) the county where the witness was served with the subpoena, or within 150 miles of the place of service, if the witness is not a resident of Texas or is a transient person; or
>
> (E) subject to the foregoing, at any other convenient place directed by the court in which the cause is pending.

(3) *Alternative means of conducting and recording.* The notice must state whether the deposition is to be taken by telephone or other remote electronic means and identify the means. If the deposition is to be recorded by nonstenographic means, the notice may include the notice required by Rule 199.1(c).

(4) *Additional attendees.* The notice may include the notice concerning additional attendees required by Rule 199.5(a)(3).

(5) *Request for production of documents.* A notice may include a request that the witness produce at the deposition documents or tangible things within the scope of discovery and within the witness's possession, custody, or control. If the witness is a nonparty, the request must comply with Rule 205 and the designation of materials required to be identified in the subpoena must be attached to, or included in, the notice. The nonparty's response to the request is governed by Rules 176 and 205. When the witness is a party or subject to the control of a party, document requests under this subdivision are governed by Rules 193 and 196.

199.3 Compelling Witness to Attend.

A party may compel the witness to attend the oral deposition by serving the witness with a subpoena under Rule 176. If the witness is a party or is retained by, employed by, or otherwise subject to the control of a party, however, service of the notice of oral deposition upon the party's attorney has the same effect as a subpoena served on the witness.

199.4 Objections to Time and Place of Oral Deposition.

A party or witness may object to the time and place designated for an oral deposition by motion for protective order or by motion to quash the notice of deposition. If the motion is filed by the third business day after service of the notice of deposition, an objection to the time and place of a deposition stays the oral deposition until the motion can be determined.

199.5 Examination, Objection, and Conduct During Oral Depositions.

(a) **Attendance**.

(1) *Witness.* The witness must remain in attendance from day to day until the deposition is begun and completed.

(2) *Attendance by party.* A party may attend an oral deposition in person, even if the deposition is taken by telephone or other remote electronic means. If a deposition is taken by telephone or other remote electronic means, the party noticing the deposition must make arrangements for all persons to attend by the same means. If the party noticing the deposition appears in person, any other party

may appear by telephone or other remote electronic means if that party makes the necessary arrangements with the deposition officer and the party noticing the deposition.

(3) *Other attendees*. If any party intends to have in attendance any persons other than the witness, parties, spouses of parties, counsel, employees of counsel, and the officer taking the oral deposition, that party must give reasonable notice to all parties, either in the notice of deposition or separately, of the identity of the other persons.

(b) **Oath; examination**. Every person whose deposition is taken by oral examination must first be placed under oath. The parties may examine and cross-examine the witness. Any party, in lieu of participating in the examination, may serve written questions in a sealed envelope on the party noticing the oral deposition, who must deliver them to the deposition officer, who must open the envelope and propound them to the witness.

(c) **Time limitation**. No side may examine or cross-examine an individual witness for more than six hours. Breaks during depositions do not count against this limitation.

(d) **Conduct during the oral deposition; conferences**. The oral deposition must be conducted in the same manner as if the testimony were being obtained in court during trial. Counsel should cooperate with and be courteous to each other and to the witness. The witness should not be evasive and should not unduly delay the examination. Private conferences between the witness and the witness's attorney during the actual taking of the deposition are improper except for the purpose of determining whether a privilege should be asserted. Private conferences may be held, however, during agreed recesses and adjournments. If the lawyers and witnesses do not comply with this rule, the court may allow in evidence at trial statements, objections, discussions, and other occurrences during the oral deposition that reflect upon the credibility of the witness or the testimony.

(e) **Objections**. Objections to questions during the oral deposition are limited to "Objection, leading" and "Objection, form." Objections to testimony during the oral deposition are limited to "Objection, non-responsive." These objections are waived if not stated as phrased during the oral deposition. All other objections need not be made or recorded during the oral deposition to be later raised with the court. The objecting party must give a clear and concise explanation of an objection if requested by the party taking the oral deposition, or the objection is waived. Argumentative or suggestive objections or explanations waive objection and may be grounds for terminating the oral deposition or assessing costs or other sanctions. The officer taking the oral deposition will not rule on objections but must record them for ruling by the court. The officer taking the oral deposition must not fail to record testimony because an objection has been made.

(f) **Instructions not to answer**. An attorney may instruct a witness not to answer a question during an oral deposition only if necessary to preserve a privilege, comply with a court order or these rules, protect a witness from an abusive question or one for which any answer would be misleading, or secure a ruling pursuant to paragraph (g). The attorney instructing the witness not to answer must give a concise, non-argumentative, non-suggestive explanation of the grounds for the instruction if requested by the party who asked the question.

(g) **Suspending the deposition**. If the time limitations for the deposition have expired or the deposition is being conducted or defended in violation of these rules, a party or witness may suspend the oral deposition for the time necessary to obtain a ruling.

(h) **Good faith required**. An attorney must not ask a question at an oral deposition solely to harass or mislead the witness, for any other improper purpose, or without a good faith legal basis at the time. An attorney must not object to a question at an oral deposition, instruct the witness not to answer a question, or suspend the deposition unless there is a good faith factual and legal basis for doing so at the time.

199.6 Hearing on Objections.

Any party may, at any reasonable time, request a hearing on an objection or privilege asserted by an instruction not to answer or suspension of the deposition; provided the failure of a party to obtain a ruling prior to trial does not waive any objection or privilege. The party seeking to avoid discovery must present any evidence necessary to support the objection or privilege either by testimony at the hearing or by affidavits served on opposing parties at least seven days before the hearing. If the court determines that an in camera review of some or all of the requested discovery is necessary to rule, answers to the deposition questions may be made in camera, to be transcribed and sealed in the event the privilege is sustained, or made in an affidavit produced to the court in a sealed wrapper.

[RULE 200. Repealed effective January 1, 1999; see, Rule 199.1 et seq.]

RULE 200. DEPOSITIONS UPON WRITTEN QUESTIONS

200.1 Procedure for Noticing Deposition Upon Written Questions.

(a) **Who may be noticed; when**. A party may take the testimony of any person or entity by deposition on written questions before any person authorized by law to take depositions on written questions. A notice of intent to take the deposition must be served on the witness and all parties at least 20 days before the deposition is taken. A deposition on written questions may be taken outside the discovery period only by agreement of the parties or with leave of court. The party noticing the deposition must also deliver to the deposition officer a copy of the notice and of all written questions to be asked during the deposition.

(b) **Content of notice**. The notice must comply with Rules 199.1(b), 199.2(b), and 199.5(a)(3). If the witness is an organization, the organization must comply with the requirements of that provision. The notice also may include a request for production of documents as permitted by Rule 199.2(b)(5), the provisions of which will govern the request, service, and response.

200.2 Compelling Witness to Attend.

A party may compel the witness to attend the deposition on written questions by serving the witness with a subpoena under Rule 176. If the witness is a party or is retained by, employed by, or otherwise subject to the control of a party, however, service of the deposition notice upon the party's attorney has the same effect as a subpoena served on the witness.

200.3 Questions and Objections.

(a) **Direct questions**. The direct questions to be propounded to the witness must be attached to the notice.

(b) **Objections and additional questions**. Within ten days after the notice and direct questions are served, any party may object to the direct questions and serve cross-questions on all other parties. Within five days after cross-questions are served, any party may object to the cross-questions and serve redirect questions on all other parties. Within three days after redirect questions are served, any party may object to the redirect questions and serve re-cross questions on all other parties. Objections to re-cross questions must be served within five days after the earlier of when re-cross questions are served or the time of the deposition on written questions.

(c) **Objections to form of questions**. Objections to the form of a question are waived unless asserted in accordance with this subdivision.

200.4 Conducting the Deposition Upon Written Questions.

The deposition officer must: take the deposition on written questions at the time and place designated; record the testimony of the witness under oath in response to the questions; and prepare, certify, and deliver the deposition transcript in accordance with Rule 203. The deposition officer has authority when necessary to summon and swear an interpreter to facilitate the taking of the deposition.

[RULE 201. Repealed effective January 1, 1999; see, Rules 176.6 and 199]

RULE 201. DEPOSITIONS IN FOREIGN JURISDICTIONS FOR USE IN TEXAS PROCEEDINGS; DEPOSITIONS IN TEXAS FOR USE IN FOREIGN PROCEEDINGS

201.1 Depositions in Foreign Jurisdictions for Use in Texas Proceedings.

(a) **Generally**. A party may take a deposition on oral examination or written questions of any person or entity located in another state or a foreign country for use in proceedings in this State. The deposition may be taken by:

(1) notice;

(2) letter rogatory, letter of request, or other such device;

(3) agreement of the parties; or

(4) court order.

(b) **By notice**. A party may take the deposition by notice in accordance with these rules as if the deposition were taken in this State, except that the deposition officer may be a person authorized to administer oaths in the place where the deposition is taken.

(c) **By letter rogatory**. On motion by a party, the court in which an action is pending must issue a letter rogatory on terms that are just and appropriate, regardless of whether any other manner of obtaining the deposition is impractical or inconvenient. The letter must:

(1) be addressed to the appropriate authority in the jurisdiction in which the deposition is to be taken;

(2) request and authorize that authority to summon the witness before the authority at a time and place stated in the letter for examination on oral or written questions; and

(3) request and authorize that authority to cause the witness's testimony to be reduced to writing and returned, together with any items marked as exhibits, to the party requesting the letter rogatory.

(d) **By letter of request or other such device**. On motion by a party, the court in which an action is pending, or the clerk of that court, must issue a letter of request or other such device in accordance with an applicable treaty or international convention on terms that are just and appropriate. The letter or other device must be issued regardless of whether any other manner of obtaining the deposition is impractical or inconvenient. The letter or other device must:

(1) be in the form prescribed by the treaty or convention under which it is issued, as presented by the movant to the court or clerk; and

(2) must state the time, place, and manner of the examination of the witness.

(e) **Objections to form of letter rogatory, letter of request, or other such device**. In issuing a letter rogatory, letter of request, or other such device, the court must set a time for objecting to the form of the device. A party must make any objection to the form of the device in writing and serve it on all other parties by the time set by the court, or the objection is waived.

(f) **Admissibility of evidence**. Evidence obtained in response to a letter rogatory, letter of request, or other such device is not inadmissible merely because it is not a verbatim transcript, or the testimony was not taken under oath, or for any similar departure from the requirements for depositions taken within this State under these rules.

(g) **Deposition by electronic means**. A deposition in another jurisdiction may be taken by telephone, video conference, teleconference, or other electronic means under the provisions of Rule 199.

201.2 Depositions in Texas for Use in Proceedings in Foreign Jurisdictions.

If a court of record of any other state or foreign jurisdiction issues a mandate, writ, or commission that requires a witness's oral or written deposition testimony in this State, the witness may be compelled to appear and testify in the same manner and by the same process used for taking testimony in a proceeding pending in this State.

[RULE 202. Repealed effective January 1, 1999; see, Rules 199.1 and 203.6]

RULE 202. DEPOSITIONS BEFORE SUIT OR TO INVESTIGATE CLAIMS

202.1 Generally.

A person may petition the court for an order authorizing the taking of a deposition on oral examination or written questions either:

(a) to perpetuate or obtain the person's own testimony or that of any other person for use in an anticipated suit; or

(b) to investigate a potential claim or suit.

202.2 Petition

The petition must:

(a) be verified;

(b) be filed in a proper court of any county:

    (1) where venue of the anticipated suit may lie, if suit is anticipated; or

    (2) where the witness resides, if no suit is yet anticipated;

(c) be in the name of the petitioner;

(d) state either:

    (1) that the petitioner anticipates the institution of a suit in which the petitioner may be a party; or

    (2) that the petitioner seeks to investigate a potential claim by or against petitioner;

(e) state the subject matter of the anticipated action, if any, and the petitioner's interest therein;

(f) if suit is anticipated, either:

    (1) state the names of the persons petitioner expects to have interests adverse to petitioner's in the anticipated suit, and the addresses and telephone numbers for such persons; or

    (2) state that the names, addresses, and telephone numbers of persons petitioner expects to have interests adverse to petitioner's in the anticipated suit cannot be ascertained through diligent inquiry, and describe those persons;

(g) state the names, addresses and telephone numbers of the persons to be deposed, the substance of the testimony that the petitioner expects to elicit from each, and the petitioner's reasons for desiring to obtain the testimony of each; and

(h) request an order authorizing the petitioner to take the depositions of the persons named in the petition.

202.3 Notice and Service.

(a) **Personal service on witnesses and persons named**. At least 15 days before the date of the hearing on the petition, the petitioner must serve the petition and a notice of the hearing - in accordance with Rule 21a - on all persons petitioner seeks to depose and, if suit is anticipated, on all persons petitioner expects to have interests adverse to petitioner's in the anticipated suit.

(b) **Service by publication on persons not named**.

(1) *Manner.* Unnamed persons described in the petition whom the petitioner expects to have interests adverse to petitioner's in the anticipated suit, if any, may be served by publication with the petition and notice of the hearing. The notice must state the place for the hearing and the time it will be held, which must be more than 14 days after the first publication of the notice. The petition and notice must be published once each week for two consecutive weeks in the newspaper of broadest circulation in the county in which the petition is filed, or if no such newspaper exists, in the newspaper of broadest circulation in the nearest county where a newspaper is published.

(2) *Objection to depositions taken on notice by publication.* Any interested party may move, in the proceeding or by bill of review, to suppress any deposition, in whole or in part, taken on notice by publication, and may also attack or oppose the deposition by any other means available.

(c) **Service in probate cases.** A petition to take a deposition in anticipation of an application for probate of a will, and notice of the hearing on the petition, may be served by posting as prescribed by Section 33(f)(2) of the Probate Code. The notice and petition must be directed to all parties interested in the testator's estate and must comply with the requirements of Section 33(c) of the Probate Code insofar as they may be applicable.

(d) **Modification by order.** As justice or necessity may require, the court may shorten or lengthen the notice periods under this rule and may extend the notice period to permit service on any expected adverse party.

202.4 Order.

(a) **Required findings.** The court must order a deposition to be taken if, but only if, it finds that:

(1) allowing the petitioner to take the requested deposition may prevent a failure or delay of justice in an anticipated suit; or

(2) the likely benefit of allowing the petitioner to take the requested deposition to investigate a potential claim outweighs the burden or expense of the procedure.

(b) **Contents.** The order must state whether a deposition will be taken on oral examination or written questions. The order may also state the time and place at which a deposition will be taken. If the order does not state the time and place at which a deposition will be taken, the petitioner must notice the deposition as required by Rules 199 or 200. The order must contain any protections the court finds necessary or appropriate to protect the witness or any person who may be affected by the procedure.

202.5 Manner of Taking and Use.

Except as otherwise provided in this rule, depositions authorized by this rule are governed by the rules applicable to depositions of non -parties in a pending suit. The scope of discovery in depositions authorized by this rule is the same as if the anticipated suit or potential claim had been filed. A court may restrict or prohibit the use of a deposition taken under this rule in a subsequent suit to protect a person who was not served with notice of the deposition from any unfair prejudice or to prevent abuse of this rule.

[RULE 203. Repealed effective January 1, 1999; see, Rules 176.8 and 215]

RULE 203. SIGNING, CERTIFICATION AND USE OF ORAL AND WRITTEN DEPOSITIONS

203.1 Signature and Changes.

(a) **Deposition transcript to be provided to witness**. The deposition officer must provide the original deposition transcript to the witness for examination and signature. If the witness is represented by an attorney at the deposition, the deposition officer must provide the transcript to the attorney instead of the witness.

(b) Changes by witness; signature. The witness may change responses as reflected in the deposition transcript by indicating the desired changes, in writing, on a separate sheet of paper, together with a statement of the reasons for making the changes. No erasures or obliterations of any kind may be made to the original deposition transcript. The witness must then sign the transcript under oath and return it to the deposition officer. If the witness does not return the transcript to the deposition officer within 20 days of the date the transcript was provided to the witness or the witness's attorney, the witness may be deemed to have waived the right to make the changes.

(c) Exceptions. The requirements of presentation and signature under this subdivision do not apply:

(1) if the witness and all parties waive the signature requirement;

(2) to depositions on written questions; or

(3) to non-stenographic recordings of oral depositions.

203.2 Certification.

The deposition officer must file with the court, serve on all parties, and attach as part of the deposition transcript or non-stenographic recording of an oral deposition a certificate duly sworn by the officer stating:

(a) that the witness was duly sworn by the officer and that the transcript or non-stenographic recording of the oral deposition is a true record of the testimony given by the witness;

(b) that the deposition transcript, if any, was submitted to the witness or to the attorney for the witness for examination and signature, the date on which the transcript was submitted, whether the witness returned the transcript, and if so, the date on which it was returned.

(c) that changes, if any, made by the witness are attached to the deposition transcript;

(d) that the deposition officer delivered the deposition transcript or nonstenographic recording of an oral deposition in accordance with Rule 203.3;

(e) the amount of time used by each party at the deposition;

(f) the amount of the deposition officer's charges for preparing the original deposition transcript, which the clerk of the court must tax as costs; and

(g) that a copy of the certificate was served on all parties and the date of service.

203.3 Delivery.

(a) Endorsement; to whom delivered. The deposition officer must endorse the title of the action and "Deposition of (name of witness)" on the original deposition transcript (or a copy, if the original was not returned) or the original nonstenographic recording of an oral deposition, and must return:

(1) the transcript to the party who asked the first question appearing in the transcript, or

(2) the recording to the party who requested it.

(b) Notice. The deposition officer must serve notice of delivery on all other parties.

(c) Inspection and copying; copies. The party receiving the original deposition transcript or non-stenographic recording must make it available upon reasonable request for inspection and copying by any other party. Any party or the witness is entitled to obtain a copy of the deposition transcript or non-stenographic recording from the deposition officer upon payment of a reasonable fee.

203.4 Exhibits.

At the request of a party, the original documents and things produced for inspection during the examination of the witness must be marked for identification by the deposition officer and annexed to the deposition transcript or non-stenographic recording. The person producing the materials may produce copies instead of originals if the party gives all other parties fair opportunity at the deposition to compare the copies with the originals. If the person offers originals rather than copies, the deposition officer must, after the conclusion of the deposition, make copies to be attached to the original deposition transcript or non-stenographic recording, and then return the originals to the person who produced them. The person who produced the originals must preserve them for hearing or trial and make them available for inspection or copying by any other party upon seven days' notice. Copies annexed to the original deposition transcript or non-stenographic recording may be used for all purposes.

203.5 Motion to Suppress.

A party may object to any errors and irregularities in the manner in which the testimony is transcribed, signed, delivered, or otherwise dealt with by the deposition officer by filing a motion to suppress all or part of the deposition. If the deposition officer complies with Rule 203.3 at least one day before the case is called to trial, with regard to a deposition transcript, or 30 days before the case is called to trial, with regard to a non-stenographic recording, the party must file and serve a motion to suppress before trial commences to preserve the objections.

203.6 Use.

(a) **Non-stenographic recording; transcription**. A non-stenographic recording of an oral deposition, or a written transcription of all or part of such a recording, may be used to the same extent as a deposition taken by stenographic means. However, the court, for good cause shown, may require that the party seeking to use a non-stenographic recording or written transcription first obtain a complete transcript of the deposition recording from a certified court reporter. The court reporter's transcription must be made from the original or a certified copy of the deposition recording. The court reporter must, to the extent applicable, comply with the provisions of this rule, except that the court reporter must deliver the original transcript to the attorney requesting the transcript, and the court reporter's certificate must include a statement that the transcript is a true record of the non-stenographic recording. The party to whom the court reporter delivers the original transcript must make the transcript available, upon reasonable request, for inspection and copying by the witness or any party.

(b) **Same proceeding**. All or part of a deposition may be used for any purpose in the same proceeding in which it was taken. If the original is not filed, a certified copy may be used. "Same proceeding" includes a proceeding in a different court but involving the same subject matter and the same parties or their representatives or successors in interest. A deposition is admissible against a party joined after the deposition was taken if:

(1) the deposition is admissible pursuant to Rule 804(b)(1) of the Rules of Evidence, or

(2) that party has had a reasonable opportunity to redepose the witness and has failed to do so.

(c) **Different proceeding**. Depositions taken in different proceedings may be used as permitted by the Rules of Evidence.

[RULE 204. Repealed effective January 1, 1999; see, Rule 199.5]

RULE 204. PHYSICAL AND MENTAL EXAMINATION

204.1 Motion and Order Required.

(a) **Motion**. A party may - no later than 30 days before the end of any applicable discovery period - move for an order compelling another party to:

(1) submit to a physical or mental examination by a qualified physician or a mental examination by a qualified psychologist; or

(2) produce for such examination a person in the other party's custody, conservatorship or legal control.

(b) **Service**. The motion and notice of hearing must be served on the person to be examined and all parties.

(c) **Requirements for obtaining order**. The court may issue an order for examination only for good cause shown and only in the following circumstances:

(1) when the mental or physical condition (including the blood group) of a party, or of a person in the custody, conservatorship or under the legal control of a party, is in controversy; or

(2) except as provided in Rule 204.4, an examination by a psychologist may be ordered when the party responding to the motion has designated a psychologist as a testifying expert or has disclosed a psychologist's records for possible use at trial.

(d) **Requirements of order**. The order must be in writing and must specify the time, place, manner, conditions, and scope of the examination and the person or persons by whom it is to be made.

204.2 Report of Examining Physician or Psychologist.

(a) **Right to report**. Upon request of the person ordered to be examined, the party causing the examination to be made must deliver to the person a copy of a detailed written report of the examining physician or psychologist setting out the findings, including results of all tests made, diagnoses and conclusions, together with like reports of all earlier examinations of the same condition. After delivery of the report, upon request of the party causing the examination, the party against whom the order is made must produce a like report of any examination made before or after the ordered examination of the same condition, unless the person examined is not a party and the party shows that the party is unable to obtain it. The court on motion may limit delivery of a report on such terms as are just. If a physician or psychologist fails or refuses to make a report the court may exclude the testimony if offered at the trial.

(b) **Agreements; relationship to other rules**. This subdivision applies to examinations made by agreement of the parties, unless the agreement expressly provides otherwise. This subdivision does not preclude discovery of a report of an examining physician or psychologist or the taking of a deposition of the physician or psychologist in accordance with the provisions of any other rule.

204.3 Effect of No Examination.

If no examination is sought either by agreement or under this subdivision, the party whose physical or mental condition is in controversy must not comment to the court or jury concerning the party's willingness to submit to an examination, or on the right or failure of any other party to seek an examination.

204.4 Cases Arising Under Titles II or V, Family Code.

In cases arising under Family Code Titles II or V, the court may - on its own initiative or on motion of a party - appoint:

(a) one or more psychologists or psychiatrists to make any and all appropriate mental examinations of the children who are the subject of the suit or of any other parties, and may make such appointment irrespective of whether a psychologist or psychiatrist has been designated by any party as a testifying expert;

(b) one or more experts who are qualified in paternity testing to take blood, body fluid, or tissue samples to conduct paternity tests as ordered by the court.

204.5 Definitions.

For the purpose of this rule, a psychologist is a person licensed or certified by a state or the District of Columbia as a psychologist.

[RULE 205. Repealed effective January 1, 1999; see, Rule 203.1 et seq.]

RULE 205. DISCOVERY FROM NON-PARTIES

205.1 Forms of Discovery; Subpoena Requirement.

A party may compel discovery from a nonparty--that is, a person who is not a party or subject to a party's control--only by obtaining a court order under Rules 196.7, 202, or 204, or by serving a subpoena compelling:

(a) an oral deposition;

(b) a deposition on written questions;

(c) a request for production of documents or tangible things, pursuant to Rule 199.2(b)(5) or Rule 200.1(b), served with a notice of deposition on oral examination or written questions; and

(d) a request for production of documents and tangible things under this rule.

205.2 Notice.

A party seeking discovery by subpoena from a nonparty must serve, on the nonparty and all parties, a copy of the form of notice required under the rules governing the applicable form of discovery. A notice of oral or written deposition must be served before or at the same time that a subpoena compelling attendance or production under the notice is served. A notice to produce documents or tangible things under Rule 205.3 must be served at least 10 days before the subpoena compelling production is served.

205.3 Production of Documents and Tangible Things Without Deposition.

(a) **Notice; subpoena**. A party may compel production of documents and tangible things from a nonparty by serving - reasonable time before the response is due but no later than 30 days before the end of any applicable discovery period - the notice required in Rule 205.2 and a subpoena compelling production or inspection of documents or tangible things.

(b) **Contents of notice**. The notice must state:

(1) the name of the person from whom production or inspection is sought to be compelled;

(2) a reasonable time and place for the production or inspection; and

(3) the items to be produced or inspected, either by individual item or by category, describing each item and category with reasonable particularity, and, if applicable, describing the desired testing and sampling with sufficient specificity to inform the nonparty of the means, manner, and procedure for testing or sampling.

(c) **Requests for production of medical or mental health records of other non-parties**. If a party requests a nonparty to produce medical or mental health records of another nonparty, the requesting party must serve the nonparty whose records are sought with the notice required under this rule. This requirement does not apply under the circumstances set forth in Rule 196.1(c)(2).

(d) **Response**. The nonparty must respond to the notice and subpoena in accordance with Rule 176.6.

(e) **Custody, inspection and copying**. The party obtaining the production must make all materials produced available for inspection by any other party on reasonable notice, and must furnish copies to any party who requests at that party's expense.

(f) **Cost of production**. A party requiring production of documents by a nonparty must reimburse the nonparty's reasonable costs of production.

[RULE 206 to 208. Repealed effective January 1, 1999]

[RULE 208a. Repealed effective April 1, 1984]

[RULE 209. Repealed effective January 1, 1999]

[RULES 210 to 214. Repealed effective April 1, 1984]

RULE 215. ABUSE OF DISCOVERY; SANCTIONS 215.1 Motion for Sanctions or Order Compelling Discovery.

A party, upon reasonable notice to other parties and all other persons affected thereby, may apply for sanctions or an order compelling discovery as follows:

(a) **Appropriate court**. On matters relating to a deposition, an application for an order to a party may be made to the court in which the action is pending, or to any district court in the district where the deposition is being taken. An application for an order to a deponent who is not a party shall be made to the court in the district where the deposition is being taken. As to all other discovery matters, an application for an order will be made to the court in which the action is pending.

(b) **Motion**.

(1) If a party or other deponent which is a corporation or other entity fails to make a designation under Rules 199.2(b)(1) or 200.1(b); or

(2) if a party, or other deponent, or a person designated to testify on behalf of a party or other deponent fails:

(A) to appear before the officer who is to take his deposition, after being served with a proper notice; or

(B) to answer a question propounded or submitted upon oral examination or upon written questions; or

(3) if a party fails:

(A) to serve answers or objections to interrogatories submitted under Rule 197, after proper service of the interrogatories; or

(B) to answer an interrogatory submitted under Rule 197; or

(C) to serve a written response to a request for inspection submitted under Rule 196, after proper service of the request; or

(D) to respond that discovery will be permitted as requested or fails to permit discovery as requested in response to a request for inspection submitted under Rule 196; the discovering party may move for an order compelling a designation, an appearance, an answer or answers, or inspection or production in accordance with the request, or apply to the court in which the action is pending for the imposition of any sanction authorized by Rule 215.2(b) without the necessity of first having obtained a court order compelling such discovery.

When taking a deposition on oral examination, the proponent of the question may complete or adjourn the examination before he applies for an order.

If the court denies the motion in whole or in part, it may make such protective order as it would have been empowered to make on a motion pursuant to Rule 192.6.

(c) **Evasive or incomplete answer**. For purposes of this subdivision an evasive or incomplete answer is to be treated as a failure to answer.

(d) **Disposition of motion to compel: award of expenses**. If the motion is granted, the court shall, after opportunity for hearing, require a party or deponent whose conduct necessitated the motion or the party or attorney advising such conduct or both of them to pay, at such time as ordered by the court, the moving party the reasonable expenses incurred in obtaining the order, including attorney fees, unless the court finds that the opposition to the motion was substantially justified or that other circumstances make an award of expenses unjust. Such an order shall be subject to review on appeal from the final judgment.

If the motion is denied, the court may, after opportunity for hearing, require the moving party or attorney advising such motion to pay to the party or deponent who opposed the motion the reasonable expenses incurred in opposing the motion, including attorney fees, unless the court finds that the making of the motion was substantially justified or that other circumstances make an award of expenses unjust.

If the motion is granted in part and denied in part, the court may apportion the reasonable expenses incurred in relation to the motion among the parties and persons in a just manner.

In determining the amount of reasonable expenses, including attorney fees, to be awarded in connection with a motion, the trial court shall award expenses which are reasonable in relation to the amount of work reasonably expended in obtaining an order compelling compliance or in opposing a motion which is denied.

(e) **Providing person's own statement**. If a party fails to comply with any person's written request for the person's own statement as provided in Rule 192.3(h), the person who made the request may move for an order compelling compliance. If the motion is granted, the movant may recover the expenses incurred in obtaining the order, including attorney fees, which are reasonable in relation to the amount of work reasonably expended in obtaining the order.

215.2 Failure to Comply with Order or with Discovery Request.

(a) **Sanctions by court in district where deposition is taken**. If a deponent fails to appear or to be sworn or to answer a question after being directed to do so by a district court in the district in which the deposition is being taken, the failure may be considered a contempt of that court.

(b) **Sanctions by court in which action is pending**. If a party or an officer, director, or managing agent of a party or a person designated under Rules 199.2(b)(1) or 200.1(b) to testify on behalf of a party fails to comply with proper discovery requests or to obey an order to provide or permit discovery, including an order made under Rules 204 or 215.1, the court in which the action is pending may, after notice and hearing, make such orders in regard to the failure as are just, and among others the following:

(1) an order disallowing any further discovery of any kind or of a particular kind by the disobedient party;

(2) an order charging all or any portion of the expenses of discovery or taxable court costs or both against the disobedient party or the attorney advising him;

(3) an order that the matters regarding which the order was made or any other designated facts shall be taken to be established for the purposes of the action in accordance with the claim of the party obtaining the order;

(4) an order refusing to allow the disobedient party to support or oppose designated claims or defenses, or prohibiting him from introducing designated matters in evidence;

(5) an order striking out pleadings or parts thereof, or staying further proceedings until the order is obeyed, or dismissing with or without prejudice the action or proceedings or any part thereof, or rendering a judgment by default against the disobedient party;

(6) in lieu of any of the foregoing orders or in addition thereto, an order treating as a contempt of court the failure to obey any orders except an order to submit to a physical or mental examination;

(7) when a party has failed to comply with an order under Rule 204 requiring him to appear or produce another for examination, such orders as are listed in paragraphs (1), (2), (3), (4) or (5) of this subdivision, unless the person failing to comply shows that he is unable to appear or to produce such person for examination.

(8) In lieu of any of the foregoing orders or in addition thereto, the court shall require the party failing to obey the order or the attorney advising him, or both, to pay, at such time as ordered by the court, the reasonable expenses, including attorney fees, caused by the failure, unless the court finds that the failure was substantially justified or that other circumstances make an award of expenses unjust. Such an order shall be subject to review on appeal from the final judgment.

(c) **Sanction against nonparty for violation of Rules 196.7 or 205.3**. If a nonparty fails to comply with an order under Rules 196.7 or 205.3, the court which made the order may treat the failure to obey as contempt of court.

215.3 Abuse of Discovery Process in Seeking, Making, or Resisting Discovery.

If the court finds a party is abusing the discovery process in seeking, making or resisting discovery or if the court finds that any interrogatory or request for inspection or production is unreasonably frivolous, oppressive, or harassing, or that a response or answer is unreasonably frivolous or made for purposes of delay, then the court in which the action is pending may, after notice and hearing, impose any appropriate sanction authorized by paragraphs (1), (2), (3), (4), (5), and (8) of Rule 215.2(b). Such order of sanction shall be subject to review on appeal from the final judgment.

215.4 Failure to Comply with Rule 198

(a) **Motion**. A party who has requested an admission under Rule 198 may move to determine the sufficiency of the answer or objection. For purposes of this subdivision an evasive or incomplete answer may be treated as a failure to answer. Unless the court determines that an objection is justified, it shall order that an answer be served. If the court determines that an answer does not comply with the requirements of Rule 198, it may order either that the matter is admitted or that an amended answer be served. The provisions of Rule 215.1(d) apply to the award of expenses incurred in relation to the motion.

(b) **Expenses on failure to admit**. If a party fails to admit the genuineness of any document or the truth of any matter as requested under Rule 198 and if the party requesting the admissions thereafter proves the genuineness of the document or the truth of the matter, he may apply to the court for an order requiring the other party to pay him the reasonable expenses incurred in making that proof, including reasonable attorney fees. The court shall make the order unless it finds that (1) the request was held objectionable pursuant to Rule 193, or (2) the admission sought was of no substantial importance, or (3) the party failing to admit had a reasonable ground to believe that he might prevail on the matter, or (4) there was other good reason for the failure to admit.

215.5 Failure of Party or Witness to Attend to or Serve Subpoena; Expenses.

(a) **Failure of party giving notice to attend**. If the party giving the notice of the taking of an oral deposition fails to attend and proceed therewith and another party attends in person or by attorney pursuant to the notice, the court may order the party giving the notice to pay such other party the reasonable expenses incurred by him and his attorney in attending, including reasonable attorney fees.

(b) **Failure of witness to attend**. If a party gives notice of the taking of an oral deposition of a witness and the witness does not attend because of the fault of the party giving the notice, if another party attends in person or by attorney because he expects the deposition of that witness to be taken, the court may order the party giving the notice to pay such other party the reasonable expenses incurred by him and his attorney in attending, including reasonable attorney fees.

215.6 Exhibits to Motions and Responses.

Motions or responses made under this rule may have exhibits attached including affidavits, discovery pleadings, or any other documents.

SECTION 10. - THE JURY IN COURT

RULE 216. REQUEST AND FEE FOR JURY TRIAL

a. **Request**. No jury trial shall be had in any civil suit, unless a written request for a jury trial is filed with the clerk of the court a reasonable time before the date set for trial of the cause on the non-jury docket, but not less than thirty days in advance.

b. **Jury Fee**. Unless otherwise provided by law, a fee of ten dollars if in the district court and five dollars if in the county court must be deposited with the clerk of the court within the time for making a written request for a jury trial. The clerk shall promptly enter a notation of the payment of such fee upon the court's docket sheet.

RULE 217. OATH OF INABILITY

The deposit for a jury fee shall not be required when the party shall within the time for making such deposit, file with the clerk his affidavit to the effect that he is unable to make such deposit, and that he can not, by the pledge of property or otherwise, obtain the money necessary for that purpose; and the court shall then order the clerk to enter the suit on the jury docket.

RULE 218. JURY DOCKET

The clerks of the district and county courts shall each keep a docket, styled "The Jury Docket," in which shall be entered in their order the cases in which jury fees have been paid or affidavit in lieu thereof has been filed as provided in the two preceding rules.

RULE 219. JURY TRIAL DAY

The court shall designate the days for taking up the jury docket and the trial of jury cases. Such order may be revoked or changed in the court's discretion.

RULE 220. WITHDRAWING CAUSE FROM JURY DOCKET

When any party has paid the fee for a jury trial, he shall not be permitted to withdraw the cause from the jury docket over the objection of the parties adversely interested. If so permitted, the court in its discretion may by an order permit him to withdraw also his jury fee deposit. Failure of a party to appear for trial shall be deemed a waiver by him of the right to trial by jury.

RULE 221. CHALLENGE TO THE ARRAY

When the jurors summoned have not been selected by jury commissioners or by drawing the names from a jury wheel, any party to a suit which is to be tried by a jury may, before the jury is drawn challenge the array upon the ground that the officer summoning the jury has acted corruptly, and has wilfully summoned jurors known to be prejudiced against the party challenging or biased in favor of the adverse party. All such challenges must be in writing setting forth distinctly the grounds of such challenge and supported by the affidavit of the party or some other credible person. When such challenge is made, the court shall hear evidence and decide without delay whether or not the challenge shall be sustained.

RULE 222. WHEN CHALLENGE IS SUSTAINED

If the challenge be sustained, the array of jurors summoned shall be discharged, and the court shall order other jurors summoned in their stead, and shall direct that the officer who summoned the persons so discharged, and on account of whose misconduct the challenge has been sustained, shall not summon any other jurors in the case.

RULE 223. JURY LIST IN CERTAIN COUNTIES

In counties governed as to juries by the laws providing for interchangeable juries, the names of the jurors shall be placed upon the general panel in the order in which they are randomly selected, and jurors shall be assigned for service from the top thereof, in the order in which they shall be needed, and jurors returned to the general panel after service in any of such courts shall be enrolled at the bottom of the list in the order of their respective return; provided, however, after such assignment to a particular court, the trial judge of such court, upon the demand prior to voir dire examination by any party or attorney in the case reached for trial in such court, shall cause the names of all members of such assigned jury panel in such case to be placed in a receptacle, shuffled, and drawn, and such names shall be transcribed in the order drawn on the jury list from which the jury is to be selected to try such case. There shall be only one shuffle and drawing by the trial judge in each case.

RULE 224. PREPARING JURY LIST

In counties not governed as to juries by the laws providing for interchangeable juries, when the parties have announced ready for trial the clerk shall write the name of each regular juror entered of record for that week on separate slips of paper, as near the same size and appearance as may be, and shall place the slips in a box and mix them well. The clerk shall draw from the box, in the presence of the court, the names of twenty-four jurors, if in the district court, or so many as there may be, if there be a less number in the box; and the names of twelve jurors if in the county court, or so many as there may be, and write the names as drawn upon two slips of paper and deliver one slip to each party to the suit or his attorney.

RULE 225. SUMMONING TALESMAN

When there are not as many as twenty- four names drawn from the box, if in the district court, or as many as twelve, if in the county court, the court shall direct the sheriff to summon such number of qualified persons as the court deems necessary to complete the panel. The names of those thus summoned shall be placed in the box and drawn and entered upon the slips as provided in the preceding rules.

RULE 226. OATH TO JURY PANEL

Before the parties or their attorneys begin the examination of the jurors whose names have thus been listed, the jurors shall be sworn by the court or under its direction, as follows: "You, and each of you, do solemnly swear that you will true answers give to all questions propounded to you concerning your qualifications as a juror, so help you God."

RULE 226a. INSTRUCTIONS TO JURY PANEL AND JURY

The court must give instructions to the jury panel and the jury as prescribed by order of the Supreme Court under this rule.

Approved Instructions

I.

That the following oral instructions, with such modifications as the circumstances of the particular case may require, shall be given by the court to the members of the jury panel after they have been sworn in as provided in Rule 226 and before the voir dire examination:

Members of the Jury Panel [or Ladies and Gentlemen of the Jury Panel]:

Thank you for being here. We are here to select a jury. Twelve [six] of you will be chosen for the jury. Even if you are not chosen for the jury, you are performing a valuable service that is your right and duty as a citizen of a free country.

Before we begin: Turn off all phones and other electronic devices. While you are in the courtroom, do not communicate with anyone through any electronic device. [For example, do not communicate by phone, text message, email message, chat room, blog, or social networking websites such as Facebook, Twitter, or Myspace.] [I will give you a number where others may contact you in case of an emergency.] Do not record or photograph any part of these court proceedings, because it is prohibited by law.

If you are chosen for the jury, your role as jurors will be to decide the disputed facts in this case. My role will be to ensure that this case is tried in accordance with the rules of law.

Here is some background about this case. This is a civil case. It is a lawsuit that is not a criminal case. The parties are as follows: The plaintiff is _____, and the defendant is

_____. Representing the plaintiff is _____, and representing the defendant is

_____. They will ask you some questions during jury selection. But before their questions begin, I must give you some instructions for jury selection.

Every juror must obey these instructions. You may be called into court to testify about any violations of these instructions. If you do not follow these instructions, you will be guilty of juror misconduct, and I might have to order a new trial and start this process over again. This would waste your time and the parties' money, and would require the taxpayers of this county to pay for another trial.

These are the instructions.

1. To avoid looking like you are friendly with one side of the case, do not mingle or talk with the lawyers, witnesses, parties, or anyone else involved in the case. You may exchange casual greetings like "hello" and "good morning." Other than that, do not talk with them at all. They have to follow these instructions too, so you should not be offended when they follow the instructions.

2. Do not accept any favors from the lawyers, witnesses, parties, or anyone else involved in the case, and do not do any favors for them. This includes favors such as giving rides and food.

3. Do not discuss this case with anyone, even your spouse or a friend, either in person or by any other means [including by phone, text message, email message, chat room, blog, or social networking websites such as Facebook, Twitter, or Myspace]. Do not allow anyone to discuss the case with you or in your hearing. If anyone tries to discuss the case with you or in your hearing, tell me immediately. We do not want you to be influenced by something other than the evidence admitted in court.

4. The parties, through their attorneys, have the right to ask you questions about your background, experiences, and attitudes. They are not trying to meddle in your affairs. They are just being thorough and trying to choose fair jurors who do not have any bias or prejudice in this particular case.

5. Remember that you took an oath that you will tell the truth, so be truthful when the lawyers ask you questions, and always give complete answers. If you do not answer a question that applies to you, that violates your oath. Sometimes a lawyer will ask a question of the whole panel instead of just one person. If the question applies to you, raise your hand and keep it raised until you are called on.

Do you understand these instructions? If you do not, please tell me now.

The lawyers will now begin to ask their questions.

II.

That the following oral and written instructions, with such modifications as the circumstances of the particular case may require, shall be given by the court to the jury immediately after the jurors are selected for the case:

Members of the Jury [or Ladies and Gentlemen]:

You have been chosen to serve on this jury. Because of the oath you have taken and your selection for the jury, you become officials of this court and active participants in our justice system.

[Hand out the written instructions.]

You have each received a set of written instructions. I am going to read them with you now. Some of them you have heard before and some are new.

1. Turn off all phones and other electronic devices. While you are in the courtroom and while you are deliberating, do not communicate with anyone through any electronic device. [For example, do not communicate by phone, text message, email message, chat room, blog, or social networking websites such as Facebook, Twitter, or Myspace.] [I will give you a number where

others may contact you in case of an emergency.] Do not post information about the case on the Internet before these court proceedings end and you are released from jury duty. Do not record or photograph any part of these court proceedings, because it is prohibited by law.

2. To avoid looking like you are friendly with one side of the case, do not mingle or talk with the lawyers, witnesses, parties, or anyone else involved in the case. You may exchange casual greetings like "hello" and "good morning." Other than that, do not talk with them at all. They have to follow these instructions too, so you should not be offended when they follow the instructions.

3. Do not accept any favors from the lawyers, witnesses, parties, or anyone else involved in the case, and do not do any favors for them. This includes favors such as giving rides and food.

4. Do not discuss this case with anyone, even your spouse or a friend, either in person or by any other means [including by phone, text message, email message, chat room, blog, or social networking websites such as Facebook, Twitter, or Myspace]. Do not allow anyone to discuss the case with you or in your hearing. If anyone tries to discuss the case with you or in your hearing, tell me immediately. We do not want you to be influenced by something other than the evidence admitted in court.

5. Do not discuss this case with anyone during the trial, not even with the other jurors, until the end of the trial. You should not discuss the case with your fellow jurors until the end of the trial so that you do not form opinions about the case before you have heard everything.

After you have heard all the evidence, received all of my instructions, and heard all of the lawyers' arguments, you will then go to the jury room to discuss the case with the other jurors and reach a verdict.

6. Do not investigate this case on your own. For example, do not:

   a. try to get information about the case, lawyers, witnesses, or issues from outside this courtroom;

   b. go to places mentioned in the case to inspect the places;

   c. inspect items mentioned in this case unless they are presented as evidence in court;

   d. look anything up in a law book, dictionary, or public record to try to learn more about the case;

   e. look anything up on the Internet to try to learn more about the case; or

   f. let anyone else do any of these things for you.

This rule is very important because we want a trial based only on evidence admitted in open court. Your conclusions about this case must be based only on what you see and hear in this courtroom because the law does not permit you to base your conclusions on information that has not been presented to you in open court. All the information must be presented in open court so the parties and their lawyers can test it and object to it. Information from other sources, like the Internet, will not go through this important process in the courtroom. In addition, information from other sources could be completely unreliable. As a result, if you investigate this case on your own, you could compromise the fairness to all parties in this case and jeopardize the results of this trial.

7. Do not tell other jurors about your own experiences or other people's experiences. For example, you may have special knowledge of something in the case, such as business, technical, or professional information. You may even have expert knowledge or opinions, or you may know what happened in this case or another similar case. Do not tell the other jurors about it. Telling other jurors about it is wrong because it means the jury will be considering things that were not admitted in court.

8. Do not consider attorneys' fees unless I tell you to. Do not guess about attorneys' fees.

9. Do not consider or guess whether any party is covered by insurance unless I tell you to.

10. During the trial, if taking notes will help focus your attention on the evidence, you may take notes using the materials the court has provided. Do not use any personal electronic devices to take notes. If taking notes will distract your attention from the evidence, you should not take notes. Your notes are for your own personal use. They are not evidence. Do not show or read your notes to anyone, including other jurors.

You must leave your notes in the jury room or with the bailiff. The bailiff is instructed not to read your notes and to give your notes to me promptly after collecting them from you. I will make sure your notes are kept in a safe, secure location and not disclosed to anyone.

[You may take your notes back into the jury room and consult them during deliberations. But keep in mind that your notes are not evidence. When you deliberate, each of you should rely on your independent recollection of the evidence and not be influenced by the fact that another juror has or has not taken notes. After you complete your deliberations, the bailiff will collect your notes.]

When you are released from jury duty, the bailiff will promptly destroy your notes so that nobody can read what you wrote.

11. I will decide matters of law in this case. It is your duty to listen to and consider the evidence and to determine fact issues that I may submit to you at the end of the trial. After you have heard all the evidence, I will give you instructions to follow as you make your decision. The instructions also will have questions for you to answer. You will not be asked and you should not consider which side will win. Instead, you will need to answer the specific questions I give you.

Every juror must obey my instructions. If you do not follow these instructions, you will be guilty of juror misconduct, and I may have to order a new trial and start this process over again. This would waste your time and the parties' money, and would require the taxpayers of this county to pay for another trial.

Do you understand these instructions? If you do not, please tell me now.

Please keep these instructions and review them as we go through this case. If anyone does not follow these instructions, tell me.

III.

Court's Charge

Before closing arguments begin, the court must give to each member of the jury a copy of the charge, which must include the following written instructions, with such modifications as the circumstances of the particular case may require:

Members of the Jury [or Ladies & Gentlemen of the Jury]:

After the closing arguments, you will go to the jury room to decide the case, answer the questions that are attached, and reach a verdict. You may discuss the case with other jurors only when you are all together in the jury room.

Remember my previous instructions: Do not discuss the case with anyone else, either in person or by any other means. Do not do any independent investigation about the case or conduct any research. Do not look up any words in dictionaries or on the Internet. Do not post information about the case on the Internet. Do not share any special knowledge or experiences with the other jurors. Do not use your phone or any other electronic device during your deliberations for any reason. [I will give you a number where others may contact you in case of an emergency.]

[Any notes you have taken are for your own personal use. You may take your notes back into the jury room and consult them during deliberations, but do not show or read your notes to your fellow jurors during your deliberations. Your notes are not evidence. Each of you should rely on your independent recollection of the evidence and not be influenced by the fact that another juror has or has not taken notes.]

[You must leave your notes with the bailiff when you are not deliberating. The bailiff will give your notes to me promptly after collecting them from you. I will make sure your notes are kept in a safe, secure location and not disclosed to anyone. After you complete your deliberations, the bailiff will collect your notes. When you are released from jury duty, the bailiff will promptly destroy your notes so that nobody can read what you wrote.]

Here are the instructions for answering the questions.

1. Do not let bias, prejudice, or sympathy play any part in your decision.

2. Base your answers only on the evidence admitted in court and on the law that is in these instructions and questions. Do not consider or discuss any evidence that was not admitted in the courtroom.

3. You are to make up your own minds about the facts. You are the sole judges of the credibility of the witnesses and the weight to give their testimony. But on matters of law, you must follow all of my instructions.

4. If my instructions use a word in a way that is different from its ordinary meaning, use the meaning I give you, which will be a proper legal definition.

5. All the questions and answers are important. No one should say that any question or answer is not important.

6. Answer "yes" or "no" to all questions unless you are told otherwise. A "yes" answer must be based on a preponderance of the evidence [unless you are told otherwise]. Whenever a question requires an answer other than "yes" or "no," your answer must be based on a preponderance of the evidence [unless you are told otherwise].

The term "preponderance of the evidence" means the greater weight of credible evidence presented in this case. If you do not find that a preponderance of the evidence supports a "yes" answer, then answer "no." A preponderance of the evidence is not measured by the number of witnesses or by the number of documents admitted in evidence. For a fact to be proved by a preponderance of the evidence, you must find that the fact is more likely true than not true.

7. Do not decide who you think should win before you answer the questions and then just answer the questions to match your decision. Answer each question carefully without considering who will win. Do not discuss or consider the effect your answers will have.

8. Do not answer questions by drawing straws or by any method of chance.

9. Some questions might ask you for a dollar amount. Do not agree in advance to decide on a dollar amount by adding up each juror's amount and then figuring the average.

10. Do not trade your answers. For example, do not say, "I will answer this question your way if you answer another question my way."

11. [Unless otherwise instructed] The answers to the questions must be based on the decision of at least 10 of the 12 [5 of the 6] jurors. The same 10 [5] jurors must agree on every answer. Do not agree to be bound by a vote of anything less than 10 [5] jurors, even if it would be a majority.

As I have said before, if you do not follow these instructions, you will be guilty of juror misconduct, and I might have to order a new trial and start this process over again. This would waste your time and the parties' money, and would require the taxpayers of this county to pay for another trial. If a juror breaks any of these rules, tell that person to stop and report it to me immediately.

[Definitions, questions, and special instructions given to the jury will be transcribed here. If exemplary damages are sought against a defendant, the jury must unanimously find, with respect to that defendant, (i) liability on at least one claim for actual damages that will support an award of exemplary damages, (ii) any additional conduct, such as malice or gross negligence, required for an award of exemplary damages, and (iii) the amount of exemplary damages to be awarded. The jury's answers to questions regarding (ii) and (iii) must be conditioned on a unanimous finding regarding (i), except in an extraordinary circumstance when the conditioning instruction would be erroneous. The jury need not be unanimous in finding the amount of actual damages. Thus, if questions regarding (ii) and (iii) are submitted to the jury for defendants D1 and D2, instructions in substantially the following form must immediately precede such questions:

Preceding question (ii):

Answer Question (ii) for D1 only if you unanimously answered "Yes" to Question[s] (i) regarding D1. Otherwise, do not answer Question (ii) for D1. [Repeat for D2.]

You are instructed that in order to answer "Yes" to [any part of] Question (ii), your answer must be unanimous. You may answer "No" to [any part of] Question (ii) only upon a vote of 10 [5] or more jurors. Otherwise, you must not answer [that part of] Question (ii).

Preceding question (iii):

Answer Question (iii) for D1 only if you answered "Yes" to Question (ii) for D1. Otherwise, do not answer Question (iii) for D1. [Repeat for D2.]

You are instructed that you must unanimously agree on the amount of any award of exemplary damages.

These examples are given by way of illustration.]

Presiding Juror:

> 1. When you go into the jury room to answer the questions, the first thing you will need to do is choose a presiding juror.

> 2. The presiding juror has these duties:

>> a. have the complete charge read aloud if it will be helpful to your deliberations;

>> b. preside over your deliberations, meaning manage the discussions, and see that you follow these instructions;

>> c. give written questions or comments to the bailiff who will give them to the judge;

>> d. write down the answers you agree on;

>> e. get the signatures for the verdict certificate; and

>> f. notify the bailiff that you have reached a verdict.

Do you understand the duties of the presiding juror? If you do not, please tell me now.

Instructions for Signing the Verdict Certificate:

> 1. [Unless otherwise instructed] You may answer the questions on a vote of 10 [5] jurors. The same 10 [5] jurors must agree on every answer in the charge. This means you may not have one group of 10 [5] jurors agree on one answer and a different group of 10 [5] jurors agree on another answer.

> 2. If 10 [5] jurors agree on every answer, those 10 [5] jurors sign the verdict.

> If 11 jurors agree on every answer, those 11 jurors sign the verdict.

> If all 12 [6] of you agree on every answer, you are unanimous and only the presiding juror signs the verdict.

> 3. All jurors should deliberate on every question. You may end up with all 12 [6] of you agreeing on some answers, while only 10 [5] or 11 of you agree on other answers. But when you sign the verdict, only those 10 [5] who agree on every answer will sign the verdict.

4. [Added if the charge requires some unanimity] There are some special instructions before Questions _____ explaining how to answer those questions. Please follow the instructions. If all 12 [6] of you answer those questions, you will need to complete a second verdict certificate for those questions.

Do you understand these instructions? If you do not, please tell me now.

_____

Judge Presiding

Verdict Certificate

Check one:

_____ Our verdict is unanimous. All 12 [6] of us have agreed to each and every answer. The presiding juror has signed the certificate for all 12 [6] of us.

_____ _____

Signature of Presiding Juror Printed Name of Presiding Juror

_____ Our verdict is not unanimous. Eleven of us have agreed to each and every answer and have signed the certificate below.

_____ Our verdict is not unanimous. Ten [Five] of us have agreed to each and every answer and have signed the certificate below.

SIGNATURE NAME PRINTED

1. _____ _____

2. _____ _____

3. _____ _____

4. _____ _____

5. _____ _____

6. _____ _____

7. _____ _____

8. _____ _____

9. _____ _____

10. _____ _____

11. _____ _____

If you have answered Question No. _____ [the exemplary damages amount], then you must sign this certificate also.

Additional Certificate

[Used when some questions require unanimous answers]

I certify that the jury was unanimous in answering the following questions. All 12 [6] of us agreed to each of the answers. The presiding juror has signed the certificate for all 12 [6] of us.

[Judge to list questions that require a unanimous answer, including the predicate liability question.]

_____ _____

Signature of Presiding Juror Printed Name of Presiding Juror

That the following oral instructions shall be given by the court to the jury after the verdict has been accepted by the court and before the jurors are released from jury duty:

Thank you for your verdict.

I have told you that the only time you may discuss the case is with the other jurors in the jury room. I now release you from jury duty. Now you may discuss the case with anyone. But you may also choose not to discuss the case; that is your right.

After you are released from jury duty, the lawyers and others may ask you questions to see if the jury followed the instructions, and they may ask you to give a sworn statement. You are free to discuss the case with them and to give a sworn statement. But you may choose not to discuss the case and not to give a sworn statement; that is your right.

RULE 227. CHALLENGE TO JUROR

A challenge to a particular juror is either a challenge for cause or a peremptory challenge. The court shall decide without delay any such challenge, and if sustained, the juror shall be discharged from the particular case. Either such challenge may be made orally on the formation of a jury to try the case.

RULE 228. "CHALLENGE FOR CAUSE" DEFINED

A challenge for cause is an objection made to a juror, alleging some fact which by law disqualifies him to serve as a juror in the case or in any case, or which in the opinion of the court, renders him an unfit person to sit on the jury. Upon such challenge the examination is not confined to the answers of the juror, but other evidence may be heard for or against the challenge.

RULE 229. CHALLENGE FOR CAUSE

When twenty-four or more jurors, if in the district court, or twelve or more, if in the county court, are drawn, and the lists of their names delivered to the parties, if either party desires to challenge any juror for cause, the challenge shall then be made. The name of a juror challenged and set aside for cause shall be erased from such lists.

RULE 230. CERTAIN QUESTIONS NOT TO BE ASKED

In examining a juror, he shall not be asked a question the answer to which may show that he has been convicted of an offense which disqualifies him, or that he stands charged by some legal accusation with theft or any felony.

RULE 231. NUMBER REDUCED BY CHALLENGES

If the challenges reduce the number of jurors to less than twenty -four, if in the district court, or to less than twelve, if in the county court, the court shall order other jurors to be drawn from the wheel or from the central jury panel or summoned, as the practice may be in the particular county, and their names written upon the list instead of those set aside for cause. Such jurors so summoned may likewise be challenged for cause.

RULE 232. MAKING PEREMPTORY CHALLENGES

If there remain on such lists not subject to challenge for cause, twenty-four names, if in the district court, or twelve names, if in the county court, the parties shall proceed to make their peremptory challenges. A peremptory challenge is made to a juror without assigning any reason therefor.

RULE 233. NUMBER OF PEREMPTORY CHALLENGES

Except as provided below, each party to a civil action is entitled to six peremptory challenges in a case tried in the district court, and to three in the county court.

Alignment of the Parties. In multiple party cases, it shall be the duty of the trial judge to decide whether any of the litigants aligned on the same side of the docket are antagonistic with respect to any issue to be submitted to the jury, before the exercise of peremptory challenges.

Definition of Side. The term "side" as used in this rule is not synonymous with "party," "litigant," or "person." Rather, "side" means one or more litigants who have common interests on the matters with which the jury is concerned.

Motion to Equalize. In multiple party cases, upon motion of any litigant made prior to the exercise of peremptory challenges, it shall be the duty of the trial judge to equalize the number of peremptory challenges so that no litigant or side is given unfair advantage as a result of the alignment of the litigants and the award of peremptory challenges to each litigant or side. In determining how the challenges should be allocated the court shall consider any matter brought to the attention of the trial judge concerning the ends of justice and the elimination of an unfair advantage.

RULE 234. LISTS RETURNED TO THE CLERK

When the parties have made or declined to make their peremptory challenges, they shall deliver their lists to the clerk. The clerk shall, if the case be in the district court, call off the first twelve names on the lists that have not been erased; and if the case be in the county court, he shall call off the first six names on the lists that have not been erased; those whose names are called shall be the jury.

RULE 235. IF JURY IS INCOMPLETE

When by peremptory challenges the jury is left incomplete, the court shall direct other jurors to be drawn or summoned to complete the jury; and such other jurors shall be impaneled as in the first instance.

RULE 236. OATH TO JURY

The jury shall be sworn by the court or under its direction, in substance as follows: "You, and each of you, do solemnly swear that in all cases between parties which shall be to you submitted, you will a true verdict render, according to the law, as it may be given you in charge by the court, and to the evidence submitted to you under the rulings of the court. So help you God."

SECTION 11. TRIAL OF CAUSES

A. Appearance and Procedure

RULE 237. APPEARANCE DAY

If a defendant, who has been duly cited, is by the citation required to answer on a day which is in term time, such day is appearance day as to him. If he is so required to answer on a day in vacation, he shall plead or answer accordingly, and the first day of the next term is appearance day as to him.

RULE 237a. CASES REMANDED FROM FEDERAL COURT

When any cause is removed to the Federal Court and is afterwards remanded to the state court, the plaintiff shall file a certified copy of the order of remand with the clerk of the state court and shall forthwith give written notice of such filing to the attorneys of record for all adverse parties. All such adverse parties shall have fifteen days from the receipt of such notice within which to file an answer. No default judgment shall be rendered against a party in a removed action remanded from federal court if that party filed an answer in federal court during removal.

RULE 238. CALL OF APPEARANCE DOCKET

On the appearance day of a particular defendant and at the hour named in the citation, or as soon thereafter as may be practicable, the court or clerk in open court shall call, in their order, all the cases on the docket in which such day is appearance day as to any defendant, or, the court or clerk failing therein, any such case shall be so called on request of the plaintiff's attorney.

RULE 239. JUDGMENT BY DEFAULT

Upon such call of the docket, or at any time after a defendant is required to answer, the plaintiff may in term time take judgment by default against such defendant if he has not previously filed an answer, and provided that the return of service shall have been on file with the clerk for the length of time required by Rule 107.

RULE 239a. NOTICE OF DEFAULT JUDGMENT

At or immediately prior to the time an interlocutory or final default judgment is rendered, the party taking the same or his attorney shall certify to the clerk in writing the last known mailing address of the party against whom the judgment is taken, which certificate shall be filed among the papers in the cause. Immediately upon the signing of the judgment, the clerk shall mail written notice thereof to the party against whom the judgment was rendered at the address shown in the certificate, and note the fact of such mailing on the docket. The notice shall state the number and style of the case, the court in which the case is pending, the names of the parties in whose favor and against whom the judgment was rendered, and the date of the signing of the judgment. Failure to comply with the provisions of this rule shall not affect the finality of the judgment.

RULE 240. WHERE ONLY SOME ANSWER

Where there are several defendants, some of whom have answered or have not been duly served and some of whom have been duly served and have made default, an interlocutory judgment by default may be entered against those who have made default, and the cause may proceed or be postponed as to the others.

RULE 241. ASSESSING DAMAGES ON LIQUIDATED DEMANDS

When a judgment by default is rendered against the defendant, or all of several defendants, if the claim is liquidated and proved by an instrument in writing, the damages shall be assessed by the court, or under its direction, and final judgment shall be rendered therefor, unless the defendant shall demand and be entitled to a trial by jury.

[RULE 242. Repealed effective December 31, 1941]

RULE 243. UNLIQUIDATED DEMANDS

If the cause of action is unliquidated or be not proved by an instrument in writing, the court shall hear evidence as to damages and shall render judgment therefor, unless the defendant shall demand and be entitled to a trial by jury in which case the judgment by default shall be noted, a writ of inquiry awarded, and the cause entered on the jury docket.

RULE 244. ON SERVICE BY PUBLICATION

Where service has been made by publication, and no answer has been filed nor appearance entered within the prescribed time, the court shall appoint an attorney to defend the suit in behalf of the defendant, and judgment shall be rendered as in other cases; but, in every such case a statement of the evidence, approved and signed by the judge, shall be filed with the papers of the cause as a part of the record thereof. The court shall allow such attorney a reasonable fee for his services, to be taxed as part of the costs.

RULE 245. ASSIGNMENT OF CASES FOR TRIAL

The court may set contested cases on written request of any party, or on the court's own motion, with reasonable notice of not less than forty-five days to the parties of a first setting for trial, or by agreement of the parties; provided, however, that when a case previously has been set for trial, the Court may reset said contested case to a later date on any reasonable notice to the parties or by agreement of the parties. Non-contested cases may be tried or disposed of at any time whether set or not, and may be set at any time for any other time.

A request for trial setting constitutes a representation that the requesting party reasonably and in good faith expects to be ready for trial by the date requested, but no additional representation concerning the completion of pretrial proceedings or of current readiness for trial shall be required in order to obtain a trial setting in a contested case.

RULE 246. CLERK TO GIVE NOTICE OF SETTINGS

The clerk shall keep a record in his office of all cases set for trial, and it shall be his duty to inform any non-resident attorney of the date of setting of any case upon request by mail from such attorney, accompanied by a return envelope properly addressed and stamped. Failure of the clerk to furnish such information on proper request shall be sufficient ground for continuance or for a new trial when it appears to the court that such failure has prevented the attorney from preparing or presenting his claim or defense.

RULE 247. TRIED WHEN SET

Every suit shall be tried when it is called, unless continued or postponed to a future day or placed at the end of the docket to be called again for trial in its regular order. No cause which has been set upon the trial docket of the court shall be taken from the trial docket for the date set except by agreement of the parties or for good cause upon motion and notice to the opposing party.

RULE 248. JURY CASES

When a jury has been demanded, questions of law, motions, exceptions to pleadings, and other unresolved pending matters shall, as far as practicable, be heard and determined by the court before the trial commences, and jurors shall be summoned to appear on the day so designated.

RULE 249. CALL OF NON-JURY DOCKET

The non -jury docket shall be taken up at such times as not unnecessarily to interfere with the dispatch of business on the jury docket.

[RULE 250. Repealed effective December 31, 1941]

SECTION 11. TRIAL OF CAUSES

B. Continuance and Change of Venue

RULE 251. CONTINUANCE

No application for a continuance shall be heard before the defendant files his defense, nor shall any continuance be granted except for sufficient cause supported by affidavit, or by consent of the parties, or by operation of law.

RULE 252. APPLICATION FOR CONTINUANCE

If the ground of such application be the want of testimony, the party applying therefor shall make affidavit that such testimony is material, showing the materiality thereof, and that he has used due diligence to procure such testimony, stating such diligence, and the cause of failure, if known; that such testimony cannot be procured from any other source; and, it if be for the absence of a witness, he shall state the name and residence of the witness, and what he expects to prove by him; and also state that the continuance is not sought for delay only, but that justice may be done; provided that, on a first application for a continuance, it shall not be necessary to show that the absent testimony cannot be procured from any other source.

The failure to obtain the deposition of any witness residing within 100 miles of the courthouse or the county in which the suit is pending shall not be regarded as want of diligence when diligence has been used to secure the personal attendance of such witness under the rules of law, unless by reason of age, infirmity or sickness, or official duty, the witness will be unable to attend the court, or unless such witness is about to leave, or has left, the State or county in which the suit is pending and will not probably be present at the trial.

RULE 253. ABSENCE OF COUNSEL AS GROUND FOR CONTINUANCE

Except as provided elsewhere in these rules, absence of counsel will not be good cause for a continuance or postponement of the cause when called for trial, except it be allowed in the discretion of the court, upon cause shown or upon matters within the knowledge or information of the judge to be stated on the record.

RULE 254. ATTENDANCE ON LEGISLATURE

In all civil actions, including matters of probate, and in all matters ancillary to such suits which require action by or the attendance of an attorney, including appeals but excluding temporary restraining orders, at any time within thirty days of a date when the legislature is to be in session, or at any time the legislature is in session, or when the legislature sits as a Constitutional Convention, it shall be mandatory that the court continue the cause if it shall appear to the court, by affidavit, that any party applying for continuance, or any attorney for any party to the cause, is a member of either branch of the legislature, and will be or is in actual attendance on a session of the same. If the member of the legislature is an attorney for a party to the cause, his affidavit shall contain a declaration that it is his intention to participate actively in the preparation and/or presentation of the case. Where a party to any cause, or an attorney for any party to a cause, is a member of the legislature, his affidavit need not be corroborated. On the filing of such affidavit, the court shall continue the cause until thirty days after adjournment of the legislature and the affidavit shall be proof of the necessity for the continuance, and the continuance shall be deemed one of right and shall not be charged against the movant upon any subsequent application for continuance.

The right to a continuance shall be mandatory, except only where the attorney was employed within ten days of the date the suit is set for trial, the right to continuance shall be discretionary.

RULE 255. CHANGE OF VENUE BY CONSENT

Upon the written consent of the parties filed with the papers of the cause, the court, by an order entered on the minutes, may transfer the same for trial to the court of any other county having jurisdiction of the subject matter of such suit.

[RULE 256. Repealed effective September 1, 1941]

RULE 257. GRANTED ON MOTION

A change of venue may be granted in civil causes upon motion of either party, supported by his own affidavit and the affidavit of at least three credible persons, residents of the county in which the suit is pending, for any following cause:

(a) That there exists in the county where the suit is pending so great a prejudice against him that he cannot obtain a fair and impartial trial.

(b) That there is a combination against him instigated by influential persons, by reason of which he cannot expect a fair and impartial trial.

(c) That an impartial trial cannot be had in the county where the action is pending.

(d) For other sufficient cause to be determined by the court.

RULE 258. SHALL BE GRANTED

Where such motion to transfer venue is duly made, it shall be granted, unless the credibility of those making such application, or their means of knowledge or the truth of the facts set out in said application are attacked by the affidavit of a credible person; when thus attacked, the issue thus formed shall be tried by the judge; and the application either granted or refused. Reasonable discovery in support of, or in opposition to, the application shall be permitted, and such discovery as is relevant, including deposition testimony on file, may be attached to, or incorporated by reference in, the affidavit of a party, a witness, or an attorney who has knowledge of such discovery.

RULE 259. TO WHAT COUNTY

If the motion under Rule 257 is granted, the cause shall be removed:

(a) If from a district court, to any county of proper venue in the same or an adjoining district;

(b) If from a county court, to any adjoining county of proper venue;

(c) If (a) or (b) are not applicable, to any county of proper venue;

(d) If a county of proper venue (other than the county of suit) cannot be found, then if from

(1) A district court, to any county in the same or an adjoining district or to any district where an impartial trial can be had;

(2) A county court, to any adjoining county or to any district where an impartial trial can be had; but the parties may agree that venue shall be changed to some other county, and the order of the court shall conform to such agreement.

[RULE 260. Repealed effective September 1, 1990]

RULE 261. TRANSCRIPT ON CHANGE

When a change of venue has been granted, the clerk shall immediately make out a correct transcript of all the orders made in said cause, certifying thereto officially under the seal of the court, and send the same, with the original papers in the cause, to the clerk of the court to which the venue has been changed.

SECTION 11. TRIAL OF CAUSES

C. The Trial

RULE 262. TRIAL BY THE COURT

The rules governing the trial of causes before a jury shall govern in trials by the court in so far as applicable.

RULE 263. AGREED CASE

Parties may submit matters in controversy to the court upon an agreed statement of facts filed with the clerk, upon which judgment shall be rendered as in other cases; and such agreed statement signed and certified by the court to be correct and the judgment rendered thereon shall constitute the record of the cause.

RULE 264. VIDEOTAPE TRIAL

By agreement of the parties, the trial court may allow that all testimony and such other evidence as may be appropriate be presented at trial by videotape. The expenses of such videotape recordings shall be taxed as costs. If any party withdraws agreement to a videotape trial, the videotape costs that have accrued will be taxed against the party withdrawing from the agreement.

RULE 265. ORDER OF PROCEEDINGS ON TRIAL BY JURY

The trial of cases before a jury shall proceed in the following order unless the court should, for good cause stated in the record, otherwise direct:

(a) The party upon whom rests the burden of proof on the whole case shall state to the jury briefly the nature of his claim or defense and what said party expects to prove and the relief sought. Immediately thereafter, the adverse party may make a similar statement, and intervenors and other parties will be accorded similar rights in the order determined by the court.

(b) The party upon whom rests the burden of proof on the whole case shall then introduce his evidence.

(c) The adverse party shall briefly state the nature of his claim or defense and what said party expects to prove and the relief sought unless he has already done so.

(d) He shall then introduce his evidence.

(e) The intervenor and other parties shall make their statement, unless they have already done so, and shall introduce their evidence.

(f) The parties shall then be confined to rebutting testimony on each side.

(g) But one counsel on each side shall examine and cross-examine the same witness, except on leave granted.

RULE 266. OPEN AND CLOSE - ADMISSION

Except as provided in Rule 269 the plaintiff shall have the right to open and conclude both in adducing his evidence and in the argument, unless the burden of proof on the whole case under the pleadings rests upon the defendant, or unless the defendant or all of the defendants, if there should be more than one, shall, after the issues of fact are settled and before the trial commences, admit that the plaintiff is entitled to recover as set forth in the petition, except so far as he may be defeated, in whole or in part, by the allegations of the answer constituting a good defense, which may be established on the trial; which admission shall be entered of record, whereupon the defendant, or the defendants, if more than one, shall have the right to open and conclude in adducing the evidence and in the argument of the cause. The admission shall not serve to admit any allegation which is inconsistent with such defense, which defense shall be one that defendant has the burden of establishing, as for example, and without excluding other defenses: accord and satisfaction, adverse possession, arbitration and award, contributory negligence, discharge in bankruptcy, duress, estoppel, failure of consideration, fraud, release, res judicata, statute of frauds, statute of limitations, waiver, and the like.

RULE 267. WITNESSES PLACED UNDER RULE

(a) At the request of either party, in a civil case, the witnesses on both sides shall be sworn and removed out of the courtroom to some place where they cannot hear the testimony as delivered by any other witness in the cause. This is termed placing witnesses under the rule.

(b) This rule does not authorize exclusion of (1) a party who is a natural person or the spouse of such natural person, or (2) an officer or employee of a party that is not a natural person and who is designated as its representative by its attorney, or (3) a person whose presence is shown by a party to be essential to the presentation of the cause.

(c) If any party be absent, the court in its discretion may exempt from the rule a representative of such party.

(d) Witnesses, when placed under Rule 614 of the Texas Rules of Civil Evidence, shall be instructed by the court that they are not to converse with each other or with any other person about the case other than the attorneys in the case, except by permission of the court, and that they are not to read any report of or comment upon the testimony in the case while under the rule.

(e) Any witness or other person violating such instructions may be punished for contempt of court.

RULE 268. MOTION FOR INSTRUCTED VERDICT

A motion for directed verdict shall state the specific grounds therefor.

RULE 269. ARGUMENT

(a) After the evidence is concluded and the charge is read, the parties may argue the case to the jury. The party having the burden of proof on the whole case, or on all matters which are submitted by the charge, shall be entitled to open and conclude the argument; where there are several parties having separate claims or defenses, the court shall prescribe the order of argument between them.

(b) In all arguments, and especially in arguments on the trial of the case, the counsel opening shall present his whole case as he relies on it, both of law and facts, and shall be heard in the concluding argument only in reply to the counsel on the other side.

(c) Counsel for an intervenor shall occupy the position in the argument assigned by the court according to the nature of the claim.

(d) Arguments on questions of law shall be addressed to the court, and counsel should state the substance of the authorities referred to without reading more from books than may be necessary to verify the statement. On a question on motions, exceptions to the evidence, and other incidental matters, the counsel will be allowed only such argument as may be necessary to present clearly the question raised, and refer to authorities on it, unless further discussion is invited by the court.

(e) Arguments on the facts should be addressed to the jury, when one is impaneled in a case that is being tried, under the supervision of the court. Counsel shall be required to confine the argument strictly to the evidence and to the arguments of opposing counsel. Mere personal criticism by counsel upon each other shall be avoided, and when indulged in shall be promptly corrected as a contempt of court.

(f) Side-bar remarks, and remarks by counsel of one side, not addressed to the court, while the counsel on the other side is examining a witness or arguing any question to the court, or addressing the jury, will be rigidly repressed by the court.

(g) The court will not be required to wait for objections to be made when the rules as to arguments are violated; but should they not be noticed and corrected by the court, opposing counsel may ask leave of the court to rise and present his point of objection. But the court shall protect counsel from any unnecessary interruption made on frivolous and unimportant grounds.

(h) It shall be the duty of every counsel to address the court from his place at the bar, and in addressing the court to rise to his feet; and while engaged in the trial of a case he shall remain at his place in the bar.

RULE 270. ADDITIONAL TESTIMONY

When it clearly appears to be necessary to the due administration of justice, the court may permit additional evidence to be offered at any time; provided that in a jury case no evidence on a controversial matter shall be received after the verdict of the jury.

SECTION 11. TRIAL OF CAUSES

D. Charge to the Jury

RULE 271. CHARGE TO THE JURY

Unless expressly waived by the parties, the trial court shall prepare and in open court deliver a written charge to the jury.

RULE 272. REQUISITES

The charge shall be in writing, signed by the court, and filed with the clerk, and shall be a part of the record of the cause. It shall be submitted to the respective parties or their attorneys for their inspection, and a reasonable time given them in which to examine and present objections thereto outside the presence of the jury, which objections shall in every instance be presented to the court in writing, or be dictated to the court reporter in the presence of the court and opposing counsel, before the charge is read to the jury. All objections not so presented shall be considered as waived. The court shall announce its rulings thereon before reading the charge to the jury and shall endorse the rulings on the objections if written or dictate same to the court reporter in the presence of counsel. Objections to the charge and the court's rulings thereon may be included as a part of any transcript or statement of facts on appeal and, when so included in either, shall constitute a sufficient bill of exception to the rulings of the court thereon. It shall be presumed, unless otherwise noted in the record, that the party making such objections presented the same at the proper time and excepted to the ruling thereon.

RULE 273. JURY SUBMISSIONS

Either party may present to the court and request written questions, definitions, and instructions to be given to the jury; and the court may give them or a part thereof, or may refuse to give them, as may be proper. Such requests shall be prepared and presented to the court and submitted to opposing counsel for examination and objection within a reasonable time after the charge is given to the parties or their attorneys for examination. A request by either party for any questions, definitions, or instructions shall be made separate and apart from such party's objections to the court's charge.

RULE 274. OBJECTIONS AND REQUESTS

A party objecting to a charge must point out distinctly the objectionable matter and the grounds of the objection. Any complaint as to a question, definition, or instruction, on account of any defect, omission, or fault in pleading, is waived unless specifically included in the objections. When the complaining party's objection, or requested question, definition, or instruction is, in the opinion of the appellate court, obscured or concealed by voluminous unfounded objections, minute differentiations or numerous unnecessary requests, such objection or request shall be untenable. No objection to one part of the charge may be adopted and applied to any other part of the charge by reference only.

RULE 275. CHARGE READ BEFORE ARGUMENT

Before the argument is begun, the trial court shall read the charge to the jury in the precise words in which it was written, including all questions, definitions, and instructions which the court may give.

RULE 276. REFUSAL OR MODIFICATION

When an instruction, question, or definition is requested and the provisions of the law have been complied with and the trial judge refuses the same, the judge shall endorse thereon "Refused," and sign the same officially. If the trial judge modifies the same the judge shall endorse thereon "Modified as follows: (stating in what particular the judge has modified the same) and given, and exception allowed" and sign the same officially. Such refused or modified instruction, question, or definition, when so endorsed shall constitute a bill of exceptions, and it shall be conclusively presumed that the party asking the same presented it at the proper time, excepted to its refusal or modification, and that all the requirements of law have been observed, and such procedure shall entitle the party requesting the same to have the action of the trial judge thereon reviewed without preparing a formal bill of exceptions.

RULE 277. SUBMISSION TO THE JURY

In all jury cases the court shall, whenever feasible, submit the cause upon broad-form questions. The court shall submit such instructions and definitions as shall be proper to enable the jury to render a verdict.

Inferential rebuttal questions shall not be submitted in the charge. The placing of the burden of proof may be accomplished by instructions rather than by inclusion in the question.

In any cause in which the jury is required to apportion the loss among the parties the court shall submit a question or questions inquiring what percentage, if any, of the negligence or causation, as the case may be, that caused the occurrence or injury in question is attributable to each of the persons found to have been culpable. The court shall also instruct the jury to answer the damage question or questions without any reduction because of the percentage of negligence or causation, if any, of the person injured. The court may predicate the damage question or questions upon affirmative findings of liability.

The court may submit a question disjunctively when it is apparent from the evidence that one or the other of the conditions or facts inquired about necessarily exists.

The court shall not in its charge comment directly on the weight of the evidence or advise the jury of the effect of their answers, but the court's charge shall not be objectionable on the ground that it incidentally constitutes a comment on the weight of the evidence or advises the jury of the effect of their answers when it is properly a part of an instruction or definition.

RULE 278. SUBMISSION OF QUESTIONS, DEFINITIONS, AND INSTRUCTIONS

The court shall submit the questions, instructions and definitions in the form provided by Rule 277, which are raised by the written pleadings and the evidence. Except in trespass to try title, statutory partition proceedings, and other special proceedings in which the pleadings are specially defined by statutes or procedural rules, a party shall not be entitled to any submission of any question raised only by a general denial and not raised by affirmative written pleading by that party. Nothing herein shall change the burden of proof from what it would have been under a general denial. A judgment shall not be reversed because of the failure to submit other and various phases or different shades of the same question. Failure to submit a question shall not be deemed a ground for reversal of the judgment, unless its submission, in substantially correct wording, has been requested in writing and tendered by the party complaining of the judgment; provided, however, that objection to such failure shall suffice in such respect if the question is one relied upon by the opposing party. Failure to submit a definition or instruction shall not be deemed a ground for reversal of the judgment unless a substantially correct definition or instruction has been requested in writing and tendered by the party complaining of the judgment.

RULE 279. OMISSIONS FROM THE CHARGE

Upon appeal all independent grounds of recovery or of defense not conclusively established under the evidence and no element of which is submitted or requested are waived. When a ground of recovery or defense consists of more than one element, if one or more of such elements necessary to sustain such ground of recovery or defense, and necessarily referable thereto, are submitted to and found by the jury, and one or more of such elements are omitted from the charge, without request or objection, and there is factually sufficient evidence to support a finding thereon, the trial court, at the request of either party, may after notice and hearing and at any time before the judgment is rendered, make and file written findings on such omitted element or elements in support of the judgment. If no such written findings are made, such omitted element or elements shall be deemed found by the court in such manner as to support the judgment. A claim that the evidence was legally or factually insufficient to warrant the submission of any question may be made for the first time after verdict, regardless of whether the submission of such question was requested by the complainant.

SECTION 11. TRIAL OF CAUSES

E. Case to the Jury

RULE 280. PRESIDING JUROR OF JURY

Each jury shall appoint one of their body presiding juror.

RULE 281. PAPERS TAKEN TO JURY ROOM

With the court's permission, the jury may take with them to the jury room any notes they took during the trial. In addition, the jury may, and on request shall, take with them in their retirement the charges and instructions, general or special, which were given and read to them, and any written evidence, except the depositions of witnesses, but shall not take with them any special charges which have been refused. Where only part of a paper has been read in evidence, the jury shall not take the same with them, unless the part so read to them is detached from that which was excluded.

RULE 282. JURY KEPT TOGETHER

The jury may either decide a case in court or retire for deliberation. If they retire, they shall be kept together in some convenient place, under the charge of an officer, until they agree upon a verdict or are discharged by the court; but the court in its discretion may permit them to separate temporarily for the night and at their meals, and for other proper purposes.

RULE 283. DUTY OF OFFICER ATTENDING JURY

The officer in charge of the jury shall not make not permit any communication to be made to them, except to inquire if they have agreed upon a verdict, unless by order of the court; and he shall not before their verdict is rendered communicate to any person the state of their deliberations or the verdict agreed upon.

RULE 284. JUDGE TO CAUTION JURY

Immediately after jurors are selected for a case, the court must instruct them to turn off their phones and other electronic devices and not to communicate with anyone through any electronic device while they are in the courtroom or while they are deliberating. The court must also instruct them that, while they are serving as jurors, they must not post any information about the case on the

Internet or search for any information outside of the courtroom, including on the Internet, to try to learn more about the case.

If jurors are permitted to separate before they are released from jury duty, either during the trial or after the case is submitted to them, the court must instruct them that it is their duty not to communicate with, or permit themselves to be addressed by, any other person about any subject relating to the case.

RULE 285. JURY MAY COMMUNICATE WITH COURT

The jury may communicate with the court by making their wish known to the officer in charge, who shall inform the court, and they may then in open court, and through their presiding juror, communicate with the court, either verbally or in writing. If the communication is to request further instructions, Rule 286 shall be followed.

RULE 286. JURY MY RECEIVE FURTHER INSTRUCTIONS

After having retired, the jury may receive further instructions from the court touching any matter of law, either at their request or upon the court's own motion. For this purpose they shall appear before the judge in open court in a body, and if the instruction is being given at their request, they shall through their presiding juror state to the court, in writing, the particular question of law upon which they desire further instruction. The court shall give such instruction in writing, but no instruction shall be given except in conformity with the rules relating to the charge. Additional argument may be allowed in the discretion of the court.

RULE 287. DISAGREEMENT AS TO EVIDENCE

If the jury disagree as to the statement of any witness, they may, upon applying to the court, have read to them from the court reporter's notes that part of such witness' testimony on the point in dispute; but, if there be no such reporter, or if his notes cannot be read to the jury, the court may cause such witness to be again brought upon the stand and the judge shall direct him to repeat his testimony as to the point in dispute, and no other, as nearly as he can in the language used on the trial; and on their notifying the court that they disagree as to any portion of a deposition or other paper not permitted to be carried with them in their retirement, the court may, in like manner, permit such portion of said deposition or paper to be again read to the jury.

RULE 288. COURT OPEN FOR JURY

The court, during the deliberations of the jury, may proceed with other business or recess from time to time, but shall be deemed open for all purposes connected with the case before the jury.

RULE 289. DISCHARGE OF JURY

The jury to whom a case has been submitted may be discharged by the court when they cannot agree and the parties consent to their discharge, or when they have been kept together for such time as to render it altogether improbable that they can agree, or when any calamity or accident may, in the opinion of the court, require it, or when by sickness or other cause their number is reduced below the number constituting the jury in such court.

The cause shall again be placed on the jury docket and shall again be set for trial as the court directs.

SECTION 11. TRIAL OF CAUSES

F. Verdict

RULE 290. DEFINITION AND SUBSTANCE

A verdict is a written declaration by a jury of its decision, comprehending the whole or all the issues submitted to the jury, and shall be either a general or special verdict, as directed, which shall be signed by the presiding juror of the jury.

A general verdict is one whereby the jury pronounces generally in favor of one or more parties to the suit upon all or any of the issues submitted to it. A special verdict is one wherein the jury finds the facts only on issues made up and submitted to them under the direction of the court.

A special verdict shall, as between the parties, be conclusive as to the facts found.

RULE 291. FORM OF VERDICT

No special form of verdict is required, and the judgment shall not be arrested or reversed for mere want of form therein if there has been substantial compliance with the requirements of the law in rendering a verdict.

RULE 292. VERDICT BY PORTION OF ORIGINAL JURY

(a) Except as provided in subsection (b), a verdict may be rendered in any cause by the concurrence, as to each and all answers made, of the same ten or more members of an original jury of twelve or of the same five or more members of an original jury of six. However, where as many as three jurors die or be disabled from sitting and there are only nine of the jurors remaining of an original jury of twelve, those remaining may render and return a verdict. If less than the original twelve or six jurors render a verdict, the verdict must be signed by each juror concurring therein.

(b) A verdict may be rendered awarding exemplary damages only if the jury was unanimous in finding liability for and the amount of exemplary damages.

RULE 293. WHEN THE JURY AGREE

When the jury agree upon a verdict, they shall be brought into the court by the proper officer, and they shall deliver their verdict to the clerk; and if they state that they have agreed, the verdict shall be read aloud by the clerk. If the verdict is in proper form, no juror objects to its accuracy, no juror represented as agreeing thereto dissents therefrom, and neither party requests a poll of the jury, the verdict shall be entered upon the minutes of the court.

RULE 294. POLLING THE JURY

Any party shall have the right to have the jury polled. A jury is polled by reading once to the jury collectively the general verdict, or the questions and answers thereto consecutively, and then calling the name of each juror separately and asking the juror if it is the juror's verdict. If any juror answers in the negative when the verdict is returned signed only by the presiding juror as a unanimous verdict, or if any juror shown by the juror's signature to agree to the verdict should answer in the negative, the jury shall be retired for further deliberation.

RULE 295. CORRECTION OF VERDICT

If the purported verdict is defective, the court may direct it to be reformed. If it is incomplete, or not responsive to the questions contained in the court's charge, or the answers to the questions are in conflict, the court shall in writing instruct the jury in open court of the nature of the incompleteness, unresponsiveness, or conflict, provide the jury such additional instructions as may be proper, and retire the jury for further deliberations.

SECTION 11. TRIAL OF CAUSES

G. Findings by the Court

RULE 296. REQUESTS FOR FINDINGS OF FACTS AND CONCLUSIONS OF LAW

In any case tried in the district or county court without a jury, any party may request the court to state in writing its findings of fact and conclusions of law. Such request shall be entitled "Request for Findings of Fact and Conclusions of Law" and shall be filed within twenty days after judgment is signed with the clerk of the court, who shall immediately call such request to the attention of the judge who tried the case. The party making the request shall serve it on all other parties in accordance with Rule 21a.

RULE 297. TIME TO FILE FINDINGS OF FACT AND CONCLUSIONS OF LAW

The court shall file its findings of fact and conclusions of law within twenty days after a timely request is filed. The court shall cause a copy of its findings and conclusions to be mailed to each party in the suit.

If the court fails to file timely findings of fact and conclusions of law, the party making the request shall, within thirty days after filing the original request, file with the clerk and serve on all other parties in accordance with Rule 21a a "Notice of Past Due Findings of Fact and Conclusions of Law" which shall be immediately called to the attention of the court by the clerk. Such notice shall state the date the original request was filed and the date the findings and conclusions were due. Upon filing this notice, the time for the court to file findings of fact and conclusions of law is extended to forty days from the date the original request was filed.

RULE 298. ADDITIONAL OR AMENDED FINDINGS OF FACT AND CONCLUSIONS OF LAW

After the court files original findings of fact and conclusions of law, any party may file with the clerk of the court a request for specified additional or amended findings or conclusions. The request for these findings shall be made within ten days after the filing of the original findings and conclusions by the court. Each request made pursuant to this rule shall be served on each party to the suit in accordance with Rule 21a.

The court shall file any additional or amended findings and conclusions that are appropriate within ten days after such request is filed, and cause a copy to be mailed to each party to the suit. No findings or conclusions shall be deemed or presumed by any failure of the court to make any additional findings or conclusions.

RULE 299. OMITTED FINDINGS

When findings of fact are filed by the trial court they shall form the basis of the judgment upon all grounds of recovery and of defense embraced therein. The judgment may not be supported upon appeal by a presumed finding upon any ground of recovery or defense, no element of which has been included in the findings of fact; but when one or more elements thereof have been found by the trial court, omitted unrequested elements, when supported by evidence, will be supplied by presumption in support of the judgment. Refusal of the court to make a finding requested shall be reviewable on appeal.

RULE 299a. FINDINGS OF FACT TO BE SEPARATELY FILED AND NOT RECITED IN A JUDGMENT

Findings of fact shall not be recited in a judgment. If there is a conflict between findings of fact recited in a judgment in violation of this rule and findings of fact made pursuant to Rules 297 and 298, the latter findings will control for appellate purposes. Findings of fact shall be filed with the clerk of the court as a document or documents separate and apart from the judgment.

SECTION 11. TRIAL OF CAUSES

H. Judgments

RULE 300. COURT TO RENDER JUDGMENT

Where a special verdict is rendered, or the conclusions of fact found by the judge are separately stated the court shall render judgment thereon unless set aside or a new trial is granted, or judgment is rendered notwithstanding verdict or jury finding under these rules.

RULE 301. JUDGMENTS

The judgment of the court shall conform to the pleadings, the nature of the case proved and the verdict, if any, and shall be so framed as to give the party all the relief to which he may be entitled either in law or equity. Provided, that upon motion and reasonable notice the court may render judgment non obstante veredicto if a directed verdict would have been proper, and provided further that the court may, upon like motion and notice, disregard any jury finding on a question that has no support in the evidence. Only one final judgment shall be rendered in any cause except where it is otherwise specially provided by law. Judgment may, in a proper case, be given for or against one or more of several plaintiffs, and for or against one or more of several defendants or intervenors.

RULE 302. ON COUNTERCLAIM

If the defendant establishes a demand against the plaintiff upon a counterclaim exceeding that established against him by the plaintiff, the court shall render judgment for defendant for such excess.

RULE 303. ON COUNTERCLAIM FOR COSTS

When a counterclaim is pleaded, the party in whose favor final judgment is rendered shall also recover the costs, unless it be made to appear on the trial that the counterclaim of the defendant was acquired after the commencement of the suit, in which case, if the plaintiff establishes a claim existing at the commencement of the suit, he shall recover his costs.

RULE 304. JUDGMENT UPON RECORD

Judgments rendered upon questions raised upon citations, pleadings, and all other proceedings, constituting the record proper as known at common law, must be entered at the date of each term when pronounced.

RULE 305. PROPOSED JUDGMENT

Any party may prepare and submit a proposed judgment to the court for signature.

Each party who submits a proposed judgment for signature shall serve the proposed judgment on all other parties to the suit who have appeared and remain in the case, in accordance with Rule 21a.

Failure to comply with this rule shall not affect the time for perfecting an appeal.

RULE 306. RECITATION OF JUDGMENT

The entry of the judgment shall contain the full names of the parties, as stated in the pleadings, for and against whom the judgment is rendered. In a suit for termination of the parent-child relationship or a suit affecting the parent-child relationship filed by a governmental entity for managing conservatorship, the judgment must state the specific grounds for termination or for appointment of the managing conservator.

RULE 306a. PERIODS TO RUN FROM SIGNING OF JUDGMENT

1. **Beginning of Periods**. The date of judgment or order is signed as shown of record shall determine the beginning of the periods prescribed by these rules for the court's plenary power to grant a new trial or to vacate, modify, correct or reform a judgment or order and for filing in the trial court the various documents that these rules authorize a party to file within such periods including, but not limited to, motions for new trial, motions to modify judgment, motions to reinstate a case dismissed for want of prosecution, motions to vacate judgment and requests for findings of fact and conclusions of law; but this rule shall not determine what constitutes rendition of a judgment or order for any other purpose.

2. **Date to Be Shown**. Judges, attorneys and clerks are directed to use their best efforts to cause all judgments, decisions and orders of any kind to be reduced to writing and signed by the trial judge with the date of signing stated therein. If the date of signing is not recited in the judgment or order, it may be shown in the record by a certificate of the judge or otherwise; provided, however, that the absence of a showing of the date in the record shall not invalidate any judgment or order.

3. **Notice of Judgment**. When the final judgment or other appealable order is signed, the clerk of the court shall immediately give notice to the parties or their attorneys of record by first-class mail advising that the judgment or order was signed. Failure to comply with the provisions of this rule shall not affect the periods mentioned in paragraph (1) of this rule, except as provided in paragraph (4).

4. **No Notice of Judgment**. If within twenty days after the judgment or other appealable order is signed, a party adversely affected by it or his attorney has neither received the notice required by paragraph (3) of this rule nor acquired actual knowledge of the order, then with respect to that party all the periods mentioned in paragraph (1) shall begin on the date that such party or his attorney received such notice or acquired actual knowledge of the signing, whichever occurred first, but in no event shall such periods begin more than ninety days after the original judgment or other appealable order was signed.

5. **Motion, Notice and Hearing**. In order to establish the application of paragraph (4) of this rule, the party adversely affected is required to prove in the trial court, on sworn motion and notice, the date on which the party or his attorney first either received a notice of the judgment or acquired actual knowledge of the signing and that this date was more than twenty days after the judgment was signed.

6. **Nunc Pro Tunc Order**. When a corrected judgment has been signed after expiration of the court's plenary power pursuant to Rule 316, the periods mentioned in paragraph (1) of this rule shall run from the date of signing the corrected judgment with repsect of any complaint that would not be applicable to the original document.

7. **When Process Served by Publication**. With respect to a motion for new trial filed more than thirty days after the judgment was signed pursuant to Rule 329 when process has been served by publication, the periods provided by paragraph (1) shall be computed as if the judgment were signed on the date of filing the motion.

[RULE 306b. Repealed effective April 1, 1984]

RULE 306c. PREMATURELY FILED DOCUMENTS

No motion for new trial or request for findings of fact and conclusions of law shall be held ineffective because prematurely filed; but every such motion shall be deemed to have been filed on the date of but subsequent to the time of signing of the judgment the motion assails, and every such request for findings of fact and conclusions of law shall be deemed to have been filed on the date of but subsequent to the time of signing of the judgment.

[RULE 306d. Repealed effective April 1, 1984]

RULE 307. EXCEPTIONS, ETC., TRANSCRIPT

In non-jury cases, where findings of fact and conclusions of law are requested and filed, and in jury cases, where a special verdict is returned, any party claiming that the findings of the court or the jury, as the case may be, do not support the judgment, may have noted in the record an exception to said judgment and thereupon take an appeal or writ of error, where such writ is allowed, without a statement of facts or further exceptions in the transcript, but the transcript in such cases shall contain the conclusions of law and fact or the special verdict and the judgment rendered thereon.

RULE 308. COURT SHALL ENFORCE ITS DECREES

The court shall cause its judgments and decrees to be carried into execution; and where the judgment is for personal property, and it is shown by the pleadings and evidence and the verdict, if any, that such property has an especial value to the plaintiff, the court may award a special writ for the seizure and delivery of such property to the plaintiff; and in such case may enforce its judgment by attachment, fine and imprisonment.

RULE 308a. IN SUITS AFFECTING THE PARENT-CHILD RELATIONSHIP

When the court has ordered child support or possession of or access to a child and it is claimed that the order has been violated, the person claiming that a violation has occurred shall make this known to the court. The court may appoint a member of the bar to investigate the claim to determine whether there is reason to believe that the court order has been violated. If the attorney in good faith believes that the order has been violated, the attorney shall take the necessary action as provided under Chapter 14, Family Code. On a finding of a violation, the court may enforce its order as provided in Chapter 14, Family Code.

Except by order of the court, no fee shall be charged by or paid to the attorney representing the claimant. If the court determines that an attorney's fee should be paid, the fee shall be adjudged against the party who violated the court's order. The fee may be assessed as costs of court, or awarded by judgment, or both.

RULE 309. IN FORECLOSURE PROCEEDINGS

Judgments for the foreclosure of mortgages and other liens shall be that the plaintiff recover his debt, damages and costs, with a foreclosure of the plaintiff's lien on the property subject thereto, and, except in judgments against executors, administrators and guardians, that an order of sale shall issue to any sheriff or any constable within the State of Texas, directing him to seize and sell the same as under execution, in satisfaction of the judgment; and, if the property cannot be found, or if the proceeds of such sale be insufficient to satisfy the judgment, then to take the money or any balance thereof remaining unpaid, out of any other property of the defendant, as in case of ordinary executions.

RULE 310. WRIT OF POSSESSION

When an order foreclosing a lien upon real estate is made in a suit having for its object the foreclosure of such lien, such order shall have all the force and effect of a writ of possession as between the parties to the foreclosure suit and any person claiming under the defendant to such suit by any right acquired pending such suit; and the court shall so direct in the judgment providing for the issuance of such order. The sheriff or other officer executing such order of sale shall proceed by virtue of such order of sale to place the purchaser of the property sold thereunder in possession thereof within thirty days after the day of sale.

RULE 311. ON APPEAL FROM PROBATE COURT

Judgment on appeal or certiorari from any county court sitting in probate shall be certified to such county court for observance.

RULE 312. ON APPEAL FROM JUSTICE COURT

Judgment on appeal or certiorari from a justice court shall be enforced by the county or district court rendering the judgment.

RULE 313. AGAINST EXECUTORS, ETC.

A judgment for the recovery of money against an executor, administrator or guardian, as such, shall state that it is to be paid in the due course of administration. No execution shall issue thereon, but it shall be certified to the county court, sitting in matters of probate, to be there enforced in accordance with law, but judgment against an executor appointed and acting under a will dispensing with the action of the county court in reference to such estate shall be enforced against the property of the testator in the hands of such executor, by execution, as in other cases.

RULE 314. CONFESSION OF JUDGMENT

Any person against whom a cause of action exists may, without process, appear in person or by attorney, and confess judgment therefor in open court as follows:

(a) A petition shall be filed and the justness of the debt or cause of action be sworn to by the person in whose favor the judgment is confessed.

(b) If the judgment is confessed by attorney, the power of attorney shall be filed and its contents be recited in the judgment.

(c) Every such judgment duly made shall operate as a release of all errors in the record thereof, but such judgment may be impeached for fraud or other equitable cause.

SECTION 11. TRIAL OF CAUSES
I. Remittitur and Correction

RULE 315. REMITTITUR

Any party in whose favor a judgment has been rendered may remit any part thereof in open court, or by executing and filing with the clerk a written remittitur signed by the party or the party's attorney of record, and duly acknowledged by the party or the party's attorney. Such remittitur shall be a part of the record of the cause. Execution shall issue for the balance only of such judgment.

RULE 316. CORRECTION OF CLERICAL MISTAKES IN JUDGMENT RECORD

Clerical mistakes in the record of any judgment may be corrected by the judge in open court according to the truth or justice of the case after notice of the motion therefor has been given to the parties interested in such judgment, as provided in Rule 21a, and thereafter the execution shall conform to the judgment as amended.

[RULES 317 - 319. Repealed effective January 1, 1988]

SECTION 11. TRIAL OF CAUSES
J. New Trials

RULE 320. MOTION AND ACTION OF COURT THEREON

New trials may be granted and judgment set aside for good cause, on motion or on the court's own motion on such terms as the court shall direct. New trials may be granted when the damages are manifestly too small or too large. When it appears to the court that a new trial should be granted on a point or points that affect only a part of the matters in controversy and that such part is clearly separable without unfairness to the parties, the court may grant a new trial as to that part only, provided that a separate trial on unliquidated damages alone shall not be ordered if liability issues are contested. Each motion for new trial shall be in writing and signed by the party or his attorney.

RULE 321. FORM

Each point relied upon in a motion for new trial or in arrest of judgment shall briefly refer to that part of the ruling of the court, charge given to the jury, or charge refused, admission or rejection of evidence, or other proceedings which are designated to be complained of, in such a way that the objection can be clearly identified and understood by the court.

RULE 322. GENERALITY TO BE AVOIDED

Grounds of objections couched in general terms - as that the court erred in its charge, in sustaining or overruling exceptions to the pleadings, and in excluding or admitting evidence, the verdict of the jury is contrary to law, and the like - shall not be considered by the court.

[RULE 323. Repealed effective January 1, 1978]

RULE 324. PREREQUISITES OF APPEAL

(a) **Motion for New Trial Not Required**. A point in a motion for new trial is not a prerequisite to a complaint on appeal in either a jury or a nonjury case, except as provided in subdivision (b).

(b) **Motion for New Trial Required**. A point in a motion for new trial is a prerequisite to the following complaints on appeal:

(1) A complaint on which evidence must be heard such as one of jury misconduct or newly discovered evidence or failure to set aside a judgment by default;

(2) A complaint of factual insufficiency of the evidence to support a jury finding;

(3) A complaint that a jury finding is against the overwhelming weight of the evidence;

(4) A complaint of inadequacy or excessiveness of the damages found by the jury; or

(5) Incurable jury argument if not otherwise ruled on by the trial court.

(c) **Judgment Notwithstanding Findings; Cross-Points**. When judgment is rendered non obstante verdicto or notwithstanding the findings of a jury on one or more questions, the appellee may bring forward by cross-point contained in his brief filed in the Court of Appeals any ground which would have vitiated the verdict or would have prevented an affirmance of the judgment had one been rendered by the trial court in harmony with the verdict, including although not limited to the ground that one or more of the jury's findings have insufficient support in the evidence or are against the overwhelming preponderance of the evidence as a matter of fact, and the ground that the verdict and judgment based thereon should be set aside because of improper argument of counsel.

The failure to bring forward by cross-points such grounds as would vitiate the verdict shall be deemed a waiver thereof; provided, however, that if a cross-point is upon a ground which requires the taking of evidence in addition to that adduced upon the trial of the cause, it is not necessary that the evidentiary hearing be held until after the appellate court determines that the cause be remanded to consider such a cross-point.

[RULE 325. Repealed effective January 1, 1978]

RULE 326. NOT MORE THAN TWO

Not more than two new trials shall be granted either party in the same cause because of insufficiency or weight of the evidence.

RULE 327. FOR JURY MISCONDUCT

(a) When the ground of a motion for new trial, supported by affidavit, is misconduct of the jury or of the officer in charge of them, or because of any communication made to the jury, or that a juror gave an erroneous or incorrect answer on voir dire examination, the court shall hear evidence thereof from the jury or others in open court, and may grant a new trial if such misconduct proved, or the communication made, or the erroneous or incorrect answer on voir dire examination, be material, and if it reasonably appears from the evidence both on the hearing of the motion and the trial of the case and from the record as a whole that injury probably resulted to the complaining party.

(b) A juror may not testify as to any matter or statement occurring during the course of the jury's deliberations or to the effect of anything upon his or any other juror's mind or emotions as influencing him to assent to or dissent from the verdict concerning his mental processes in connection therewith, except that a juror may testify whether any outside influence was improperly brought to bear upon any juror. Nor may his affidavit or evidence of any statement by him concerning a matter about which he would be precluded from testifying be received for these purposes.

[RULE 328. Repealed effective January 1, 1988]

RULE 329. MOTION FOR NEW TRIAL ON JUDGMENT FOLLOWING CITATION BY PUBLICATION

In cases in which judgment has been rendered on service of process by publication, when the defendant has not appeared in person or by attorney of his own selection:

(a) The court may grant a new trial upon petition of the defendant showing good cause, supported by affidavit, filed within two years after such judgment was signed. The parties adversely interested in such judgment shall be cited as in other cases.

(b) Execution of such judgment shall not be suspended unless the party applying therefor shall give a good and sufficient bond payable to the plaintiff in the judgment, in an amount fixed in accordance with Appellate Rule 47 relating to supersedeas bonds, to be approved by the clerk, and conditioned that the party will prosecute his petition for new trial to effect and will perform such judgment as may be rendered by the court should its decision be against him.

(c) If property has been sold under the judgment and execution before the process was suspended, the defendant shall not recover the property so sold, but shall have judgment against the plaintiff in the judgment for the proceeds of such sale.

(d) If the motion is filed more than thirty days after the judgment was signed, the time period shall be computed pursuant to Rule 306a(7).

RULE 329a. COUNTY COURT CASES

If a case or other matter is on trial or in the process of hearing when the term of the county court expires, such trial, hearing or other matter may be proceeded with at the next or any subsequent term of court and no motion or plea shall be considered as waived or overruled, because not acted upon at the term of court at which it was filed, but may be acted upon at any time the judge may fix or at which it may have been postponed or continued by agreement of the parties with leave of the court. This subdivision is not applicable to original or amended motions for new trial which are governed by Rule 329b.

RULE 329b. TIME FOR FILING MOTIONS

The following rules shall be applicable to motions for new trial and motions to modify, correct, or reform judgments (other than motions to correct the record under Rule 316) in all district and county courts:

(a) A motion for new trial, if filed, shall be filed prior to or within thirty days after the judgment or other order complained of is signed.

(b) One or more amended motions for new trial may be filed without leave of court before any preceding motion for new trial filed by the movant is overruled and within thirty days after the judgment or other order complained of is signed.

(c) In the event an original or amended motion for new trial or a motion to modify, correct or reform a judgment is not determined by written order signed within seventy-five days after the judgment was signed, it shall be considered overruled by operation of law on expiration of that period.

(d) The trial court, regardless of whether an appeal has been perfected, has plenary power to grant a new trial or to vacate, modify, correct, or reform the judgment within thirty days after the judgment is signed.

(e) If a motion for new trial is timely filed by any party, the trial court, regardless of whether an appeal has been perfected, has plenary power to grant a new trial or to vacate, modify, correct, or reform the judgment until thirty days after all such timely-filed motions are overruled, either by a written and signed order or by operation of law, whichever occurs first.

(f) On expiration of the time within which the trial court has plenary power, a judgment cannot be set aside by the trial court except by bill of review for sufficient cause, filed within the time allowed by law; provided that the court may at any time correct a clerical error in the record of a judgment and render judgment nunc pro tunc under Rule 316, and may also sign an order declaring a previous judgment or order to be void because signed after the court's plenary power had expired.

(g) A motion to modify, correct, or reform a judgment (as distinguished from motion to correct the record of a judgment under Rule 316), if filed, shall be filed and determined within the time prescribed by this rule for a motion for new trial and shall extend the trial court's plenary power and the time for perfecting an appeal in the same manner as a motion for new trial. Each such motion shall be in writing and signed by the party or his attorney and shall specify the respects in which the judgment should be modified, corrected, or reformed. The overruling of such a motion shall not preclude the filing of a motion for new trial, nor shall the overruling of a motion for new trial preclude the filing of a motion to modify, correct, or reform.

(h) If a judgment is modified, corrected or reformed in any respect, the time for appeal shall run from the time the modified, corrected, or reformed judgment is signed, but if a correction is made pursuant to Rule 316 after expiration of the period of plenary power provided by this rule, no complaint shall be heard on appeal that could have been presented in an appeal from the original judgment.

SECTION 11. TRIAL OF CAUSES

K. Certain District Courts

RULE 330. RULES OF PRACTICE AND PROCEDURE IN CERTAIN DISTRICT COURTS

The following rules of practice and procedure shall govern and be followed in all civil actions in district courts in counties where the only district court of said county vested with civil jurisdiction, or all the district courts thereof having civil jurisdiction, have successive terms in said county throughout the year, without more than two days intervening between any of such terms, whether or not any one or more of such district courts include one or more other counties within its jurisdiction.

(a) **Appealed Cases**. In cases appealed to said district courts from inferior courts, the appeal, including transcript, shall be filed in the district court within thirty (30) days after the rendition of the judgment or order appealed from, and the appellee shall enter his appearance on the docket or answer to said appeal on or before ten o'clock a.m. of the Monday next after the expiration of twenty (20) days from the date the appeal is filed in the district court.

(b) [Repealed]

(c) **Postponement or Continuance**. Cases may be postponed or continued by agreement with the approval of the court, or upon the court's own motion or for cause. When a case is called for trial and only one party is ready, the court may for good cause either continue the case for the term or postpone and reset it for a later day in the same or succeeding term.

(d) **Cases May Be Reset**. A case that is set and reached for trial may be postponed for a later day in the term or continued and reset for a day certain in the succeeding term on the same grounds as an application for continuance would be granted in other district courts. After any case has been set and reached in its due order and called for trial two (2) or more times and not tried, the court may dismiss the same unless the parties agree to a postponement or continuance but the court shall respect written agreements of counsel for postponement and continuance if filed in the case when or before it is called for trial unless to do so will unreasonably delay or interfere with other business of the court.

(e) **Exchange and Transfer**. Where in such county there are two or more district courts having civil jurisdiction, the judges of such courts may, in their discretion, exchange benches or districts from time to time, and may transfer cases and other proceedings from one court to another, and any of them may in his own courtroom try and determine any case or proceeding pending in another court without having the case transferred, or may sit in any other of said courts and there hear and determine any case there pending, and every judgment and order shall be entered in the minutes of the court in which the case is pending and at the time the judgment or order is rendered, and two (2) or more judges may try different cases in the same court at the same time, and each may occupy his own courtroom or the room of any other court. The judge of any such court may issue restraining orders and injunctions returnable to any other judge or court, and any judge may transfer any case or proceeding pending in his court to any other of said courts, and the judge of any court to which a case or proceeding is transferred shall receive and try the same, and in turn shall have power in his discretion to transfer any such case to any other of said courts and any other judge may in his courtroom try any case pending in any other of such courts.

(f) **Cases Transferred to Judges Not Occupied**. Where in such counties there are two or more district courts having civil jurisdiction, when the judge of any such court shall become disengaged, he shall notify the presiding judge, and the presiding judge shall transfer to the court of the disengaged judge the next case which is ready for trial in any of said courts. Any judge not engaged in his own court may try any case in any other court.

(g) **Judge May Hear Only Part of Case**. Where in such counties there are two or more district courts having civil jurisdiction, any judge may hear any part of any case or proceeding pending in any of said courts and determine the same, or may hear and determine any question in any case, and any other judge may complete the hearing and render judgment in the case.

(h) **Any Judge May Hear Dilatory Pleas**. Where in such county there are two or more district courts having civil jurisdiction, any judge may hear and determine motions, petitions for injunction, applications for appointment of receivers, interventions, pleas of privilege, pleas in abatement, all dilatory pleas and special exceptions, motions for a new trial and all preliminary matters, questions and proceedings and may enter judgment or order thereon in the court in which the case is pending without having the case transferred to the court of the judge acting, and the judge in whose court the case is pending may thereafter proceed to hear, complete and determine the case or other matter, or any part thereof, and render final judgment therein. Any judgment rendered or action taken by any judge in any of said courts in the county shall be valid and binding.

(i) **Acts in Succeeding Terms**. If a case or other matter is on trial, or in the process of hearing when the term of court expires, such trial, hearing or other matter may be proceeded with at the next or any subsequent term of court and no motion or plea shall be considered as waived or overruled, because not acted upon at the term of court at which it was filed, but may be acted upon at any time the judge may fix or at which it may have been postponed or continued by agreement of the parties with leave of the court. This subdivision is not applicable to original or amended motions for new trial which are governed by Rule 329b.

[RULE 331. Repealed effective January 1, 1988]

SECTION 12. REVIEW BY DISTRICT COURTS OF COUNTY COURT RULINGS

[RULES 332-351. Repealed effective January 1, 1976]

PART III - RULES OF PROCEDURE FOR THE COURTS OF APPEALS

SECTION 1. PERFECTING APPEAL

[RULES 352 to 358. Repealed effective September 1, 1986] [RULE 359. Repealed effective April 1, 1984]

[RULE 360. Repealed effective September 1, 1986] [RULES 361 to 362. Repealed effective April 1, 1984]

[RULES 363 to 369a. Repealed effective September 1, 1986]

SECTION 2. RECORD ON APPEAL

[RULE 370. Repealed effective January 1, 1981]

[RULES 371 to 373. Repealed effective September 1, 1986]

[RULE 374. Repealed effective January 1, 1978]

[RULES 375 to 382. Repealed effective September 1, 1986]

SECTION 3. PROCEEDINGS IN THE COURTS OF APPEALS

[RULES 383 to 389a. Repealed effective September 1, 1986]

[RULE 390. Repealed effective April 1, 1984]

[RULE 391. Repealed effective March 1, 1950]

[RULE 392. Repealed effective April 1, 1984]

[RULES 393 to 414. Repealed effective September 1, 1986]

[RULES 415 to 417. Repealed effective April 1, 1984]

[RULE 418. Repealed effective October 1, 1984]

[RULES 419 to 420. Repealed effective September 1, 1986]

[RULE 421. Repealed effective January 1, 1981]

[RULES 422 to 423. Repealed effective September 1, 1986]

[RULES 424 to 427. Repealed effective April 1, 1984]

[RULES 429 to 429. Repealed effective September 1, 1986]

[RULES 430 to 432. Repealed effective April 1, 1984]

SECTION 4. JUDGMENT

[RULES 433 to 442. Repealed effective September 1, 1986]

[RULES 443 to 444. Repealed effective April 1, 1984]

[RULE 445. Repealed effective January 1, 1978]

[RULES 446 to 448. Repealed effective September 1, 1986]

[RULES 449 to 450. Repealed effective April 1, 1984]

SECTION 5. OPINIONS

[RULES 451 to 452. Repealed effective September 1, 1986]

[RULES 453 to 455. Repealed effective April 1, 1984]

[RULES 456 to 457. Repealed effective September 1, 1986]

SECTION 6. REHEARING

[RULE 458. Repealed effective September 1, 1986]

[RULE 459. Repealed effective December 31, 1941]

[RULE 460. Repealed effective September 1, 1986]

SECTION 7. CERTIFICATION OF QUESTIONS

[RULES 461 to 462. Repealed effective September 1, 1986]

[RULES 463 to 464. Repealed effective April 1, 1984]

[RULE 465. Renumbered as Rule 462 effective April 1, 1984]

[RULE 466. Repealed effective September 1, 1986]

SECTION 8. APPLICTION FOR WRIT OF ERROR

[RULE 467. Repealed effective April 1, 1984]

[RULES 468 to 470. Repealed effective September 1, 1986]

[RULE 471. Repealed effective April 1, 1984]

[RULE 472. Repealed effective September 1, 1986]

[RULE 473. Repealed effective April 1, 1984]

PART IV - RULES OF PRACTICE FOR THE SUPREME COURT

SECTION 1. PROCEEDINGS IN THE SUPREME COURT

[RULES 474 to 481. Repealed effective September 1, 1986]

[RULE 482. Repealed effective April 1, 1984]

[RULES 483 to 486. Repealed effective September 1, 1986]

[RULE 487. Repealed effective February 1, 1946]

[RULES 488 to 493. Repealed effective September 1, 1986]

[RULE 492. Repealed effective February 1, 1946]

[RULES 495 to 499a. Repealed effective September 1, 1986]

SECTION 2. JUDGMENT

[RULES 500 to 505. Repealed effective September 1, 1986]

[RULE 506. Repealed effective April 1, 1984]

[RULE 507. Repealed effective September 1, 1986]

[RULE 508. Repealed effective April 1, 1984]

[RULE 509. Repealed effective January 1, 1978]

[RULE 510. Repealed effective September 1, 1986]

[RULES 511 to 513. Repealed effective April 1, 1984]

[RULE 514. Repealed effective September 1, 1986]

SECTION 3. REHEARING

[RULE 515. Repealed effective September 1, 1986]

[RULE 516. Repealed effective April 1, 1984]

SECTION 4. COMMISSION OF APPEALS (REPEALED)

[RULES 518 to 522. Repealed effective February 1, 1946]

PART V - RULES OF PRACTICE IN JUSTICE COURTS

[RULES 523 to 591. Repealed effective August 31, 2013]

RULE 500. GENERAL RULES

RULE 500.1. CONSTRUCTION OF RULES

Unless otherwise expressly provided, in Part V of these Rules of Civil Procedure:

(a) the past, present, and future tense each includes the other;

(b) the term "it" includes a person of either gender or an entity; and

(c) the singular and plural each includes the other.

RULE 500.2. DEFINITIONS

In Part V of these Rules of Civil Procedure:

(a) "Answer" is the written response that a party who is sued must file with the court after being served with a citation.

(b) "Citation" is the court-issued document required to be served upon a party to inform the party that it has been sued.

(c) "Claim" is the legal theory and alleged facts that, if proven, entitle a party to relief against another party in court.

(d) "Clerk" is a person designated by the judge as a justice court clerk, or the judge if there is no clerk available.

(e) "Counterclaim" is a claim brought by a party who has been sued against the party who filed the lawsuit, for example, a defendant suing a plaintiff.

(f) "County court" is the county court, statutory county court, or district court in a particular county with jurisdiction over appeals of civil cases from justice court.

(g) "Cross-claim" is a claim brought by one party against another party on the same side of a lawsuit. For example, if a plaintiff sues two defendants, the defendants can seek relief against each other by means of a cross-claim.

(h) "Default judgment" is a judgment awarded to a plaintiff when the defendant fails to answer and dispute the plaintiff's claims in the lawsuit.

(i) "Defendant" is a party who is sued, including a plaintiff against whom a counterclaim is filed.

(j) "Defense" is an assertion by a defendant that the plaintiff is not entitled to relief from the court.

(k) "Discovery" is the process through which parties obtain information from each other in order to prepare for trial or enforce a judgment. The term does not refer to any information that a party is entitled to under applicable law.

(l) "Dismissed without prejudice" means a case has been dismissed but has not been finally decided and may be refiled.

(m) "Dismissed with prejudice" means a case has been dismissed and finally decided and may not be refiled.

(n) "Judge" is a justice of the peace.

(o) "Judgment" is a final order by the court that states the relief, if any, a party is entitled to or must provide.

(p) "Jurisdiction" is the authority of the court to hear and decide a case.

(q) "Motion" is a request that the court make a specified ruling or order.

(r) "Notice" is a document prepared and delivered by the court or a party stating that something is required of the party receiving the notice.

(s) "Party" is a person or entity involved in the case that is either suing or being sued, including all plaintiffs, defendants, and third parties that have been joined in the case.

(t) "Petition" is a formal written application stating a party's claims and requesting relief from the court. It is the first document filed with the court to begin a lawsuit.

(u) "Plaintiff" is a party who sues, including a defendant who files a counterclaim.

(v) "Pleading" is a written document filed by a party, including a petition and an answer, that states a claim or defense and outlines the relief sought.

(w) "Relief" is the remedy a party requests from the court, such as the recovery of money or the return of property.

(x) "Serve" and "service" are delivery of citation as required by Rule 501.2, or of a document as required by Rule 501.4.

(y) "Sworn" means signed in front of someone authorized to take oaths, such as a notary, or signed under penalty of perjury. Filing a false sworn document can result in criminal prosecution.

(z) "Third party claim" is a claim brought by a party being sued against someone who is not yet a party to the case.

RULE 500.3. APPLICATION OF RULES IN JUSTICE COURT CASES

(a) **Small Claims Case**. A small claims case is a lawsuit brought for the recovery of money damages, civil penalties, personal property, or other relief allowed by law. The claim can be for no more than $10,000, excluding statutory interest and court costs but including attorney fees, if any. Small claims cases are governed by Rules 500-507 of Part V of the Rules of Civil Procedure.

(b) **Debt Claim Case**. A debt claim case is a lawsuit brought to recover a debt by an assignee of a claim, a debt collector or collection agency, a financial institution, or a person or entity primarily engaged in the business of lending money at interest. The claim can be for no more than $10,000, excluding statutory interest and court costs but including attorney fees, if any. Debt claim cases in justice court are governed by Rules 500-507 and 508 of Part V of the Rules of Civil Procedure. To the extent of any conflict between Rule 508 and the rest of Part V, Rule 508 applies.

(c) **Repair and Remedy Case**. A repair and remedy case is a lawsuit filed by a residential tenant under Chapter 92, Subchapter B of the Texas Property Code to enforce the landlord's duty to repair or remedy a condition materially affecting the physical health or safety of an ordinary tenant. The relief sought can be for no more than $10,000, excluding statutory interest and court costs but including attorney fees, if any. Repair and remedy cases are governed by Rules 500-507 and 509 of Part V of the Rules of Civil Procedure. To the extent of any conflict between Rule 509 and the rest of Part V, Rule 509 applies.

(d) **Eviction Case**. An eviction case is a lawsuit brought to recover possession of real property under Chapter 24 of the Texas Property Code, often by a landlord against a tenant. A claim for rent may be joined with an eviction case if the amount of rent due and unpaid is not more than $10,000, excluding statutory interest and court costs but including attorney fees, if any. Eviction cases are governed by Rules 500-507 and 510 of Part V of the Rules of Civil Procedure. To the extent of any conflict between Rule 510 and the rest of Part V, Rule 510 applies.

(e) **Application of Other Rules**. The other Rules of Civil Procedure and the Rules of Evidence do not apply except:

> (1) when the judge hearing the case determines that a particular rule must be followed to ensure that the proceedings are fair to all parties; or

> (2) when otherwise specifically provided by law or these rules.

(f) **Examination of Rules**. The court must make the Rules of Civil Procedure and the Rules of Evidence available for examination, either in paper form or electronically, during the court's business hours.

RULE 500.4. REPRESENTATION IN JUSTICE COURT CASES

(a) Representation of an Individual. An individual may:

> (1) represent himself or herself;

> (2) be represented by an authorized agent in an eviction case; or

> (3) be represented by an attorney.

(b) Representation of a Corporation or Other Entity. A corporation or other entity may:

> (1) be represented by an employee, owner, officer, or partner of the entity who is not an attorney;

> (2) be represented by a property manager or other authorized agent in an eviction case; or

> (3) be represented by an attorney.

(c) Assisted Representation. The court may, for good cause, allow an individual representing himself or herself to be assisted in court by a family member or other individual who is not being compensated.

RULE 500.5. COMPUTATION OF TIME; TIMELY FILING

(a) **Computation of Time**. To compute a time period in these rules:

> (1) exclude the day of the event that triggers the period;

> (2) count every day, including Saturdays, Sundays, and legal holidays; and

> (3) include the last day of the period, but

>> (A) if the last day is a Saturday, Sunday, or legal holiday, the time period is extended to the next day that is not a Saturday, Sunday, or legal holiday; and

(B) if the last day for filing falls on a day during which the court is closed before 5:00 p.m., the time period is extended to the court's next business day.

(b) **Timely Filing by Mail**. Any document required to be filed by a given date is considered timely filed if deposited in the U.S. mail on or before that date, and received within 10 days of the due date. A legible postmark affixed by the United States Postal Service is evidence of the date of mailing.

(c) **Extensions**. The judge may, for good cause shown, extend any time period under these rules except those relating to new trial and appeal.

RULE 500.6. JUDGE TO DEVELOP THE CASE

In order to develop the facts of the case, a judge may question a witness or party and may summon any person or party to appear as a witness when the judge considers it necessary to ensure a correct judgment and a speedy disposition.

RULE 500.7. EXCLUSION OF WITNESSES

The court must, on a party's request, or may, on its own initiative, order witnesses excluded so that they cannot hear the testimony of other witnesses. This rule does not authorize the exclusion of:

(a) a party who is a natural person or the spouse of such natural person;

(b) an officer or employee designated as a representative of a party who is not a natural person; or

(c) a person whose presence is shown by a party to be essential to the presentation of the party's case.

RULE 500.8. SUBPOENAS

(a) **Use**. A subpoena may be used by a party or the judge to command a person or entity to attend and give testimony at a hearing or trial. A person may not be required by subpoena to appear in a county that is more than 150 miles from where the person resides or is served.

(b) **Who Can Issue**. A subpoena may be issued by the clerk of the justice court or an attorney authorized to practice in the State of Texas, as an officer of the court.

(c) **Form**. Every subpoena must be issued in the name of the "State of Texas" and must:

(1) state the style of the suit and its case number;

(2) state the court in which the suit is pending;

(3) state the date on which the subpoena is issued;

(4) identify the person to whom the subpoena is directed;

(5) state the date, time, place, and nature of the action required by the person to whom the subpoena is directed;

(6) identify the party at whose instance the subpoena is issued, and the party's attorney of record, if any;

(7) state that "Failure by any person without adequate excuse to obey a subpoena served upon that person may be deemed a contempt of court from which the subpoena is issued and may be punished by fine or confinement, or both"; and

(8) be signed by the person issuing the subpoena.

(d) **Service: Where, By Whom, How**. A subpoena may be served at any place within the State of Texas by any sheriff or constable of the State of Texas, or by any person who is not a party and is 18 years of age or older. A subpoena must be served by delivering a copy to the witness and tendering to that person any fees required by law. If the witness is a party and is represented by an attorney of record in the proceeding, the subpoena may be served on the witness's attorney of record. Proof of service must be made by filing either:

(1) the witness's signed written memorandum attached to the subpoena showing that the witness accepted the subpoena; or

(2) a statement by the person who made the service stating the date, time, and manner of service, and the name of the person served.

(e) **Compliance Required**. A person commanded by subpoena to appear and give testimony must remain at the hearing or trial from day to day until discharged by the court or by the party summoning the witness. If a subpoena commanding testimony is directed to a corporation, partnership, association, governmental agency, or other organization, and the matters on which examination is requested are described with reasonable particularity, the organization must designate one or more persons to testify on its behalf as to matters known or reasonably available to the organization.

(f) **Objection**. A person commanded to attend and give testimony at a hearing or trial may object or move for a protective order before the court at or before the time and place specified for compliance. A party causing a subpoena to issue must take reasonable steps to avoid imposing undue burden or expense on the person served. In ruling on objections or motions for protection, the court must provide a person served with a subpoena an adequate time for compliance and protection from undue burden or expense. The court may impose reasonable conditions on compliance with a subpoena, including compensating the witness for undue hardship.

(g) **Enforcement**. Failure by any person without adequate excuse to obey a subpoena served upon that person may be deemed a contempt of the court from which the subpoena is issued or of a district court in the county in which the subpoena is served, and may be punished by fine or confinement, or both. A fine may not be imposed, nor a person served with a subpoena attached, for failure to comply with a subpoena without proof of service and proof by affidavit of the party requesting the subpoena or the party's attorney of record that all fees due the witness by law were paid or tendered.

RULE 500.9. DISCOVERY

(a) **Pretrial Discovery**. Pretrial discovery is limited to that which the judge considers reasonable and necessary. Any requests for pretrial discovery must be presented to the court for approval by written motion. The motion must be served on the responding party. Unless a hearing is requested, the judge may rule on the motion without a hearing. The discovery request must not be served on the responding party unless the judge issues a signed order approving the request. Failure to comply with a discovery order can result in sanctions, including dismissal of the case or an order to pay the other party's discovery expenses.

(b) **Post-judgment Discovery**. Post-judgment discovery is not required to be filed with the court. The party requesting discovery must give the responding party at least 30 days to respond to a post-judgment discovery request. The responding party may file a written objection with the court within 30 days of receiving the request. If an objection is filed, the judge must hold a hearing to determine if the request is valid. If the objection is denied, the judge must order the party to respond to the request. If the objection is upheld, the judge may reform the request or dismiss it entirely.

RULE 501. CITATION AND SERVICE

RULE 501.1. CITATION

(a) **Issuance**. When a petition is filed with a justice court to initiate a suit, the clerk must promptly issue a citation and deliver the citation as directed by the plaintiff. The plaintiff is responsible for obtaining service on the defendant of the citation and a copy of the petition with any documents filed with the petition. Upon request, separate or additional citations must be issued by the clerk. The clerk must retain a copy of the citation in the court's file.

(b) **Form**. The citation must:

(1) be styled "The State of Texas";

(2) be signed by the clerk under seal of court or by the judge;

(3) contain the name, location, and address of the court;

(4) show the date of filing of the petition;

(5) show the date of issuance of the citation;

(6) show the file number and names of parties;

(7) be directed to the defendant;

(8) show the name and address of attorney for plaintiff, or if the plaintiff does not have an attorney, the address of plaintiff; and

(9) notify defendant that if the defendant fails to file an answer, judgment by default may be rendered for the relief demanded in the petition.

(c) **Notice.** The citation must include the following notice to the defendant in boldface type: "You have been sued. You may employ an attorney to help you in defending against this lawsuit. But you are not required to employ an attorney. You or your attorney must file an answer with the court. Your answer is due by the end of the 14th day after the day you were served with these papers. If the 14th day is a Saturday, Sunday, or legal holiday, your answer is due by the end of the first day following the 14th day that is not a Saturday, Sunday, or legal holiday. Do not ignore these papers. If you do not file an answer by the due date, a default judgment may be taken against you. For further information, consult Part V of the Texas Rules of Civil Procedure, which is available online and also at the court listed on this citation."

(d) **Copies.** The plaintiff must provide enough copies to be served on each defendant. If the plaintiff fails to do so, the clerk may make copies and charge the plaintiff the allowable copying cost.

RULE 501.2. SERVICE OF CITATION

(a) **Who May Serve.** No person who is a party to or interested in the outcome of the suit may serve citation in that suit, and, unless otherwise authorized by written court order, only a sheriff or constable may serve a citation in an eviction case, a writ that requires the actual taking of possession of a person, property or thing, or process requiring that an enforcement action be physically enforced by the person delivering the process. Other citations may be served by:

(1) a sheriff or constable;

(2) a process server certified under order of the Supreme Court;

(3) the clerk of the court, if the citation is served by registered or certified mail; or

(4) a person authorized by court order who is 18 years of age or older.

(b) **Method of Service.** Citation must be served by:

(1) delivering a copy of the citation with a copy of the petition attached to the defendant in person, after endorsing the date of delivery on the citation; or

(2) mailing a copy of the citation with a copy of the petition attached to the defendant by registered or certified mail, restricted delivery, with return receipt or electronic return receipt requested.

(c) **Service Fees.** A plaintiff must pay all fees for service unless the plaintiff has filed a Statement of Inability to Afford Payment of Court Costs with the court. If the plaintiff has filed a Statement, the plaintiff must arrange for the citation to be served by a sheriff, constable, or court clerk.

(d) **Service on Sunday.** A citation cannot be served on a Sunday except in attachment, garnishment, sequestration, or distress proceedings.

(e) **Alternative Service of Citation**. If the methods under (b) are insufficient to serve the defendant, the plaintiff, or the constable, sheriff, process server certified under order of the Supreme Court, or other person authorized to serve process, may make a request for alternative service. This request must include a sworn statement describing the methods attempted under (b) and stating the defendant's usual place of business or residence, or other place where the defendant can probably be found. The court may authorize the following types of alternative service:

(1) mailing a copy of the citation with a copy of the petition attached by first class mail to the defendant at a specified address, and also leaving a copy of the citation with petition attached at the defendant's residence or other place where the defendant can probably be found with any person found there who is at least 16 years of age; or

(2) mailing a copy of the citation with a copy of the petition attached by first class mail to the defendant at a specified address, and also serving by any other method that the court finds is reasonably likely to provide the defendant with notice of the suit.

(f) **Service by Publication**. In the event that service of citation by publication is necessary, the process is governed by the rules in county and district court.

RULE 501.3. DUTIES OF OFFICER OR PERSON RECEIVING CITATION; RETURN OF SERVICE

(a) **Endorsement; Execution; Return**. The officer or authorized person to whom process is delivered must:

(1) endorse on the process the date and hour on which he or she received it;

(2) execute and return the same without delay; and

(3) complete a return of service, which may, but need not, be endorsed on or attached to the citation.

(b) **Contents of Return**. The return, together with any document to which it is attached, must include the following information:

(1) the case number and case name;

(2) the court in which the case is filed;

(3) a description of what was served;

(4) the date and time the process was received for service;

(5) the person or entity served;

(6) the address served;

(7) the date of service or attempted service;

(8) the manner of delivery of service or attempted service;

(9) the name of the person who served or attempted service;

(10) if the person named in (9) is a process server certified under Supreme Court Order, his or her identification number and the expiration date of his or her certification; and

(11) any other information required by rule or law.

(c) **Citation by Mail**. When the citation is served by registered or certified mail as authorized by Rule 501.2(b)(2), the return by the officer or authorized person must also contain the receipt with the addressee's signature.

(d) **Failure to Serve**. When the officer or authorized person has not served the citation, the return must show the diligence used by the officer or authorized person to execute the same and the cause of failure to execute it, and where the defendant is to be found, if ascertainable.

(e) **Signature**. The officer or authorized person who serves or attempts to serve a citation must sign the return. If the return is signed by a person other than a sheriff, constable, or clerk of the court, the return must either be verified or be signed under penalty of perjury. A return signed under penalty of perjury must contain the statement below in substantially the following form:

"My name is (First) (Middle) (Last) , my date of birth is (Month) (Day), (Year) , and my address is (Street), (City), (State) (Zip Code), (Country) . I declare under penalty of perjury that the foregoing is true and correct.

Executed in County, State of , on the day of (Month) , (Year) .

Declarant"

(f) **Alternative Service**. Where citation is executed by an alternative method as authorized by 501.2(e), proof of service must be made in the manner ordered by the court.

(g) **Filing Return**. The return and any document to which it is attached must be filed with the court and may be filed electronically or by fax, if those methods of filing are available.

(h) **Prerequisite for Default Judgment**. No default judgment may be granted in any case until proof of service as provided by this rule, or as ordered by the court in the event citation is executed by an alternative method under 501.2(e), has been on file with the clerk of the court 3 days, exclusive of the day of filing and the day of judgment.

RULE 501.4. SERVICE OF PAPERS OTHER THAN CITATION

(a) **Method of Service**. Other than a citation or oral motions made during trial or when all parties are present, every notice required by these rules, and every pleading, plea, motion, application to the court for an order, or other form of request, must be served on all other parties in one of the following ways:

(1) *In person*. A copy may be delivered to the party to be served, or the party's duly authorized agent or attorney of record, in person or by agent.

(2) *Mail or courier*. A copy may be sent by courier-receipted delivery or by certified or registered mail, to the party's last known address. Service by certified or registered mail is complete when the document is properly addressed and deposited in the United States mail, postage prepaid.

(3) *Fax*. A copy may be faxed to the recipient's current fax number. Service by fax after 5:00 p.m. local time of the recipient will be deemed to have been served on the following day.

(4) *Email*. A copy may be sent to an email address expressly provided by the receiving party, if the party has consented to email service in writing. Service by email after 5:00 p.m. local time of the recipient will be deemed to have been served on the following day.

(5) *Other*. A copy may be delivered in any other manner directed by the court.

(b) **Timing**. If a document is served by mail, 3 days will be added to the length of time a party has to respond to the document. Notice of any hearing requested by a party must be served on all other parties not less than 3 days before the time specified for the hearing.

(c) **Who May Serve**. Documents other than a citation may be served by a party to the suit, an attorney of record, a sheriff or constable, or by any other person competent to testify.

(d) **Certificate of Service**. The party or the party's attorney of record must include in writing on all documents filed a signed statement describing the manner in which the document was served on the other party or parties and the date of service. A certificate by a party or the party's attorney of record, or the return of the officer, or the sworn statement of any other person showing service of a notice is proof of service.

(e) **Failure to Serve**. A party may offer evidence or testimony that a notice or document was not received, or, if service was by mail, that it was not received within 3 days from the date of mailing, and upon so finding, the court may extend the time for taking the action required of the party or grant other relief as it deems just.

RULE 502. INSTITUTION OF SUIT

RULE 502.1. PLEADINGS AND MOTIONS MUST BE WRITTEN, SIGNED, AND FILED

Except for oral motions made during trial or when all parties are present, every pleading, plea, motion, application to the court for an order, or other form of request must be written and signed by the party or its attorney and must be filed with the court. A document may be filed with the court by personal or commercial delivery, by mail, or electronically, if the court allows electronic filing. Electronic filing is governed by Rule 21.

RULE 502.2. PETITION

(a) **Contents**. To initiate a lawsuit, a petition must be filed with the court. A petition must contain:

(1) the name of the plaintiff;

(2) the name, address, telephone number, and fax number, if any, of the plaintiff's attorney, if applicable, or the address, telephone number, and fax number, if any, of the plaintiff;

(3) the name, address, and telephone number, if known, of the defendant;

(4) the amount of money, if any, the plaintiff seeks;

(5) a description and claimed value of any personal property the plaintiff seeks;

(6) a description of any other relief reqested;

(7) the basis for the plaintiff's claim against the defendant; and

(8) if the plaintiff consents to email service of the answer and any other motions or pleadings, a statement consenting to email service and email contact information.

(b) **Justice Court Civil Case Information Sheet**. A justice court civil case information sheet, in the form promulgated by the Supreme Court of Texas, must accompany the filing of a petition and must be signed by the plaintiff or the plaintiff's attorney. The justice court civil case information sheet is for data collection for statistical and administrative purposes and does not affect any substantive right. The court may not reject a pleading because the pleading is not accompanied by a justice court civil case information sheet.

RULE 502.3. FEES; INABILITY TO AFFORD FEES

(a) **Fees and Statement of Inability to Afford Payment of Court Costs**. On filing the petition, the plaintiff must pay the appropriate filing fee and service fees, if any, with the court. A plaintiff who is unable to afford to pay the fees must file a Statement of Inability to Afford Payment of Court Costs. The Statement must either be sworn to before a notary or made under penalty of perjury. Upon filing the Statement, the clerk must docket the action, issue citation, and provide any other customary services.

(b) **Supreme Court Form; Contents of Statement**. The plaintiff must use the form Statement approved by the Supreme Court, or the Statement must include the information required by the Court-approved form. The clerk must make the form available to all persons without charge or request.

(c) **Certificate of Legal-Aid Provider**. If the party is represented by an attorney who is providing free legal services because of the party's indigence, without contingency, and the attorney is providing services either directly or by referral from a legal-aid provider described in Rule 145(e)(2), the attorney may file a certificate confirming that the provider screened the party for eligibility under the income and asset guidelines established by the provider. A Statement that is accompanied by the certificate of a legal-aid provider may not be contested under (d).

(d) **Contest**. Unless a certificate is filed under (c), the defendant may file a contest of the Statement at any time within 7 days after the day the defendant's answer is due. If the Statement attests to receipt of government entitlement based on indigence, the Statement may only be contested with regard to the veracity of the attestation. If contested, the judge must hold a hearing to determine the plaintiff's ability to afford the fees. At the hearing, the burden is on the plaintiff to prove the inability to afford fees. The judge may, regardless of whether the defendant contests the Statement, examine the Statement and conduct a hearing to determine the plaintiff's ability to afford fees. If the judge determines that the plaintiff is able to afford the fees, the judge must enter a written order listing the reasons for the determination, and the plaintiff must pay the fees in the time specified in the order or the case will be dismissed without prejudice.

RULE 502.4. VENUE — WHERE A LAWSUIT MAY BE BROUGHT

(a) **Applicable Law**. Laws specifying the venue – the county and precinct where a lawsuit may be brought – are found in Chapter 15, Subchapter E of the Texas Civil Practice and Remedies Code, which is available online and for examination during the court's business hours.

(b) **General Rule**. Generally, a defendant in a small claims case as described in Rule 500.3(a) or a debt claim case as described in Rule 500.3(b) is entitled to be sued in one of the following venues:

(1) the county and precinct where the defendant resides;

(2) the county and precinct where the incident, or the majority of incidents, that gave rise to the claim occurred;

(3) the county and precinct where the contract or agreement, if any, that gave rise to the claim was to be performed; or

(4) the county and precinct where the property is located, in a suit to recover personal property.

(c) **Non-Resident Defendant; Defendant's Residence Unknown**. If the defendant is a non-resident of Texas, or if defendant's residence is unknown, the plaintiff may file the suit in the county and precinct where the plaintiff resides.

(d) **Motion to Transfer Venue**. If a plaintiff files suit in an improper venue, a defendant may challenge the venue selected by filing a motion to transfer venue. The motion must be filed before trial, no later than 21 days after the day the defendant's answer is filed, and must contain a sworn statement that the venue chosen by the plaintiff is improper and a specific county and precinct of proper venue to which transfer is sought. If the defendant fails to name a county and precinct, the court must instruct the defendant to do so and allow the defendant 7 days to cure the defect. If the defendant fails to correct the defect, the motion will be denied, and the case will proceed in the county and precinct where it was originally filed.

(1) *Procedure.*

(A) Judge to Set Hearing. If a defendant files a motion to transfer venue, the judge must set a hearing on the motion.

(B) Response. A plaintiff may file a response to a defendant's motion to transfer venue.

(C) Hearing. The parties may present evidence at the hearing. A witness may testify at a hearing, either in person or, with permission of the court, by means of telephone or an electronic communication system.

(D) Judge's Decision. If the motion is granted, the judge must sign an order designating the court to which the case will be transferred. If the motion is denied, the case will be heard in the court in which the plaintiff initially filed suit.

(E) Review. Motions for rehearing and interlocutory appeals of the judge's ruling on venue are not permitted.

(F) Time for Trial of the Case. No trial may be held until at least the 14th day after the judge's ruling on the motion to transfer venue.

(G) Order. An order granting a motion to transfer venue must state the reason for the transfer and the name of the court to which the transfer is made. When such an order of transfer is made, the judge who issued the order must immediately make out a true and correct transcript of all the entries made on the docket in the case, certify the transcript, and send the transcript, with a certified copy of the bill of costs and the original papers in the case, to the court in the precinct to which the case has been transferred. The court receiving the case must then notify the plaintiff that the case has been received and, if the case is transferred to a different county, that the plaintiff has 14 days after receiving the notice to pay the filing fee in the new court, or file a Statement of Inability to Afford Payment of Court Costs. The plaintiff is not entitled to a refund of any fees already paid. Failure to pay the fee or file a Statement will result in dismissal of the case without prejudice.

(e) **Fair Trial Venue Change**. If a party believes it cannot get a fair trial in a specific precinct or before a specific judge, the party may file a sworn motion stating such, supported by the sworn statements of two other credible persons, and specifying if the party is requesting a change of location or a change of judge. Except for good cause shown, this motion must be filed no less than 7 days before trial. If the party seeks a change of judge, the judge must exchange benches with another qualified justice of the peace, or if no judge is available to exchange benches, the county judge must appoint a visiting judge to hear the case. If the party seeks a change in location, the case must be transferred to the nearest justice court in the county that is not subject to the same or some other disqualification. If there is only one justice of the peace precinct in the county, then the judge must exchange benches with another qualified justice of the peace, or if no judge is available to exchange benches, the county judge must appoint a visiting judge to hear the case. In cases where exclusive jurisdiction is within a specific precinct, as in eviction cases, the only remedy available is a change of judge. A party may apply for relief under this rule only one time in any given lawsuit.

(f) **Transfer of Venue by Consent**. On the written consent of all parties or their attorneys, filed with the court, venue must be transferred to the court of any other justice of the peace of the county, or any other county.

RULE 502.5. ANSWER

(a) **Requirements**. A defendant must file with the court a written answer to a lawsuit as directed by the citation and must also serve a copy of the answer on the plaintiff. The answer must contain:

(1) the name of the defendant;

(2) the name, address, telephone number, and fax number, if any, of the defendant's attorney, if applicable, or the address, telephone number, and fax number, if any, of the defendant; and

(3) if the defendant consents to email service, a statement consenting to email service and email contact information.

(b) **General Denial**. An answer that denies all of the plaintiff's allegations without specifying the reasons is sufficient to constitute an answer or appearance and does not bar the defendant from raising any defense at trial.

(c) **Answer Docketed**. The defendant's appearance must be noted on the court's docket.

(d) **Due Date**. Unless the defendant is served by publication, the defendant's answer is due by the end of the 14th day after the day the defendant was served with the citation and petition, but

(1) if the 14th day is a Saturday, Sunday, or legal holiday, the answer is due on the next day that is not a Saturday, Sunday, or legal holiday; and

(2) if the 14th day falls on a day during which the court is closed before 5:00 p.m., the answer is due on the court's next business day.

(e) **Due Date When Defendant Served by Publication**. If a defendant is served by publication, the defendant's answer is due by the end of the 42nd day after the day the citation was issued, but

(1) if the 42nd day is a Saturday, Sunday, or legal holiday, the answer is due on the next day that is not a Saturday, Sunday, or legal holiday; and

(2) if the 42nd day falls on a day during which the court is closed before 5:00 p.m., the answer is due on the court's next business day.

RULE 502.6. COUNTERCLAIM; CROSS-CLAIM; THIRD PARTY CLAIM

(a) **Counterclaim**. A defendant may file a petition stating as a counterclaim any claim against a plaintiff that is within the jurisdiction of the justice court, whether or not related to the claims in the plaintiff's petition. The defendant must file a counterclaim petition as provided in Rule 502.2, and must pay a filing fee or provide a Statement of Inability to Afford Payment of Court Costs. The court need not generate a citation for a counterclaim and no answer to the counterclaim need be filed. The defendant must serve a copy of the counterclaim as provided by Rule 501.4.

(b) **Cross-Claim**. A plaintiff seeking relief against another plaintiff, or a defendant seeking relief against another defendant may file a cross-claim. The filing party must file a cross-claim petition as provided in Rule 502.2, and must pay a filing fee or provide a Statement of Inability to Afford Payment of Court Costs. A citation must be issued and served as provided by Rule 501.2 on any party that has not yet filed a petition or an answer, as appropriate. If the party filed against has filed a petition or an answer, the filing party must serve the cross-claim as provided by Rule 501.4.

(c) **Third Party Claim**. A defendant seeking to bring another party into a lawsuit who may be liable for all or part of the plaintiff's claim against the defendant may file a petition as provided in Rule 502.2, and must pay a filing fee or provide a Statement of Inability to Afford Payment of Court Costs. A citation must be issued and served as provided by Rule 501.2.

RULE 502.7. AMENDING AND CLARIFYING PLEADINGS

(a) **Amending Pleadings**. A party may withdraw something from or add something to a pleading, as long as the amended pleading is filed and served as provided by Rule 501.4 not less than 7 days before trial. The court may allow a pleading to be amended less than 7 days before trial if the amendment will not operate as a surprise to the opposing party.

(b) **Insufficient Pleadings**. A party may file a motion with the court asking that another party be required to clarify a pleading. The court must determine if the pleading is sufficient to place all parties on notice of the issues in the lawsuit, and may hold a hearing to make that determination. If the court determines a pleading is insufficient, the court must order the party to amend the pleading and set a date by which the party must amend. If a party fails to comply with the court's order, the pleading may be stricken.

RULE 503. DEFAULT JUDGMENT; PRE-TRIAL MATTERS; TRIAL

RULE 503.1. IF DEFENDANT FAILS TO ANSWER

(a) **Default Judgment**. If the defendant fails to file an answer by the date stated in Rule 502.5, the judge must ensure that service was proper, and may hold a hearing for this purpose. If it is determined that service was proper, the judge must render a default judgment in the following manner:

(1) *Claim Based on Written Document.* If the claim is based on a written document signed by the defendant, and a copy of the document has been filed with the court and served on the defendant, along with a sworn statement from the plaintiff that this is a true and accurate copy of the document and the relief sought is owed, and all payments, offsets or credits due to the defendant have been accounted for, the judge must render judgment for the plaintiff in the requested amount, without any necessity for a hearing. The plaintiff's attorney may also submit affidavits supporting an award of attorney fees to which the plaintiff is entitled, if any.

(2) *Other Cases.* Except as provided in (1), a plaintiff who seeks a default judgment against a defendant must request a hearing, orally or in writing. The plaintiff must appear at the hearing and

provide evidence of its damages. If the plaintiff proves its damages, the judge must render judgment for the plaintiff in the amount proven. If the plaintiff is unable to prove its damages, the judge must render judgment in favor of the defendant. With the permission of the court, a party may appear at a hearing by means of telephone or an electronic communication system.

(b) **Appearance**. If a defendant files an answer or otherwise appears in a case before a default judgment is signed by the judge, the judge must not enter a default judgment and the case must be set for trial as described in Rule 503.3.

(c) **Post-Answer Default**. If a defendant who has answered fails to appear for trial, the court may proceed to hear evidence on liability and damages and render judgment accordingly.

(d) **Notice**. The plaintiff requesting a default judgment must provide to the clerk in writing the last known mailing address of the defendant at or before the time the judgment is signed. When a default judgment is signed, the clerk must immediately mail written notice of the judgment to the defendant at the address provided by the plaintiff, and note the fact of such mailing on the docket. The notice must state the number and style of the case, the court in which the case is pending, the names of the parties in whose favor and against whom the judgment was rendered, and the date the judgment was signed. Failure to comply with the provisions of this rule does not affect the finality of the judgment.

RULE 503.2. SUMMARY DISPOSITION

(a) **Motion**. A party may file a sworn motion for summary disposition of all or part of a claim or defense without a trial. The motion must set out all supporting facts. All documents on which the motion relies must be attached. The motion must be granted if it shows that:

(1) there are no genuinely disputed facts that would prevent a judgment in favor of the party;

(2) there is no evidence of one or more essential elements of a defense which the defendant must prove to defeat the plaintiff's claim; or

(3) there is no evidence of one or more essential elements of the plaintiff's claim.

(b) **Response**. The party opposing the motion may file a sworn written response to the motion.

(c) **Hearing**. The court must not consider a motion for summary disposition until it has been on file for at least 14 days. The judge may consider evidence offered by the parties at the hearing. By agreement of the parties, the judge may decide the motion and response without a hearing.

(d) **Order**. The judge may enter judgment as to the entire case or may specify the facts that are established and direct such further proceedings in the case as are just.

RULE 503.3. SETTINGS AND NOTICE; POSTPONING TRIAL

(a) **Settings and Notice**. After the defendant answers, the case will be set on a trial docket at the discretion of the judge. The court must send a notice of the date, time, and place of this setting to all parties at their address of record no less than 45 days before the setting date, unless the judge determines that an earlier setting is required in the interest of justice. Reasonable notice of all subsequent settings must be sent to all parties at their addresses of record.

(b) **Postponing Trial**. A party may file a motion requesting that the trial be postponed. The motion must state why a postponement is necessary. The judge, for good cause, may postpone any trial for a reasonable time.

RULE 503.4. PRETRIAL CONFERENCE

(a) **Conference Set; Issues**. If all parties have appeared in a lawsuit, the court, at any party's request or on its own, may set a case for a pretrial conference. Reasonable notice must be sent to all parties at their addresses of record. Appropriate issues for the pretrial conference include:

(1) discovery;

(2) the amendment or clarification of pleadings;

(3) the admission of facts and documents to streamline the trial process;

(4) a limitation on the number of witnesses at trial;

(5) the identification of facts, if any, which are not in dispute between the parties;

(6) mediation or other alternative dispute resolution services;

(7) the possibility of settlement;

(8) trial setting dates that are amenable to the court and all parties;

(9) the appointment of interpreters, if needed;

(10) the application of a Rule of Civil Procedure not in Part V or a Rule of Evidence; and

(11) any other issue that the court deems appropriate.

(b) **Eviction Cases**. The court must not schedule a pretrial conference in an eviction case if it would delay trial.

RULE 503.5. ALTERNATIVE DISPUTE RESOLUTION

(a) **State Policy**. The policy of this state is to encourage the peaceable resolution of disputes through alternative dispute resolution, including mediation, and the early settlement of pending litigation through voluntary settlement procedures. For that purpose, the judge may order any case to mediation or another appropriate and generally accepted alternative dispute resolution process.

(b) **Eviction Cases**. The court must not order mediation or any other alternative dispute resolution process in an eviction case if it would delay trial.

RULE 503.6. TRIAL

(a) **Docket Called**. On the day of the trial setting, the judge must call all of the cases set for trial that day.

(b) **If Plaintiff Fails to Appear**. If the plaintiff fails to appear when the case is called for trial, the judge may postpone or dismiss the suit.

(c) **If Defendant Fails to Appear**. If the defendant fails to appear when the case is called for trial, the judge may postpone the case, or may proceed to take evidence. If the plaintiff proves its case, judgment must be awarded for the relief proven. If the plaintiff fails to prove its case, judgment must be rendered against the plaintiff.

RULE 504. JURY

RULE 504.1. JURY TRIAL DEMANDED

(a) **Demand**. Any party is entitled to a trial by jury. A written demand for a jury must be filed no later than 14 days before the date a case is set for trial. If the demand is not timely, the right to a jury is waived unless the late filing is excused by the judge for good cause.

(b) **Jury Fee**. Unless otherwise provided by law, a party demanding a jury must pay a fee of $22.00 or must file a Statement of Inability to Afford Payment of Court Costs at or before the time the party files a written request for a jury.

(c) **Withdrawal of Demand**. If a party who demands a jury and pays the fee withdraws the demand, the case will remain on the jury docket unless all other parties present agree to try the case without a jury. A party that withdraws its jury demand is not entitled to a refund of the jury fee.

(d) **No Demand**. If no party timely demands a jury and pays the fee, the judge will try the case without a jury.

RULE 504.2. EMPANELING THE JURY

(a) **Drawing Jury and Oath**. If no method of electronic draw has been implemented, the judge must write the names of all prospective jurors present on separate slips of paper as nearly alike as may be, place them in a box, mix them well, and then draw the names one by one from the box. The judge must list the names drawn and deliver a copy to each of the parties or their attorneys.

(b) **Oath**. After the draw, the judge must swear the panel as follows: "You solemnly swear or affirm that you will give true and correct answers to all questions asked of you concerning your qualifications as a juror."

(c) **Questioning the Jury**. The judge, the parties, or their attorneys will be allowed to question jurors as to their ability to serve impartially in the trial but may not ask the jurors how they will rule in the case. The judge will have discretion to allow or disallow specific questions and determine the amount of time each side will have for this process.

(d) **Challenge for Cause**. A party may challenge any juror for cause. A challenge for cause is an objection made to a juror alleging some fact, such as a bias or prejudice, that disqualifies the juror from serving in the case or that renders the juror unfit to sit on the jury. The challenge must be made during jury questioning. The party must explain to the judge why the juror should be excluded from the jury. The judge must evaluate the questions and answers given and either grant or deny the challenge. When a challenge for cause has been sustained, the juror must be excused.

(e) **Challenges Not for Cause**. After the judge determines any challenges for cause, each party may select up to 3 jurors to excuse for any reason or no reason at all. But no prospective juror may be excused for membership in a constitutionally protected class.

(f) **The Jury**. After all challenges, the first 6 prospective jurors remaining on the list constitute the jury to try the case.

(g) **If Jury Is Incomplete**. If challenges reduce the number of prospective jurors below 6, the judge may direct the sheriff or constable to summon others and allow them to be questioned and challenged by the parties as before, until at least 6 remain.

(h) **Jury Sworn**. When the jury has been selected, the judge must require them to take substantially the following oath: "You solemnly swear or affirm that you will render a true verdict according to the law and the evidence presented."

RULE 504.3. JURY NOT CHARGED

The judge must not charge the jury.

RULE 504.4. JURY VERDICT FOR SPECIFIC ARTICLES

When the suit is for the recovery of specific articles and the jury finds for the plaintiff, the jury must assess the value of each article separately, according to the evidence presented at trial.

RULE 505. JUDGMENT; NEW TRIAL

RULE 505.1. JUDGMENT

(a) **Judgment Upon Jury Verdict**. Where a jury has returned a verdict, the judge must announce the verdict in open court, note it in the court's docket, and render judgment accordingly. The judge may render judgment on the verdict or, if the verdict is contrary to the law or the evidence, judgment notwithstanding the verdict.

(b) **Case Tried by Judge**. When a case has been tried before the judge without a jury, the judge must announce the decision in open court, note the decision in the court's docket, and render judgment accordingly.

(c) **Form**. A judgment must:

(1) clearly state the determination of the rights of the parties in the case;

(2) state who must pay the costs;

(3) be signed by the judge; and

(4) be dated the date of the judge's signature.

(d) **Costs**. The judge must award costs allowed by law to the successful party.

(e) **Judgment for Specific Articles**. Where the judgment is for the recovery of specific articles, the judgment must order that the plaintiff recover such specific articles, if they can be found, and if not, then their value as assessed by the judge or jury with interest at the prevailing post-judgment interest rate.

RULE 505.2. ENFORCEMENT OF JUDGMENT

Justice court judgments are enforceable in the same method as in county and district court, except as provided by law. When the judgment is for personal property, the court may award a special writ for the seizure and delivery of such property to the plaintiff, and may, in addition to the other relief granted in such cases, enforce its judgment by attachment or fine.

RULE 505.3. MOTION TO SET ASIDE; MOTION TO REINSTATE; MOTION FOR NEW TRIAL

(a) **Motion to Reinstate after Dismissal**. A plaintiff whose case is dismissed may file a motion to reinstate the case no later than 14 days after the dismissal order is signed. The plaintiff must serve the defendant with a copy of the motion no later than the next business day using a method approved under Rule 501.4. The court may reinstate the case for good cause shown.

(b) **Motion to Set Aside Default**. A defendant against whom a default judgment is granted may file a motion to set aside the judgment no later than 14 days after the judgment is signed. The defendant must serve the plaintiff with a copy of the motion no later than the next business day using a method approved under Rule 501.4. The court may set aside the judgment and set the case for trial for good cause shown.

(c) **Motion for New Trial**. A party may file a motion for a new trial no later than 14 days after the judgment is signed. The party must serve all other parties with a copy of the motion no later than the next business day using a method approved under Rule 501.4. The judge may grant a new trial upon a showing that justice was not done in the trial of the case. Only one new trial may be granted to either party.

(d) **Motion Not Required**. Failure to file a motion under this rule does not affect a party's right to appeal the underlying judgment.

(e) **Motion Denied as a Matter of Law**. If the judge has not ruled on a motion to set aside, motion to reinstate, or motion for new trial, the motion is automatically denied at 5:00 p.m. on the 21st day after the day the judgment was signed.

RULE 506. APPEAL

RULE 506.1. APPEAL

(a) **How Taken; Time**. A party may appeal a judgment by filing a bond, making a cash deposit, or filing a Statement of Inability to Afford Payment of Court Costs with the justice court within 21 days after the judgment is signed or the motion to reinstate, motion to set aside, or motion for new trial, if any, is denied.

(b) **Amount of Bond; Sureties; Terms**. A plaintiff must file a $500 bond. A defendant must file a bond in an amount equal to twice the amount of the judgment. The bond must be supported by a surety or sureties approved by the judge. The bond must be payable to the appellee and must be conditioned on the appellant's prosecution of its appeal to effect and payment of any judgment and all costs rendered against it on appeal.

(c) **Cash Deposit in Lieu of Bond**. In lieu of filing a bond, an appellant may deposit with the clerk of the court cash in the amount required of the bond. The deposit must be payable to the appellee and must be conditioned on the appellant's prosecution of its appeal to effect and payment of any judgment and all costs rendered against it on appeal.

(d) **Statement of Inability to Afford Payment of Court Costs**.

(1) *Filing*. An appellant who cannot furnish a bond or pay a cash deposit in the amount required may instead file a Statement of Inability to Afford Payment of Court Costs. The Statement must be on the form approved by the Supreme Court or include the information required by the Court-approved form and may be the same one that was filed with the petition.

(2) *Contest*. The Statement may be contested as provided in Rule 502.3(d) within 7 days after the opposing party receives notice that the Statement was filed.

(3) *Appeal If Contest Sustained*. If the contest is sustained, the appellant may appeal that decision by filing notice with the justice court within 7 days of that court's written order. The justice court must then forward all related documents to the county court for resolution. The county court must set the matter for hearing within 14 days and hear the contest de novo, as if there had been no previous hearing, and if the appeal is granted, must direct the justice court to transmit to the clerk of the county court the transcript, records, and papers of the case, as provided in these rules.

(4) *If No Appeal or If Appeal Overruled*. If the appellant does not appeal the ruling sustaining the contest, or if the county court denies the appeal, the appellant may, within five days, post an appeal bond or make a cash deposit in compliance with this rule.

(e) **Notice to Other Parties Required**. If a Statement of Inability to Afford Payment of Court Costs is filed, the court must provide notice to all other parties that the Statement was filed no later than the next business day. Within 7 days of filing a bond or making a cash deposit, an appellant must serve written notice of the appeal on all other parties using a method approved under Rule 501.4.

(f) **No Default on Appeal Without Compliance With Rule**. The county court to which an appeal is taken must not render default judgment against any party without first determining that the appellant has fully complied with this rule.

(g) **No Dismissal of Appeal Without Opportunity for Correction**. An appeal must not be dismissed for defects or irregularities in procedure, either of form or substance, without allowing the appellant, after 7 days' notice from the court, the opportunity to correct such defect.

(h) **Appeal Perfected**. An appeal is perfected when a bond, cash deposit, or Statement of Inability to Afford Payment of Court Costs is filed in accordance with this rule.

(i) **Costs**. The appellant must pay the costs on appeal to a county court in accordance with Rule 143a.

RULE 506.2. RECORD ON APPEAL

When an appeal has been perfected from the justice court, the judge must immediately send to the clerk of the county court a certified copy of all docket entries, a certified copy of the bill of costs, and the original papers in the case.

RULE 506.3. TRIAL DE NOVO

The case must be tried de novo in the county court. A trial de novo is a new trial in which the entire case is presented as if there had been no previous trial.

RULE 506.4. WRIT OF CERTIORARI

(a) **Application**. Except in eviction cases, after final judgment in a case tried in justice court, a party may apply to the county court for a writ of certiorari.

(b) **Grounds**. An application must be granted only if it contains a sworn statement setting forth facts showing that either:

(1) the justice court did not have jurisdiction; or

(2) the final determination of the suit worked an injustice to the applicant that was not caused by the applicant's own inexcusable neglect.

(c) **Bond, Cash Deposit, or Sworn Statement of Indigency to Pay Required**. If the application is granted, a writ of certiorari must not issue until the applicant has filed a bond, made a cash deposit, or filed a Statement of Inability to Afford Payment of Court Costs that complies with Rule 145.

(d) **Time for Filing**. An application for writ of certiorari must be filed within 90 days after the date the final judgment is signed.

(e) **Contents of Writ**. The writ of certiorari must command the justice court to immediately make and certify a copy of the entries in the case on the docket, and immediately transmit the transcript of the proceedings in the justice court, together with the original papers and a bill of costs, to the proper court.

(f) **Clerk to Issue Writ and Citation**. When the application is granted and the bond, cash deposit, or Statement of Inability to Afford Payment of Court Costs has been filed, the clerk must issue a writ of certiorari to the justice court and citation to the adverse party.

(g) **Stay of Proceedings**. When the writ of certiorari is served on the justice court, the court must stay further proceedings on the judgment and comply with the writ.

(h) **Cause Docketed**. The action must be docketed in the name of the original plaintiff, as plaintiff, and of the original defendant, as defendant.

(i) **Motion to Dismiss**. Within 30 days after the service of citation on the writ of certiorari, the adverse party may move to dismiss the certiorari for want of sufficient cause appearing in the affidavit, or for want of sufficient bond. If the certiorari is dismissed, the judgment must direct the justice court to proceed with the execution of the judgment below.

(j) **Amendment of Bond or Oath**. The affidavit or bond may be amended at the discretion of the court in which it is filed.

(k) **Trial De Novo**. The case must be tried de novo in the county court and judgment must be rendered as in cases appealed from justice courts. A trial de novo is a new trial in which the entire case is presented as if there had been no previous trial.

RULE 507. ADMINISTRATIVE RULES FOR JUDGES AND COURT PERSONNEL

RULE 507.1. PLENARY POWER

A justice court loses plenary power over a case when an appeal is perfected or if no appeal is perfected, 21 days after the later of the date judgment is signed or the date a motion to set aside, motion to reinstate, or motion for new trial, if any, is denied.

RULE 507.2. FORMS

The court may provide forms to enable a party to file documents that comply with these rules. No party may be forced to use the court's forms.

RULE 507.3. DOCKET AND OTHER RECORDS

(a) **Docket**. Each judge must keep a civil docket in a permanent record containing the following information:

(1) the title of all suits commenced before the court;

(2) the date when the first process was issued against the defendant, when returnable, and the nature of that process;

(3) the date when the parties, or either of them, appeared before the court, either with or without a citation;

(4) a description of the petition and any documents filed with the petition;

(5) every adjournment, stating at whose request and to what time;

(6) the date of the trial, stating whether the same was by a jury or by the judge;

(7) the verdict of the jury, if any;

(8) the judgment signed by the judge and the date the judgment was signed;

(9) all applications for setting aside judgments or granting new trials and the orders of the judge thereon, with the date;

(10) the date of issuing execution, to whom directed and delivered, and the amount of debt, damages and costs and, when any execution is returned, the date of the return and the manner in which it was executed; and

(11) all stays and appeals that may be taken, and the date when taken, the amount of the bond and the names of the sureties.

(b) **Other Records**. The judge must also keep copies of all documents filed; other dockets, books, and records as may be required by law or these rules; and a fee book in which all costs accruing in every suit commenced before the court are taxed.

(c) **Form of Records**. All records required to be kept under this rule may be maintained electronically.

RULE 507.4. ISSUANCE OF WRITS

Every writ from the justice courts must be in writing and be issued and signed by the judge officially. The style thereof must be "The State of Texas." It must, except where otherwise specially provided by law or these rules, be directed to the person or party upon whom it is to be served, be made returnable to the court, and note the date of its issuance.

RULE 508. DEBT CLAIM CASES

RULE 508.1. APPLICATION

Rule 508 applies to a claim for the recovery of a debt brought by an assignee of a claim, a financial institution, a debt collector or collection agency, or a person or entity primarily engaged in the business of lending money at interest.

RULE 508.2. PETITION

(a) **Contents**. In addition to the information required by Rule 502.2, a petition filed in a lawsuit governed by this rule must contain the following information:

(1) *Credit Accounts*. In a claim based upon a credit card, revolving credit, or open account, the petition must state:

(A) the account name or credit card name;

(B) the account number (which may be masked);

(C) the date of issue or origination of the account, if known;

(D) the date of charge-off or breach of the account, if known;

(E) the amount owed as of a date certain; and

(F) whether the plaintiff seeks ongoing interest.

(2) *Personal and Business Loans*. In a claim based upon a promissory note or other promise to pay a specific amount as of a date certain, the petition must state:

(A) the date and amount of the original loan;

(B) whether the repayment of the debt was accelerated, if known;

(C) the date final payment was due;

(D) the amount due as of the final payment date;

(E) the amount owed as of a date certain; and

(F) whether plaintiff seeks ongoing interest.

(3) *Ongoing Interest*. If a plaintiff seeks ongoing interest, the petition must state:

(A) the effective interest rate claimed;

(B) whether the interest rate is based upon contract or statute; and

(C) the dollar amount of interest claimed as of a date certain.

(4) *Assigned Debt*. If the debt that is the subject of the claim has been assigned or transferred, the petition must state:

(A) that the debt claim has been transferred or assigned;

(B) the date of the transfer or assignment;

(C) the name of any prior holders of the debt; and

(D) the name or a description of the original creditor.

RULE 508.3. DEFAULT JUDGMENT

(a) **Generally**. If the defendant does not file an answer to a claim by the answer date or otherwise appear in the case, the judge must promptly render a default judgment upon the plaintiff's proof of the amount of damages.

(b) **Proof of the Amount of Damages**.

(1) *Evidence Must Be Served or Submitted*. Evidence of plaintiff's damages must either be attached to the petition and served on the defendant or submitted to the court after defendant's failure to answer by the answer date.

(2) *Form of Evidence*. Evidence of plaintiff's damages may be offered in a sworn statement or in live testimony. The evidence offered may include documentary evidence.

(3) *Establishment of the Amount of Damages*. The amount of damages is established by evidence:

(A) that the account or loan was issued to the defendant and the defendant is obligated to pay it;

(B) that the account was closed or the defendant breached the terms of the account or loan agreement;

(C) of the amount due on the account or loan as of a date certain after all payment credits and offsets have been applied; and

(D) that the plaintiff owns the account or loan and, if applicable, how the plaintiff acquired the account or loan.

(4) *Documentary Evidence Offered By Sworn Statement*. Documentary evidence may be considered if it is attached to a sworn statement made by the plaintiff or its representative, a prior holder of the debt or its representative, or the original creditor or its representative, that attests to the following:

(A) the documents were kept in the regular course of business;

(B) it was the regular course of business for an employee or representative with knowledge of the act recorded to make the record or to transmit information to be included in such record;

(C) the documents were created at or near the time or reasonably soon thereafter; and

(D) the documents attached are the original or exact duplicates of the original.

(5) *Consideration of Sworn Statement.* A judge is not required to accept a sworn statement if the source of information or the method or circumstances of preparation indicate lack of trustworthiness. But a judge may not reject a sworn statement only because it is not made by the original creditor or because the documents attested to were created by a third party and subsequently incorporated into and relied upon by the business of the plaintiff.

(c) **Hearing**. The judge may enter a default judgment without a hearing if the plaintiff submits sufficient written evidence of its damages and should do so to avoid undue expense and delay. Otherwise, the plaintiff may request a default judgment hearing at which the plaintiff must appear, in person or by telephonic or electronic means, and prove its damages. If the plaintiff proves its damages, the judge must render judgment for the plaintiff in the amount proven. If the plaintiff is unable to prove its damages, the judge must render judgment in favor of the defendant.

(d) **Appearance**. If the defendant files an answer or otherwise appears in a case before a default judgment is signed by the judge, the judge must not render a default judgment and must set the case for trial.

(e) **Post-Answer Default**. If a defendant who has answered fails to appear for trial, the court may proceed to hear evidence on liability and damages and render judgment accordingly.

RULE 509. REPAIR AND REMEDY CASES

RULE 509.1. APPLICABILITY OF RULE

Rule 509 applies to a lawsuit filed in a justice court by a residential tenant under Chapter 92, Subchapter B of the Texas Property Code to enforce the landlord's duty to repair or remedy a condition materially affecting the physical health or safety of an ordinary tenant.

RULE 509.2. CONTENTS OF PETITION; COPIES; FORMS AND AMENDMENTS

(a) **Contents of Petition**. The petition must be in writing and must include the following:

(1) the street address of the residential rental property;

(2) a statement indicating whether the tenant has received in writing the name and business street address of the landlord and landlord's management company;

(3) to the extent known and applicable, the name, business street address, and telephone number of the landlord and the landlord's management company, on-premises manager, and rent collector serving the residential rental property;

(4) for all notices the tenant gave to the landlord requesting that the condition be repaired or remedied:

(A) the date of the notice;

(B) the name of the person to whom the notice was given or the place where the notice was given;

(C) whether the tenant's lease is in writing and requires written notice;

(D) whether the notice was in writing or oral;

(E) whether any written notice was given by certified mail, return receipt requested, or by registered mail; and

(F) whether the rent was current or had been timely tendered at the time notice was given;

(5) a description of the property condition materially affecting the physical health or safety of an ordinary tenant that the tenant seeks to have repaired or remedied;

(6) a statement of the relief requested by the tenant, including an order to repair or remedy a condition, a reduction in rent, actual damages, civil penalties, attorney's fees, and court costs;

(7) if the petition includes a request to reduce the rent:

(A) the amount of rent paid by the tenant, the amount of rent paid by the government, if known, the rental period, and when the rent is due; and

(B) the amount of the requested rent reduction and the date it should begin;

(8) a statement that the total relief requested does not exceed $10,000, excluding interest and court costs but including attorney's fees; and

(9) the tenant's name, address, and telephone number.

(b) **Copies**. The tenant must provide the court with copies of the petition and any attachments to the petition for service on the landlord.

(c) **Forms and Amendments**. A petition substantially in the form promulgated by the Supreme Court is sufficient. A suit may not be dismissed for a defect in the petition unless the tenant is given an opportunity to correct the defect and does not promptly correct it.

RULE 509.3. CITATION: ISSUANCE; APPEARANCE DATE; ANSWER

(a) **Issuance**. When the tenant files a written petition with a justice court, the judge must immediately issue citation directed to the landlord, commanding the landlord to appear before such judge at the time and place named in the citation.

(b) **Appearance Date; Answer**. The appearance date on the citation must not be less than 10 days nor more than 21 days after the petition is filed. For purposes of this rule, the appearance date on the citation is the trial date. The landlord may, but is not required to, file a written answer on or before the appearance date.

RULE 509.4. SERVICE AND RETURN OF CITATION; ALTERNATIVE SERVICE OF CITATION

(a) **Service and Return of Citation**. The sheriff, constable, or other person authorized by Rule 501.2 who receives the citation must serve the citation by delivering a copy of it, along with a copy of the petition and any attachments, to the landlord at least 6 days before the appearance date. At least one day before the appearance date, the person serving the citation must file a return of service with the court that issued the citation. The citation must be issued, served, and returned in like manner as ordinary citations issued from a justice court.

(b) **Alternative Service of Citation**.

(1) If the petition does not include the landlord's name and business street address, or if, after making diligent efforts on at least two occasions, the officer or authorized person is unsuccessful in serving the citation on the landlord under (a), the officer or authorized person must serve the citation by delivering a copy of the citation, petition, and any attachments to:

(A) the landlord's management company if the tenant has received written notice of the name and business street address of the landlord's management company; or

(B) if (b)(1)(A) does not apply and the tenant has not received the landlord's name and business street address in writing, the landlord's authorized agent for service of process, which may be the landlord's management company, on-premise manager, or rent collector serving the residential rental property.

(2) If the officer or authorized person is unsuccessful in serving citation under (b)(1) after making diligent efforts on at least two occasions at either the business street address of the landlord's

management company, if (b)(1)(A) applies, or at each available business street address of the landlord's authorized agent for service of process, if (b)(1)(B) applies, the officer or authorized person must execute and file in the justice court a sworn statement that the officer or authorized person made diligent efforts to serve the citation on at least two occasions at all available business street addresses of the landlord and, to the extent applicable, the landlord's management company, on-premises manager, and rent collector serving the residential rental property, providing the times, dates, and places of each attempted service. The judge may then authorize the officer or authorized person to serve citation by:

(A) delivering a copy of the citation, petition, and any attachments to someone over the age of 16 years, at any business street address listed in the petition, or, if nobody answers the door at a business street address, either placing the citation, petition, and any attachments through a door mail chute or slipping them under the front door, and if neither of these latter methods is practical, affixing the citation, petition, and any attachments to the front door or main entry to the business street address;

(B) within 24 hours of complying with (b)(2)(A), sending by first class mail a true copy of the citation, petition, and any attachments addressed to the landlord at the landlord's business street address provided in the petition; and

(C) noting on the return of the citation the date of delivery under (b)(2)(A) and the date of mailing under (b)(2)(B).

The delivery and mailing to the business street address under (b)(2)(A)-(B) must occur at least 6 days before the appearance date. At least one day before the appearance date, a return of service must be completed and filed in accordance with Rule 501.3 with the court that issued the citation. It is not necessary for the tenant to request the alternative service authorized by this rule.

RULE 509.5. DOCKETING AND TRIAL; FAILURE TO APPEAR

(a) **Docketing and Trial**. The case must be docketed and tried as other cases. The judge may develop the facts of the case in order to ensure justice.

(b) **Failure to Appear**.

(1) If the tenant appears at trial and the landlord has been duly served and fails to appear at trial, the judge may proceed to hear evidence. If the tenant establishes that the tenant is entitled to recover, the judge must render judgment against the landlord in accordance with the evidence.

(2) If the tenant fails to appear for trial, the judge may dismiss the lawsuit.

RULE 509.6. JUDGMENT: AMOUNT; FORM AND CONTENT; ISSUANCE AND SERVICE; FAILURE TO COMPLY

(a) **Amount**. Judgment may be rendered against the landlord for failure to repair or remedy a condition at the residential rental property if the total judgment does not exceed $10,000, excluding interest and court costs but including attorney's fees. Any party who prevails in a lawsuit brought under these rules may recover the party's court costs and reasonable attorney's fees as allowed by law.

(b) **Form and Content**.

(1) The judgment must be in writing, signed, and dated and must include the names of the parties to the proceeding and the street address of the residential rental property where the condition is to be repaired or remedied.

(2) In the judgment, the judge may:

(A) order the landlord to take reasonable action to repair or remedy the condition;

(B) order a reduction in the tenant's rent, from the date of the first repair notice, in proportion to the reduced rental value resulting from the condition until the condition is repaired or remedied;

(C) award a civil penalty of one month's rent plus $500;

(D) award the tenant's actual damages; and

(E) award court costs and attorney's fees, excluding any attorney's fees for a claim for damages relating to a personal injury.

(3) If the judge orders the landlord to repair or remedy a condition, the judgment must include in reasonable detail the actions the landlord must take to repair or remedy the condition and the date when the repair or remedy must be completed.

(4) If the judge orders a reduction in the tenant's rent, the judgment must state:

(A) the amount of the rent the tenant must pay, if any;

(B) the frequency with which the tenant must pay the rent;

(C) the condition justifying the reduction of rent;

(D) the effective date of the order reducing rent;

(E) that the order reducing rent will terminate on the date the condition is repaired or remedied; and

(F) that on the day the condition is repaired or remedied, the landlord must give the tenant written notice, served in accordance with Rule 501.4, that the condition justifying the reduction of rent has been repaired or remedied and the rent will revert to the rent amount specified in the lease.

(c) **Issuance and Service**. The judge must issue the judgment. The judgment may be served on the landlord in open court or by any means provided in Rule 501.4 at an address listed in the citation, the address listed on any answer, or such other address the landlord furnishes to the court in writing. Unless the judge serves the landlord in open court or by other means provided in Rule 501.4, the sheriff, constable, or other authorized person who serves the landlord must promptly file a return of service in the justice court.

(d) **Failure to Comply**. If the landlord fails to comply with an order to repair or remedy a condition or reduce the tenant's rent, the failure is grounds for citing the landlord for contempt of court under Section 21.002 of the Texas Government Code.

RULE 509.7. COUNTERCLAIMS

Counterclaims and the joinder of suits against third parties are not permitted in suits under these rules. Compulsory counterclaims may be brought in a separate suit. Any potential causes of action, including a compulsory counterclaim, that are not asserted because of this rule are not precluded.

RULE 509.8. APPEAL: TIME AND MANNER; PERFECTION; EFFECT; COSTS; TRIAL ON APPEAL

(a) **Time and Manner**. Either party may appeal the decision of the justice court to a statutory county court or, if there is no statutory county court with jurisdiction, a county court or district court with jurisdiction by filing a written notice of appeal with the justice court within 21 days after the date the judge signs the judgment. If the judgment is amended in any respect, any party has the right to appeal within 21 days after the date the judge signs the new judgment, in the same manner set out in this rule.

(b) **Perfection**. The posting of an appeal bond is not required for an appeal under this rule, and the appeal is considered perfected with the filing of a notice of appeal. Otherwise, the appeal is in the manner provided by law for appeal from a justice court.

(c) **Effect**. The timely filing of a notice of appeal stays the enforcement of any order to repair or remedy a condition or reduce the tenant's rent, as well as any other actions.

(d) **Costs**. The appellant must pay the costs on appeal to a county court in accordance with Rule 143a.

(e) **Trial on Appeal**. On appeal, the parties are entitled to a trial de novo. A trial de novo is a new trial in which the entire case is presented as if there had been no previous trial. Either party is entitled to trial by jury on timely request and payment of a fee, if required. An appeal of a judgment of a justice court under these rules takes precedence in the county court and may be held at any time after the eighth day after the date the transcript is filed in the county court.

RULE 509.9. EFFECT OF WRIT OF POSSESSION

If a judgment for the landlord for possession of the residential rental property becomes final, any order to repair or remedy a condition is vacated and unenforceable.

RULE 510. EVICTION CASES

RULE 510.1. APPLICATION

Rule 510 applies to a lawsuit to recover possession of real property under Chapter 24 of the Texas Property Code.

RULE 510.2. COMPUTATION OF TIME FOR EVICTION CASES

Rule 500.5 applies to the computation of time in an eviction case. But if a document is filed by mail and not received by the court by the due date, the court may take any action authorized by these rules, including issuing a writ of possession requiring a tenant to leave the property.

RULE 510.3. PETITION

(a) **Contents**. In addition to the requirements of Rule 502.2, a petition in an eviction case must be sworn to by the plaintiff and must contain:

(1) a description, including the address, if any, of the premises that the plaintiff seeks possession of;

(2) a description of the facts and the grounds for eviction;

(3) a description of when and how notice to vacate was delivered;

(4) the total amount of rent due and unpaid at the time of filing, if any; and

(5) a statement that attorney fees are being sought, if applicable.

(b) **Where Filed**. The petition must be filed in the precinct where the premises is located. If it is filed elsewhere, the judge must dismiss the case. The plaintiff will not be entitled to a refund of the filing fee, but will be refunded any service fees paid if the case is dismissed before service is attempted.

(c) **Defendants Named**. If the eviction is based on a written residential lease, the plaintiff must name as defendants all tenants obligated under the lease residing at the premises whom plaintiff seeks to evict. No judgment or writ of possession may issue or be executed against a tenant obligated under a lease and residing at the premises who is not named in the petition and served with citation.

(d) **Claim for Rent**. A claim for rent within the justice court's jurisdiction may be asserted in an eviction case.

(e) **Only Issue**. The court must adjudicate the right to actual possession and not title. Counterclaims and the joinder of suits against third parties are not permitted in eviction cases. A claim that is not asserted because of this rule can be brought in a separate suit in a court of proper jurisdiction.

RULE 510.4. ISSUANCE, SERVICE, AND RETURN OF CITATION

(a) **Issuance of Citation; Contents**. When a petition is filed, the court must immediately issue citation directed to each defendant. The citation must:

(1) be styled "The State of Texas";

(2) be signed by the clerk under seal of court or by the judge;

(3) contain the name, location, and address of the court;

(4) state the date of filing of the petition;

(5) state the date of issuance of the citation;

(6) state the file number and names of parties;

(7) state the plaintiff's cause of action and relief sought;

(8) be directed to the defendant;

(9) state the name and address of attorney for plaintiff, or if the plaintiff does not have an attorney, the address of plaintiff;

(10) state the day the defendant must appear in person for trial at the court issuing citation, which must not be less than 10 days nor more than 21 days after the petition is filed;

(11) notify the defendant that if the defendant fails to appear in person for trial, judgment by default may be rendered for the relief demanded in the petition;

(12) inform the defendant that, upon timely request and payment of a jury fee no later than 3 days before the day set for trial, the case will be heard by a jury;

(13) contain all warnings required by Chapter 24 of the Texas Property Code; and

(14) include the following statement: "For further information, consult Part V of the Texas Rules of Civil Procedure, which is available online and also at the court listed on this citation."

(b) **Service and Return of Citation**.

(1) Who May Serve. Unless otherwise authorized by written court order, citation must be served by a sheriff or constable.

(2) Method of Service. The constable, sheriff, or other person authorized by written court order receiving the citation must execute it by delivering a copy with a copy of the petition attached to the defendant, or by leaving a copy with a copy of the petition attached with some person, other than the plaintiff, over the age of 16 years, at the defendant's usual place of residence, at least 6 days before the day set for trial.

(3) Return of Service. At least one day before the day set for trial, the constable, sheriff, or other person authorized by written court order must complete and file a return of service in accordance with Rule 501.3 with the court that issued the citation.

(c) **Alternative Service by Delivery to the Premises**.

(1) *When Allowed*. The citation may be served by delivery to the premises if:

(A) the constable, sheriff, or other person authorized by written court order is unsuccessful in serving the citation under (b);

(B) the petition lists all home and work addresses of the defendant that are known to the plaintiff and states that the plaintiff knows of no other home or work addresses of the defendant in the county where the premises are located; and

(C) the constable, sheriff, or other person authorized files a sworn statement that it has made diligent efforts to serve such citation on at least two occasions at all addresses of the defendant in the county where the premises are located, stating the times and places of attempted service.

(2) *Authorization*. The judge must promptly consider a sworn statement filed under (1)(C) and determine whether citation may be served by delivery to the premises. The plaintiff is not required to make a request or motion for alternative service.

(3) *Method*. If the judge authorizes service by delivery to the premises, the constable, sheriff, or other person authorized by written court order must, at least 6 days before the day set for trial:

(A) deliver a copy of the citation with a copy of the petition attached to the premises by placing it through a door mail chute or slipping it under the front door; if neither method is possible, the officer may securely affix the citation to the front door or main entry to the premises; and

(B) deposit in the mail a copy of the citation with a copy of the petition attached, addressed to defendant at the premises and sent by first class mail.

(4) *Notation on Return*. The constable, sheriff, or other person authorized by written court order must note on the return of service the date the citation was delivered and the date it was deposited in the mail.

RULE 510.5. REQUEST FOR IMMEDIATE POSSESSION

(a) **Immediate Possession Bond**. The plaintiff may, at the time of filing the petition or at any time prior to final judgment, file a possession bond to be approved by the judge in the probable amount of costs of suit and damages that may result to defendant in the event that the suit has been improperly instituted, and conditioned that the plaintiff will pay defendant all such costs and damages that are adjudged against plaintiff.

(b) **Notice to Defendant**. The court must notify a defendant that the plaintiff has filed a possession bond. The notice must be served in the same manner as service of citation and must inform the defendant that if the defendant does not file an answer or appear for trial, and judgment for possession is granted by default, an officer will place the plaintiff in possession of the property on or after the 7th day after the date defendant is served with the notice.

(c) **Time for Issuance and Execution of Writ**. If judgment for possession is rendered by default and a possession bond has been filed, approved, and served under this rule, a writ of possession must issue immediately upon demand and payment of any required fees. The writ must not be executed before the 7th day after the date defendant is served with notice under (b).

(d) **Effect of Appearance**. If the defendant files an answer or appears at trial, no writ of possession may issue before the 6th day after the date a judgment for possession is signed or the day following the deadline for the defendant to appeal the judgment, whichever is later.

RULE 510.6. TRIAL DATE; ANSWER; DEFAULT JUDGMENT

(a) **Trial Date and Answer**. The defendant must appear for trial on the day set for trial in the citation. The defendant may, but is not required to, file a written answer with the court on or before the day set for trial in the citation.

(b) **Default Judgment**. If the defendant fails to appear at trial and fails to file an answer before the case is called for trial, and proof of service has been filed in accordance with Rule 510.4, the allegations of the complaint must be taken as admitted and judgment by default rendered accordingly. If a defendant who has answered fails to appear for trial, the court may proceed to hear evidence and render judgment accordingly.

(c) **Notice of Default**. When a default judgment is signed, the clerk must immediately mail written notice of the judgment by first class mail to the defendant at the address of the premises.

RULE 510.7. TRIAL

(a) **Trial**. An eviction case will be docketed and tried as other cases. No eviction trial may be held less than 6 days after service under Rule 510.4 has been obtained.

(b) **Jury Trial Demanded**. Any party may file a written demand for trial by jury by making a request to the court at least 3 days before the trial date. The demand must be accompanied by payment of a jury fee or by filing a Statement of Inability to Afford Payment of Court Costs. If a jury is demanded by either party, the jury will be impaneled and sworn as in other cases; and after hearing the evidence it will return its verdict in favor of the plaintiff or the defendant. If no jury is timely demanded by either party, the judge will try the case.

(c) **Limit on Postponement**. Trial in an eviction case must not be postponed for more than 7 days total unless both parties agree in writing.

RULE 510.8. JUDGMENT; WRIT; NO NEW TRIAL

(a) **Judgment Upon Jury Verdict**. Where a jury has returned a verdict, the judge may render judgment on the verdict or, if the verdict is contrary to the law or the evidence, judgment notwithstanding the verdict.

(b) **Judgment for Plaintiff**. If the judgment is in favor of the plaintiff, the judge must render judgment for plaintiff for possession of the premises, costs, delinquent rent as of the date of entry of judgment, if any, and attorney fees if recoverable by law.

(c) **Judgment for Defendant**. If the judgment is in favor of the defendant, the judge must render judgment for defendant against the plaintiff for costs and attorney fees if recoverable by law.

(d) **Writ**. If the judgment or verdict is in favor of the plaintiff, the judge must award a writ of possession upon demand of the plaintiff and payment of any required fees.

(1) *Time to Issue*. Except as provided by Rule 510.5, no writ of possession may issue before the 6th day after the date a judgment for possession is signed or the day following the deadline for the defendant to appeal the judgment, whichever is later. A writ of possession may not issue more than 60 days after a judgment for possession is signed. For good cause, the court may extend the deadline for issuance to 90 days after a judgment for possession is signed.

(2) *Time to Execute*. A writ of possession may not be executed after the 90th day after a judgment for possession is signed.

(3) *Effect of Appeal*. A writ of possession must not issue if an appeal is perfected and, if applicable, rent is paid into the registry, as required by these rules.

(e) **No Motion For New Trial**. No motion for new trial may be filed.

RULE 510.9. APPEAL

(a) **How Taken; Time**. A party may appeal a judgment in an eviction case by filing a bond, making a cash deposit, or filing a Statement of Inability to Afford Payment of Court Costs with the justice court within 5 days after the judgment is signed.

(b) **Amount of Security; Terms**. The justice court judge will set the amount of the bond or cash deposit to include the items enumerated in Rule 510.11. The bond or cash deposit must be payable to the appellee and must be conditioned on the appellant's prosecution of its appeal to effect and payment of any judgment and all costs rendered against it on appeal.

(c) **Statement of Inability to Afford Payment of Court Costs**.

(1) *Filing*. An appellant who cannot furnish a bond or pay a cash deposit in the amount required may instead file a Statement of Inability to Afford Payment of Court Costs. The Statement must be on the form approved by the Supreme Court or include the information required by the Court-approved form.

(2) *Contest*. The Statement may be contested as provided in Rule 502.3(d) within 5 days after the opposing party receives notice that the Statement was filed.

(3) *Appeal If Contest Sustained*. If the contest is sustained, the appellant may appeal that decision by filing notice with the justice court within 5 days of that court's written order. The justice court must then forward all related documents to the county court for resolution. The county court must set the matter for hearing within 5 days and hear the contest de novo, as if there had been no previous hearing, and, if the appeal is granted, must direct the justice court to transmit to the clerk of the county court the transcript, records, and papers of the case, as provided in these rules.

(4) *If No Appeal or If Appeal Overruled.* If the appellant does not appeal the ruling sustaining the contest, or if the county court denies the appeal, the appellant may, within one business day, post an appeal bond or make a cash deposit in compliance with this rule.

(5) *Payment of Rent in Nonpayment of Rent Appeals.*

(A) Notice. If a defendant appeals an eviction for nonpayment of rent by filing a Statement of Inability to Afford Payment of Court Costs, the justice court must provide to the defendant a written notice at the time the Statement is filed that contains the following information in bold or conspicuous type:

(i) the amount of the initial deposit of rent, equal to one rental period's rent under the terms of the rental agreement, that the defendant must pay into the justice court registry;

(ii) whether the initial deposit must be paid in cash, cashier's check, or money order, and to whom the cashier's check or money order, if applicable, must be made payable;

(iii) the calendar date by which the initial deposit must be paid into the justice court registry, which must be within 5 days of the date the Statement is filed; and

(iv) a statement that failure to pay the required amount into the justice court registry by the required date may result in the court issuing a writ of possession without hearing.

(B) Defendant May Remain in Possession. A defendant who appeals an eviction for nonpayment of rent by filing a Statement of Inability to Afford Payment of Court Costs is entitled to stay in possession of the premises during the pendency of the appeal by complying with the following procedure:

(i) Within 5 days of the date that the defendant files a Statement of Inability to Afford Payment of Court Costs, it must pay into the justice court registry the amount set forth in the notice provided at the time the defendant filed the Statement. If the defendant was provided with notice and fails to pay the designated amount into the justice court registry within 5 days, and the transcript has not been transmitted to the county clerk, the plaintiff is entitled, upon request and payment of the applicable fee, to a writ of possession, which the justice court must issue immediately and without hearing.

(ii) During the appeal process as rent becomes due under the rental agreement, the defendant must pay the designated amount into the county court registry within 5 days of the rental due date under the terms of the rental agreement.

(iii) If a government agency is responsible for all or a portion of the rent, the defendant must pay only that portion of the rent determined by the justice court to be paid during appeal. Either party may contest the portion of the rent that the justice court determines must be paid into the county court registry by filing a contest within 5 days after the judgment is signed. If a contest is filed, the justice court must notify the parties and hold a hearing on the contest within 5 days. If the defendant objects to the justice court's ruling at the hearing, the defendant is required to pay only the portion claimed to be owed by the defendant until the issue is tried in county court.

(iv) If the defendant fails to pay the designated amount into the court registry within the time limits prescribed by these rules, the plaintiff may file a sworn motion that the defendant is in default in county court. The plaintiff must notify the defendant of the motion and the hearing date. Upon a showing that the defendant is in default, the court must issue a writ of possession.

(v) The plaintiff may withdraw any or all rent in the county court registry upon sworn motion and hearing, prior to final determination of the case, showing just cause; dismissal of the appeal; or order of the court after final hearing.(vi) All hearings and motions under this subparagraph are entitled to precedence in the county court.

(d) **Notice to Other Parties Required**. If a Statement of Inability to Afford Payment of Court Costs is filed, the court must provide notice to all other parties that the Statement was filed no later than the next business day. Within 5 days of filing a bond or making a cash deposit, an appellant must serve written notice of the appeal on all other parties using a method approved under Rule 501.4.

(e) **No Default on Appeal Without Compliance With Rule**. No judgment may be taken by default against the adverse party in the court to which the case has been appealed without first showing substantial compliance with this rule.

(f) **Appeal Perfected**. An appeal is perfected when a bond, cash deposit, or Statement of Inability to Afford Payment of Court Costs is filed in accordance with this rule.

RULE 510.10. RECORD ON APPEAL; DOCKETING; TRIAL DE NOVO

(a) **Preparation and Transmission of Record**. Unless otherwise provided by law or these rules, when an appeal has been perfected, the judge must stay all further proceedings on the judgment and must immediately send to the clerk of the county court a certified copy of all docket entries, a certified copy of the bill of costs, and the original papers in the case together with any money in the court registry, including sums tendered pursuant to Rule 510.9(c)(5)(B).

(b) **Docketing; Notice**. The county clerk must docket the case and must immediately notify the parties of the date of receipt of the transcript and the docket number of the case. The notice must advise the defendant that it must file a written answer in the county court within 8 days if one was not filed in the justice court.

(c) **Trial De Novo**. The case must be tried de novo in the county court. A trial de novo is a new trial in which the entire case is presented as if there had been no previous trial. The trial, as well as any hearings and motions, is entitled to precedence in the county court.

RULE 510.11. DAMAGES ON APPEAL

On the trial of the case in the county court the appellant or appellee will be permitted to plead, prove and recover his damages, if any, suffered for withholding or defending possession of the premises during the pendency of the appeal. Damages may include but are not limited to loss of rentals during the pendency of the appeal and attorney fees in the justice and county courts provided, as to attorney fees, that the requirements of Section 24.006 of the Texas Property Code have been met. Only the party prevailing in the county court will be entitled to recover damages against the adverse party. The prevailing party will also be entitled to recover court costs and to recover against the sureties on the appeal bond in cases where the adverse party has executed an appeal bond.

RULE 510.12. JUDGMENT BY DEFAULT ON APPEAL

An eviction case appealed to county court will be subject to trial at any time after the expiration of 8 days after the date the transcript is filed in the county court. If the defendant has filed a written answer in the justice court, it must be taken to constitute his appearance and answer in the county court and may be amended as in other cases. If the defendant made no answer in writing in the justice court and fails to file a written answer within 8 days after the transcript is filed in the county court, the allegations of the complaint may be taken as admitted and judgment by default may be entered accordingly.

RULE 510.13. WRIT OF POSSESSION ON APPEAL

The writ of possession, or execution, or both, will be issued by the clerk of the county court according to the judgment rendered, and the same will be executed by the sheriff or constable, as in other cases. The judgment of the county court may not be stayed unless within 10 days from the judgment the appellant files a supersedeas bond in an amount set by the county court pursuant to Section 24.007 of the Texas Property Code.

PART VI - RULES RELATING TO ANCILLARY PROCEEDINGS

SECTION 1. ATTACHMENT

RULE 592. APPLICATION FOR WIT OF ATTACHMENT AND ORDER

Either at the commencement of a suit or at any time during its progress the plaintiff may file an application for the issuance of a writ of attachment. Such application shall be supported by affidavits of the plaintiff, his agent, his attorney, or other persons having knowledge of relevant facts. The application shall comply with all statutory requirements and shall state the grounds for issuing the writ and the specific facts relied upon by the plaintiff to warrant the required findings by the court. The writ shall not be quashed because two or more grounds are stated conjunctively or disjunctively. The application and any affidavits shall be made on personal knowledge and shall set forth such facts as would be admissible in evidence; provided that facts may be stated based upon information and belief if the grounds of such belief are specifically stated.

No writ shall issue except upon written order of the court after a hearing, which may be ex parte. The court, in its order granting the application, shall make specific findings of facts to support the statutory grounds found to exist, and shall specify the maximum value of property that may be attached, and the amount of bond required of plaintiff, and, further shall command that the attached property be kept safe and preserved subject to further orders of the court. Such bond shall be in an amount which, in the opinion of the court, will adequately compensate the defendant in the event plaintiff fails to prosecute his suit to effect, and to pay all damages and costs which may be adjudged against him for wrongfully suing out the writ of attachment. The court shall further find in its order the amount of bond required of defendant to replevy, which, unless the defendant chooses to exercise his option as provided in Rule 599, shall be the amount of plaintiff's claim, one year's accrual of interest if allowed by law on the claim, and the estimated costs of court. The order may direct the issuance of several writs at the same time, or in succession, to be sent to different counties.

RULE 592a. BOND FOR ATTACHMENT

No writ of attachment shall issue until the party applying therefor has filed with the officer authorized to issue such writ a bond payable to the defendant in the amount fixed by the court's order, with sufficient surety or sureties as provided by statute to be approved by such officer, conditioned that the plaintiff will prosecute his suit to effect and pay to the extent of the penal amount of the bond all damages and costs as may be adjudged against him for wrongfully suing out such writ of attachment.

After notice to the opposite party, either before or after the issuance of the writ, the defendant or plaintiff may file a motion to increase or reduce the amount of such bond, or to question the sufficiency of the sureties thereon, in the court in which such suit is pending. Upon hearing, the court shall enter its order with respect to such bond and sufficiency of the sureties.

RULE 592b. FORM OF ATTACHMENT BOND

The following form of bond may be used:

"The State of Texas,

County of _____,

"We, the undersigned, as principal, and and as sureties, acknowledge ourselves bound to pay to C.D. the sum of dollars, conditioned that the above bound plaintiff in attachment against the said C.D., defendant, will prosecute his said suit to effect, and that he will pay all such damages and costs to the extent of penal amount of this bond as shall be adjudged against him for wrongfully suing out such attachment. Witness our hands this _____ day of _____, 20___ ."

RULE 593. REQUISITES FOR WRIT

A writ of attachment shall be directed to the sheriff or any constable within the State of Texas. It shall command him to attach and hold, unless replevied, subject to the further order of the court, so much of the property of the defendant, of a reasonable value in approximately the amount fixed by the court, as shall be found within his county.

RULE 594. FORM OF WRIT

The following form of writ may be issued:

"The State of Texas.

"To the Sheriff or any Constable of any County of the State of Texas, greeting:

"We command you that you attach forthwith so much of the property of C.D., if it be found in your county, repleviable on security, as shall be of value sufficient to make the sum of _____dollars, and the probable costs of suit, to satisfy the demand of A.B., and that you keep and secure in your hands the property so attached, unless replevied, that the same may be liable to further proceedings thereon to be had before our court in _____, County of _____. You will true return make of this writ on or before 10 a.m. of Monday, the _____day of _____, 20___ , showing how you have executed the same."

RULE 595. SEVERAL WRITS

Several writs of attachment may, at the option of the plaintiff, be issued at the same time, or in succession and sent to different counties, until sufficient property shall be attached to satisfy the writ.

RULE 596. DELIVERY OF WRIT

The writ of attachment shall be dated and tested as other writs, and may be delivered to the sheriff or constable by the officer issuing it, or he may deliver it to the plaintiff, his agent or attorney, for that purpose.

RULE 597. DUTY OF OFFICER

The sheriff or constable receiving the writ shall immediately proceed to execute the same by levying upon so much of the property of the defendant subject to the writ, and found within his county, as may be sufficient to satisfy the command of the writ.

RULE 598. LEVY, HOW MADE

The writ of attachment shall be levied in the same manner as is, or may be, the writ of execution upon similar property.

RULE 598a. SERVICE OF WRIT ON DEFENDANT

The defendant shall be served in any manner prescribed for service of citation, or as provided in Rule 21a, with a copy of the writ of attachment, the application, accompanying affidavits, and orders of the court as soon as practicable following the levy of the writ. There shall be prominently displayed on the face of the copy of the writ served on the defendant, in ten-point type and in a manner calculated to advise a reasonably attentive person of its contents, the following:

"To _____, Defendant:

"You are hereby notified that certain properties alleged to be owned by you have been attached. If you claim any rights in such property, you are advised:

"YOU HAVE A RIGHT TO REGAIN POSSESSION OF THE PROPERTY BY FILING A REPLEVY BOND. YOU HAVE A RIGHT TO SEEK TO REGAIN POSSESSION OF THE PROPERTY BY FILING WITH THE COURT A MOTION TO DISSOLVE THIS WRIT."

RULE 599. DEFENDANT MAY REPLEVY

At any time before judgment, should the attached property not have been previously claimed or sold, the defendant may replevy the same, or any part thereof, or the proceeds from the sale of the property if it has been sold under order of the court, by giving bond with sufficient surety or sureties as provided by statute, to be approved by the officer who levied the writ, payable to plaintiff, in the amount fixed by the court's order, or, at the defendant's option, for the value of the property sought to be replevied (to be estimated by the officer), plus one year's interest thereon at the legal rate from the date of the bond, conditioned that the defendant shall satisfy, to the extent of the penal amount of the bond, any judgment which may be rendered against him in such action.

On reasonable notice to the opposing party (which may be less than three days) either party shall have the right to prompt judicial review of the amount of bond required, denial of bond, sufficiency of sureties, and estimated value of the property, by the court which authorized issuance of the writ. The court's determination may be made upon the basis of affidavits, if uncontroverted, setting forth such facts as would be admissible in evidence; otherwise, the parties shall submit evidence. The court shall forthwith enter its order either approving or modifying the requirements of the officer or of the court's prior order, and such order of the court shall supersede and control with respect to such matters.

On reasonable notice to the opposing party (which may be less than three days) the defendant shall have the right to move the court for a substitution of property, of equal value as that attached, for the property attached. Provided that there has been located sufficient property of the defendants to satisfy the order of attachment, the court may authorize substitution of one or more items of defendant's property for all or for part of the property attached. The court shall first make findings as to the value of the property to be substituted. If property is substituted, the property released from attachment shall be delivered to defendant, if such property is personal property, and all liens upon such property from the original order of attachment or modification thereof shall be terminated. Attachment of substituted property shall be deemed to have existed from the date of levy on the original property attached, and no property on which liens have become affixed since the date of levy on the original property may be substituted.

RULE 600. SALE OF PERISHABLE PROPERTY

Whenever personal property which has been attached shall not have been claimed or replevied, the judge, or justice of the peace, out of whose court the writ was issued, may, either in term time or in vacation, order the same to be sold, when it shall be made to appear that such property is in danger of serious and immediate waste or decay, or that the keeping of the same until the trial will necessarily be attended with such expense or deterioration in value as greatly to lessen the amount likely to be realized therefrom.

RULE 601. TO PROTECT INTERESTS

In determining whether the property attached is perishable, and the necessity or advantage or ordering a sale thereof, the judge or justice of the peace may act upon affidavits in writing or oral testimony, and may by a preliminary order entered of record, with or without notice to the parties as the urgency of the case in his opinion requires, direct the sheriff or constable to sell such property at public auction for cash, and thereupon the officer shall sell it accordingly.

RULE 602. BOND OF APPLICANT FOR SALE

If the application for an order of sale be filed by any person or party other than the defendant from whose possession the property was taken by levy, the court shall not grant such order unless the applicant shall file with such court a bond payable to such defendant, with two or more good and sufficient sureties, to be approved by said court, conditioned that they will be responsible to the defendant for such damages as he may sustain in case such sale be illegally and unjustly applied for, or be illegally and unjustly made.

RULE 603. PROCEDURE FOR SALE

Such sale of attached perishable personal property shall be conducted in the same manner as sales of personal property under execution; provided, however, that the time of the sale, and at the time of advertisement thereof, may be fixed by the judge or justice of the peace at a time earlier than ten days, according to the exigency of the case, and in such event notice thereof shall be given in such manner as directed by the order.

RULE 604. RETURN OF SALE

The officer making such sale of perishable property shall promptly pay the proceeds of such sale to the clerk of such court or justice of the peace, as the case may be, and shall make written return of the order of sale signed by him officially, stating the time and place of the sale, the name of the purchaser, and the amount of money received, with an itemized account of the expenses attending the sale. Such return shall be filed with the papers of the case.

RULE 605. JUDGE MAY MAKE NECESSARY ORDERS

When the perishable personal property levied on under the attachment writ has not been claimed or replevied, the judge or justice of the peace may make such orders, either in term time or vacation, as may be necessary for its preservation or use.

RULE 606. RETURN OF WRIT

The officer executing the writ of attachment shall return the writ, with his action endorsed thereon, or attached thereto, signed by him officially, to the court from which it issued, at or before 10 o'clock a.m. of the Monday next after the expiration of fifteen days from the date of issuance of the writ. Such return shall describe the property attached with sufficient certainty to identify it, and state when the same was attached, and whether any personal property attached remains still in his hands, and, if not, the disposition made of the same. When property has been replevied he shall deliver the replevy bond to the clerk or justice of the peace to be filed with the papers of the cause.

RULE 607. REPORT OF DISPOSITION OF PROPERTY

When the property levied on is claimed, replevied or sold, or otherwise disposed of after the writ has been returned, the officer having the custody of the same shall immediately make a report in writing, signed by him officially, to the clerk, or justice of the peace, as the case may be, showing such disposition of the property. Such report shall be filed among the papers of the cause.

RULE 608. DISSOLUTION OR MODIFICATION OF WRIT OF ATTACHMENT

A defendant whose property has been attached or any intervening party who claims an interest in such property, may by sworn written motion, seek to vacate, dissolve, or modify the writ, and the order directing its issuance, for any grounds or cause, extrinsic or intrinsic. Such motion shall admit or deny each finding of the order directing the issuance of the writ except where the movant is unable to admit or deny the finding, in which case movant shall set forth the reasons why he cannot admit or deny. Unless the parties agree to an extension of time, the motion shall be heard promptly, after reasonable notice to the plaintiff (which may be less than three days), and the issue shall be determined not later than ten days after the motion is filed. The filing of the motion shall stay any further proceedings under the writ, except for any orders concerning the care, preservation, or sale of perishable property, until a hearing is had and the issue is determined. The writ shall be dissolved unless at such hearing, the plaintiff shall prove the grounds relied upon for its issuance, but the court may modify its previous order granting the writ and the writ issued pursuant thereto. The movant shall, however, have the burden to prove that the reasonable value of the property attached exceeds the amount necessary to secure the debt, interest for one year, and probable costs. He shall also have the burden to prove the facts to justify substitution of property.

The court's determination may be made upon the basis of affidavits, if uncontroverted, setting forth such facts as would be admissible in evidence; otherwise, the parties shall submit evidence. The court may make all such orders, including orders concerning the care, preservation, or disposition of the property (or the proceeds therefrom if the same has been sold), as justice may require. If the movant has given a replevy bond, an order to vacate or dissolve the writ shall vacate the replevy bond and discharge the sureties thereon, and if the court modifies its order or the writ issued pursuant thereto, it shall make such further orders with respect to the bond as may be consistent with its modification.

RULE 609. AMENDMENT

Clerical errors in the affidavit, bond, or writ of attachment, or the officer's return thereof, may upon application in writing to the judge or justice of the court in which the suit is filed, and after notice to the opponent, be amended in such manner and on such terms as the judge or justice shall authorize by an order entered in the minutes of the court or noted on the docket of the justice of the peace, provided the amendment does not change or add to the grounds of such attachment as stated in the affidavit, and provided such amendment appears to the judge or justice to be in furtherance of justice.

SECTION 2. DISTRESS WARRANT

RULE 610. APPLICATION FOR DISTRESS WARRANT AND ORDER

Either at the commencement of a suit or at any time during its progress the plaintiff may file an application for the issuance of a distress warrant with the justice of the peace. Such application may be supported by affidavits of the plaintiff, his agent, his attorney, or other persons having knowledge of relevant facts, but shall include a statement that the amount sued for is rent, or advances prescribed by statute, or shall produce a writing signed by the tenant to that effect, and shall further swear that such warrant is not sued out for the purpose of vexing and harassing the defendant. The application shall comply with all statutory requirements and shall state the grounds for issuing the warrant and the specific facts relied upon by the plaintiff to warrant the required findings by the justice of the peace. The warrant shall not be quashed because two or more grounds are stated conjunctively or disjunctively. The application and any affidavits shall be made on personal knowledge and shall set forth such facts as would be admissible in evidence provided that facts may be stated based upon information and belief if the grounds of such belief are specifically stated.

No warrant shall issue before final judgment except on written order of the justice of the peace after a hearing, which may be ex parte. Such warrant shall be made returnable to a court having jurisdiction of the amount in controversy. The justice of the peace in his order granting the application shall make specific findings of fact to support the statutory grounds found to exist, and shall specify the maximum value of property that may be seized, and the amount of bond required of plaintiff, and, further shall command that property be kept safe and preserved subject to further orders of the court having jurisdiction. Such bond shall be in an amount which, in the opinion of the court, shall adequately compensate defendant in the event plaintiff fails to prosecute his suit to effect, and pay all damages and costs as shall be adjudged against him for wrongfully suing out the warrant. The justice of the peace shall further find in his order the amount of bond required to replevy, which, unless the defendant chooses to exercise his option as provided in Rule 614, shall be the amount of plaintiff's claim, one year's accrual of interest if allowed by law on the claim, and the estimated costs of court. The order may direct the issuance of several warrants at the same time, or in succession, to be sent to different counties.

RULE 611. BOND FOR DISTRESS WARRANT

No distress warrant shall issue before final judgment until the party applying therefor has filed with the justice of the peace authorized to issue such warrant a bond payable to the defendant in an amount approved by the justice of the peace, with sufficient surety or sureties as provided by statute, conditioned that the plaintiff will prosecute his suit to effect and pay all damages and costs as may be adjudged against him for wrongfully suing out such warrant.

After notice to the opposite party, either before or after the issuance of the warrant, the defendant or plaintiff may file a motion to increase or reduce the amount of such bond, or to question the sufficiency of the sureties thereon, in a court having jurisdiction of the subject matter. Upon hearing, the court shall enter its order with respect to such bond and sufficiency of the sureties.

RULE 612. REQUISITES FOR WARRANT

A distress warrant shall be directed to the sheriff or any constable within the State of Texas. It shall command him to attach and hold, unless replevied, subject to the further orders of the court having jurisdiction, so much of the property of the defendant, not exempt by statute, of reasonable value in approximately the amount fixed by the justice of the peace, as shall be found within his county.

RULE 613. SERVICE OF WARRANT ON DEFENDANT

The defendant shall be served in any manner prescribed for service of citation, or as provided in Rule 21a, with a copy of the distress warrant, the application, accompanying affidavits, and orders of the justice of the peace as soon as practicable following the levy of the warrant. There shall be prominently displayed on the face of the copy of the warrant served on the defendant, in 10-point type and in a manner calculated to advise a reasonably attentive person of its contents, the following:

To _____, Defendant:

You are hereby notified that certain properties alleged to be owned by you have been seized. If you claim any rights in such property, you are advised:

"YOU HAVE A RIGHT TO REGAIN POSSESSION OF THE PROPERTY BY FILING A REPLEVY BOND. YOU HAVE A RIGHT TO SEEK TO REGAIN POSSESSION OF THE PROPERTY BY FILING WITH THE COURT A MOTION TO DISSOLVE THIS WARRANT."

RULE 614. DEFENDANT MAY REPLEVY

At any time before judgment, should the seized property not have been previously claimed or sold, the defendant may replevy the same, or any part thereof, or the proceeds from the sale of the property if it has been sold under order of the court, by giving bond with sufficient surety or sureties as provided by statute, to be approved by a court having jurisdiction of the amount in controversy payable to plaintiff in double the amount of the plaintiff's debt, or, at the defendant's option for not less than the value of the property sought to be replevied, plus one year's interest thereon at the legal rate from the date of the bond, conditioned that the defendant shall satisfy to the extent of the penal amount of the bond any judgment which may be rendered against him in such action.

On reasonable notice to the opposing party (which may be less than three days) either party shall have the right to prompt judicial review of the amount of bond required, denial of bond, sufficiency of sureties, and estimated value of the property, by a court having jurisdiction of the amount in controversy. The court's determination may be made upon the basis of affidavits if uncontroverted setting forth such facts as would be admissible in evidence, otherwise the parties shall submit evidence. The court shall forthwith enter its order either approving or modifying the requirements of the order of the justice of the peace, and such order of the court shall supersede and control with respect to such matters.

On reasonable notice to the opposing party (which may be less than three days) the defendant shall have the right to move the court for a substitution of property, of equal value as that attached, for the property seized. Provided that there has been located sufficient property of the defendant's to satisfy the order of seizure, the court may authorize substitution of one or more items of defendant's property for all or part of the property seized. The court shall first make findings as to the value of the property to be substituted. If property is substituted, the property released from seizure shall be delivered to defendant, if such property is personal property, and all liens upon such property from the original order of seizure or modification thereof shall be terminated. Seizure of substituted property shall be deemed to have existed from the date of levy on the original property seized, and no property on which liens have become affixed since the date of levy on the original property may be substituted.

RULE 614a. DISSOLUTION OR MODIFICATION OF DISTRESS WARRANT

A defendant whose property has been seized or any intervening claimant who claims an interest in such property, may by sworn written motion, seek to vacate, dissolve, or modify the seizure, and the order directing its issuance, for any grounds or cause, extrinsic or intrinsic. Such motion shall admit or deny each finding of the order directing the issuance of the warrant except where the movant is unable to admit or deny the finding, in which case movant shall set forth the reasons why he cannot admit or deny. Unless the parties agree to an extension of time, the motion shall be heard promptly, after reasonable notice to the plaintiff (which may be less than three days), and the issue shall be determined not later than 10 days after the motion is filed. The filing of the motion shall stay any further proceedings under the warrant, except for any orders concerning the care, preservation, or sale of any perishable property, until a hearing is had, and the issue is determined. The warrant shall be dissolved unless, at such hearing, the plaintiff shall prove the specific facts alleged and the grounds relied upon for its issuance, but the court may modify the order of the justice of the peace granting the warrant and the warrant issued pursuant thereto. The movant shall however have the burden to prove that the reasonable value of the property seized exceeds the amount necessary to secure the debt, interest for one year, and probable costs. He shall also have the burden to prove the facts to justify substitution of property.

The court's determination may be made upon the basis of affidavits setting forth such facts as would be admissible in evidence, but additional evidence, if tendered by either party shall be received and considered. The court may make all such orders, including orders concerning the care, preservation, or disposition of the property (or the proceeds therefrom if the same has been sold), as justice may require. If the movant has given a replevy bond, an order to vacate or dissolve the warrant shall vacate the replevy bond and discharge the sureties thereon, and if the court modifies the order of the justice of the peace of the warrant issue pursuant thereto, it shall make such further orders with respect to the bond as may be consistent with its modification.

RULE 615. SALE OF PERISHABLE PROPERTY

Whenever personal property which has been levied on under a distress warrant shall not have been claimed or replevied, the judge, or justice of the peace, to whose court such writ is made returnable may, either in term time or in vacation, order the same to be sold, when it shall be made to appear that such property is in danger of serious and immediate waste or decay, or that the keeping of the same until the trial will necessarily be attended with such expense or deterioration in value as greatly to lessen the amount likely to be realized therefrom.

RULE 616. TO PROTECT INTERESTS

In determining whether the property levied upon is perishable, and the necessity or advantage of ordering a sale thereof, the judge or justice of the peace may act upon affidavits in writing or oral testimony, and may by a preliminary order entered of record with or without notice to the parties as the urgency of the case in his opinion requires, direct the sheriff or constable to sell such property at public auction for cash, and thereupon the sheriff or constable shall sell it accordingly. If the application for an order of sale be filed by any person or party other than the defendant from whose possession the property was taken by levy, the court shall not grant such order, unless the applicant shall file with such court a bond payable to such defendant, with two or more good and sufficient sureties, to be approved by said court, conditioned that they will be responsible to the defendant for such damages as he may sustain in case such sale be illegally and unjustly applied for, or be illegally and unjustly made.

RULE 617. PROCEDURE FOR SALE

Such sale of perishable property shall be conducted in the same manner as sales of personal property under execution; provided, however, that the time of the sale, and the time of advertisement thereof, may be fixed by the judge or justice of the peace at a time earlier than ten days, according to the exigency of the case, and in such event notice thereof shall be given in such manner as directed by the order.

RULE 618. RETURN OF SALE

The officer making such sale of perishable property shall promptly pay the proceeds of such sale to the clerk of such court or to the justice of the peace, as the case may be, and shall make written return of the order of sale, signed by him officially, stating the time and place of the sale, the name of the purchaser, and the amount of money received, with an itemized account of the expenses attending the sale. Such return shall be filed with the papers of the case.

RULE 619. CITATION FOR DEFENDANT

The justice at the time he issues the warrant shall issue a citation to the defendant requiring him to answer before such justice at the first day of the next succeeding term of court, stating the time and place of holding the same, if he has jurisdiction to finally try the cause, and upon its being returned served, to proceed to judgment as in ordinary cases; and, if he has not such jurisdiction, the citation shall require the defendant to answer before the court to which the warrant was made returnable at or before ten o'clock a.m. of the Monday next after the expiration of twenty days from the date of service thereof, stating the place of holding the court, and shall be returned with the other papers to such court. If the defendant has removed from the county without service, the proper officer shall state this fact in his return on the citation; and the court shall proceed to try the case ex parte, and may enter judgment.

RULE 620. PETITION

When the warrant is made returnable to the district or county court, the plaintiff shall file his petition within ten days from the date of the issuance of the writ.

SECTION 3. EXECUTIONS

RULE 621. ENFORCEMENT OF JUDGMENT

The judgments of the district, county, and justice courts shall be enforced by execution or other appropriate process. Such execution or other process shall be returnable in thirty, sixty, or ninety days as requested by the plaintiff, his agent or attorney.

RULE 621a. DISCOVERY AND ENFORCEMENT OF JUDGMENT

At any time after rendition of judgment, and so long as said judgment has not been suspended by a supersedeas bond or by order of a proper court and has not become dormant as provided by Article 3773, V.A.T.S., the successful party may, for the purpose of obtaining information to aid in the enforcement of such judgment, initiate and maintain in the trial court in the same suit in which said judgment was rendered any discovery proceeding authorized by these rules for pre-trial matters. Also, at any time after rendition of judgment, either party may, for the purpose of obtaining information relevant to motions allowed by Texas Rules of Appellate Procedure 47 and 49 initiate and maintain in the trial court in the same suit in which said judgment was rendered any discovery proceeding authorized by these rules for pre- trial matters. The rules governing and related to such pre- trial discovery proceedings shall apply in like manner to discovery proceedings after judgment. The rights herein granted to the parties shall inure to their successors or assignees, in whole or in part. Judicial supervision of such discovery proceedings after judgment shall be the same as that provided by law or these rules for pre-trial discovery and proceedings insofar as applicable.

RULE 622. EXECUTION

An execution is a process of the court from which it is issued. The clerk of the district or county court or the justice of the peace, as the case may be, shall tax the costs in every case in which a final judgment has been rendered and shall issue execution to enforce such judgment and collect such costs. The execution and subsequent executions shall not be addressed to a particular county, but shall be addressed to any sheriff or any constable within the State of Texas.

RULE 623. ON DEATH OF EXECUTOR

When an executor, administrator, guardian or trustee of an express trust dies, or ceases to be such executor, administrator, guardian or trustee after judgment, execution shall issue on such judgment in the name of his successor, upon an affidavit of such death or termination being filed with the clerk of the court or the justice of the peace, as the case may be, together with the certificate of the appointment of such successor under the hand and seal of the clerk of the court wherein the appointment was made.

RULE 624. ON DEATH OF NOMINAL PLAINTIFF

When a person in whose favor a judgment is rendered for the use of another dies after judgment, execution shall issue in the name of the party for whose use the suit was brought upon an affidavit of such death being filed with the clerk of the court or the justice of the peace.

RULE 625. ON MONEY OF DECEASED

If a sole defendant dies after judgment for money against him, execution shall not issue thereon, but the judgment may be proved up and paid in due course of administration.

RULE 626. ON PROPERTY OF DECEASED

In any case of judgment other than a money judgment, where the sole defendant, or one or more of several joint defendants, shall die after judgment, upon an affidavit of such death being filed with the clerk, together with the certificate of the appointment of a representative of such decedent under the hand and seal of the clerk of the court wherein such appointment was made, the proper process on such judgment shall issue against such representative.

RULE 627. TIME FOR ISSUANCE

If no supersedeas bond or notice of appeal, as required of agencies exempt from filing bonds, has been filed and approved, the clerk of the court or justice of the peace shall issue the execution upon such judgment upon application of the successful party or his attorney after the expiration of thirty days from the time a final judgment is signed. If a timely motion for new trial or in arrest of judgment is filed, the clerk shall issue the execution upon the judgment on application of the party or his attorney after the expiration of thirty days from the time the order overruling the motion is signed or from the time the motion is overruled by operation of law.

RULE 628. EXECUTION WITHIN THIRTY DAYS

Such execution may be issued at any time before the thirtieth day upon the filing of an affidavit by the plaintiff in the judgment or his agent or attorney that the defendant is about to remove his personal property subject to execution by law out of the county, or is about to transfer or secrete such personal property for the purpose of defrauding his creditors.

RULE 629. REQUISITES OF EXECUTION

The style of the execution shall be "The State of Texas." It shall be directed to any sheriff or any constable within the State of Texas. It shall be signed by the clerk or justice officially, and bear the seal of the court, if issued out of the district or county court, and shall require the officer to execute it according to its terms, and to make the costs which have been adjudged against the defendant in execution and the further costs of executing the writ. It shall describe the judgment, stating the court in which, and the time when, rendered, and the names of the parties in whose favor and against whom the judgment was rendered. A correct copy of the bill of costs taxed against the defendant in execution shall be attached to the writ. It shall require the officer to return it within thirty, sixty, or ninety days, as directed by the plaintiff or his attorney.

RULE 630. EXECUTION ON JUDGMENT FOR MONEY

When an execution is issued upon a judgment for a sum of money, or directing the payment simply of a sum of money, it must specify in the body thereof the sum recovered or directed to be paid and the sum actually due when it is issued and the rate of interest upon the sum due. It must require the officer to satisfy the judgment and costs out of the property of the judgment debtor subject to execution by law.

RULE 631. EXECUTION FOR SALE OF PARTICULAR PROPERTY

An execution issued upon a judgment for the sale of particular chattels or personal property or real estate, must particularly describe the property, and shall direct the officer to make the sale by previously giving the public notice of the time and place of sale required by law and these rules.

RULE 632. EXECUTION FOR DELIVERY OF CERTAIN PROPERTY

An execution issued upon a judgment for the delivery of the possession of a chattel or personal property, or for the delivery of the possession of real property, shall particularly describe the property, and designate the party to whom the judgment awards the possession. The writ shall require the officer to deliver the possession of the property to the party entitled thereto.

RULE 633. EXECUTION FOR POSSESSION OR VALUE OF PERSONAL PROPERTY

If the judgment be for the recovery of personal property or its value, the writ shall command the officer, in case a delivery thereof cannot be had, to levy and collect the value thereof for which the judgment was recovered, to be specified therein, out of any property of the party against whom judgment was rendered, liable to execution.

RULE 634. EXECUTION SUPERSEDED

The clerk or justice of the peace shall immediately issue a writ of supersedeas suspending all further proceedings under any execution previously issued when a supersedeas bond is afterward filed and approved within the time prescribed by law or these rules.

RULE 635. STAY OF EXECUTION IN JUSTICE COURT

At any time within ten days after the rendition of any judgment in a justice court, the justice may grant a stay of execution thereof for three months from the date of such judgment, if the person against whom such judgment was rendered shall, with one or more good and sufficient sureties, to be approved by the justice, appear before him and acknowledge themselves and each of them bound to the successful party in such judgment for the full amount thereof, with interest and costs, which acknowledgment shall be entered in writing on the docket, and signed by the persons binding themselves as sureties; provided, no such stay of execution shall be granted unless the party applying therefor shall first file an affidavit with the justice that he has not the money with which to pay such judgment, and that the enforcement of same by execution prior to three months would be a hardship upon him and would cause a sacrifice of his property which would not likely be caused should said execution be stayed. Such acknowledgment shall be entered by the justice on his docket and shall constitute a judgment against the defendant and such sureties, upon which execution shall issue in case the same is not paid on or before the expiration of such day.

RULE 636. INDORSEMENTS BY OFFICER

The officer receiving the execution shall indorse thereon the exact hour and day when he received it. If he receives more than one on the same day against the same person he shall number them as received.

RULE 637. LEVY OF EXECUTION

When an execution is delivered to an officer he shall proceed without delay to levy the same upon the property of the defendant found within his county not exempt from execution, unless otherwise directed by the plaintiff, his agent or attorney. The officer shall first call upon the defendant, if he can be found, or, if absent, upon his agent within the county, if known, to point out property to be levied upon, and the levy shall first be made upon the property designated by the defendant, or his agent. If in the opinion of the officer the property so designated will not sell for enough to satisfy the execution and costs of sale, he shall require an additional designation by the defendant. If no property be thus designated by the defendant, the officer shall levy the execution upon any property of the defendant subject to execution.

RULE 638. PROPERTY NOT TO BE DESIGNATED

A defendant in execution shall not point out property which he has sold, mortgaged or conveyed in trust, or property exempt from forced sale.

RULE 639. LEVY

In order to make a levy on real estate, it shall not be necessary for the officer to go upon the ground but is shall be sufficient for him to indorse such levy on the writ. Levy upon personal property is made by taking possession thereof, when the defendant in execution is entitled to the possession. Where the defendant in execution has an interest in personal property, but is not entitled to the possession thereof, a levy is made thereon by giving notice thereof to the person who is entitled to the possession, or one of them where there are several.

RULE 640. LEVY ON STOCK RUNNING AT LARGE

A levy upon livestock running at large in a range, and which cannot be herded and penned without great inconvenience and expense, may be made by designating by reasonable estimate the number of animals and describing them by their marks and brands, or either; such levy shall be made in the presence of two or more credible persons, and notice thereof shall be given in writing to the owner or his herder or agent, if residing within the county and known to the officer.

RULE 641. LEVY ON SHARES OF STOCK

A levy upon shares of stock of any corporation or joint stock company for which a certificate is outstanding is made by the officer seizing and taking possession of such certificate. Provided, however, that nothing herein shall be construed as restricting any rights granted under Section 8.317 of the Texas Uniform Commercial Code.

[RULE 642. Repealed effective January 1, 1976]

RULE 643. LEVY ON GOODS PLEDGED OR MORTGAGED

Goods and chattels pledged, assigned or mortgaged as security for any debt or contract, may be levied upon and sold on execution against the person making the pledge, assignment or mortgage subject thereto; and the purchaser shall be entitled to the possession when it is held by the pledgee, assignee or mortgagee, on complying with the conditions of the pledge, assignment or mortgage.

RULE 644. MAY GIVE DELIVERY BOND

Any personal property taken in execution may be returned to the defendant by the officer upon the delivery by the defendant to him of a bond, payable to the plaintiff, with two or more good and sufficient sureties, to be approved by the officer, conditioned that the property shall be delivered to the officer at the time and place named in the bond, to be sold according to law, or for the payment to the officer of a fair value thereof, which shall be stated in the bond.

RULE 645. PROPERTY MAY BE SOLD BY DEFENDANT

Where property has been replevied, as provided in the preceding rule, the defendant may sell or dispose of the same, paying the officer the stipulated value thereof.

RULE 646. FORFEITED DELIVERY BOND

In case of the non-delivery of the property according to the terms of the delivery bond, and non-payment of the value thereof, the officer shall forthwith indorse the bond "Forfeited" and return the same to the clerk of the court or the justice of the peace from which the execution issued; whereupon, if the judgment remain unsatisfied in whole or in part, the clerk or justice shall issue execution against the principal debtor and the sureties on the bond for the amount due, not exceeding the stipulated value of the property, upon which execution no delivery bond shall be taken, which instruction shall be indorsed by the clerk or justice on the execution.

RULE 646a. SALE OF REAL PROPERTY

Real property taken by virtue of any execution shall be sold at public auction, at the courthouse door of the county, unless the court orders that such sale be at the place where the real property is situated, on the first Tuesday of the month, between the hours of ten o'clock, a.m. and four o'clock, p.m.

RULE 647. NOTICE OF SALE OF REAL ESTATE

The time and place of sale of real estate under execution, order of sale, or venditioni exponas, shall be advertised by the officer by having the notice thereof published in the English language once a week for three consecutive weeks preceding such sale, in some newspaper published in said county. The first of said publications shall appear not less than twenty days immediately preceding the day of sale. Said notice shall contain a statement of the authority by virtue of which the sale is to be made, the time of levy, and the time and place of sale; it shall also contain a brief description of the property to be sold, and shall give the number of acres, original survey, locality in the county, and the name by which the land is most generally known, but it shall not be necessary for it to contain field notes. Publishers of newspapers shall charge the legal rate of Two (2) Cents per word for the first insertion of such publication and One (1) Cent per word for such subsequent insertions, or such newspapers shall be entitled to charge for such publication at a rate equal to but not in excess of the published word or line rate of that newspaper for such class of advertising. If there be no newspaper published in the county, or none which will publish the notice of sale for the compensation herein fixed, the officer shall then post such notice in writing in three public places in the county, one of which shall be at the courthouse door of such county, for at least twenty days successively next before the day of sale. The officer making the levy shall give the defendant, or his attorney, written notice of such sale, either in person or by mail, which notice shall substantially conform to the foregoing requirements.

RULE 648. "COURTHOUSE DOOR" DEFINED

By the term "courthouse door" of a county is meant either of the principal entrances to the house provided by the proper authority for the holding of the district court. If from any cause there is no such house, the door of the house where the district court was last held in that county shall be deemed to be the courthouse door. Where the courthouse, or house used by the court, has been destroyed by fire or other cause, and another has not been designated by the proper authority, the place where such house stood shall be deemed to be the courthouse door.

RULE 649. SALE OF PERSONAL PROPERTY

Personal property levied on under execution shall be offered for sale on the premises where it is taken in execution, or at the courthouse door of the county, or at some other place if, owing to the nature of the property, it is more convenient to exhibit it to purchasers at such place. Personal property susceptible of being exhibited shall not be sold unless the same be present and subject to the view of those attending the sale, except shares of stock in joint stock or incorporated companies, and in cases where the defendant in execution has merely an interest without right to the exclusive possession in which case the interest of defendant may be sold and conveyed without the presence or delivery of the property. When a levy is made upon livestock running at large on the range, it is not necessary that such stock, or any part thereof, be present at the place of sale, and the purchaser at such sale is authorized to gather and pen such stock and select therefrom the number purchased by him.

RULE 650. NOTICE OF SALE OF PERSONAL PROPERTY

Previous notice of the time and place of the sale of any personal property levied on under execution shall be given by posting notice thereof for ten days successively immediately prior to the date of sale at the courthouse door of any county and at the place where the sale is to be made.

RULE 651. WHEN EXECUTION IS NOT SATISFIED

When the property levied upon does not sell for enough to satisfy the execution, the officer shall proceed anew, as in the first instance, to make the residue.

RULE 652. PURCHASER FAILING TO COMPLY

If any person shall bid off property at any sale made by virtue of an execution, and shall fail to comply with the terms of the sale, he shall be liable to pay the plaintiff in execution twenty per cent on the value of the property thus bid off, besides costs, to be recovered on motion, five days notice of such motion being given to such purchaser; and should the property on a second sale bring less than on the former, he shall be liable to pay to the defendant in execution all loss which he sustains thereby, to be recovered on motion as above provided.

RULE 653. RESALE OF PROPERTY

When the terms of the sale shall not be complied with by the bidder the levying officer shall proceed to sell the same property again on the same day, if there be sufficient time; but if not, he shall readvertise and sell the same as in the first instance.

RULE 654. RETURN OF EXECUTION

The levying officer shall make due return of the execution, in writing and signed by him officially, stating concisely what such officer has done in pursuance of the requirements of the writ and of the law. The return shall be filed with the clerk of the court or the justice of the peace as the case may be. The execution shall be returned forthwith if satisfied by the collection of the money or if ordered by the plaintiff or his attorney indorsed thereon.

RULE 655. RETURN OF EXECUTION BY MAIL

When an execution is placed in the hands of an officer of a county other than the one in which the judgment is rendered, return may be made by mail; but money cannot be thus sent except by direction of the party entitled to receive the same or his attorney of record.

RULE 656. EXECUTION DOCKET

The clerk of each court shall keep an execution docket in which he shall enter a statement of all executions as they are issued by him, specifying the names of the parties, the amount of the judgment, the amount due thereon, the rate of interest when it exceeds six per cent, the costs, the date of issuing the execution, to whom delivered, and the return of the officer thereon, with the date of such return. Such docket entries shall be taken and deemed to be a record. The clerk shall keep an index and cross-index to the execution docket. When execution is in favor or against several persons, it shall be indexed in the name of each person. Any clerk who shall fail to keep said execution docket and index thereto, or shall neglect to make the entries therein, shall be liable upon his official bond to any person injured for the amount of damages sustained by such neglect.

SECTION 4. GARNISHMENT

RULE 657. JUDGMENT FINAL FOR GARNISHMENT

In the case mentioned in subsection 3, section 63.001, Civil Practice and Remedies Code, the judgment whether based upon a liquidated demand or an unliquidated demand, shall be deemed final and subsisting for the purpose of garnishment from and after the date it is signed, unless a supersedeas bond shall have been approved and filed in accordance with Texas Rule of Appellate Procedure 47.

RULE 658. APPLICATION FOR WRIT OF GARNISHMENT AND ORDER

Either at the commencement of a suit or at any time during its progress the plaintiff may file an application for a writ of garnishment. Such application shall be supported by affidavits of the plaintiff, his agent, his attorney, or other person having knowledge of relevant facts. The application shall comply with all statutory requirements and shall state the grounds for issuing the writ and the specific facts relied upon by the plaintiff to warrant the required findings by the court. The writ shall not be quashed because two or more grounds are stated conjunctively or disjunctively. The application and any affidavits shall be made on personal knowledge and shall set forth such facts as would be admissible in evidence; provided that facts may be stated based upon information and belief if the grounds of such belief are specifically stated.

No writ shall issue before final judgment except upon written order of the court after a hearing, which may be ex parte. The court in its order granting the application shall make specific findings of facts to support the statutory grounds found to exist, and shall specify the maximum value of property or indebtedness that may be garnished and the amount of bond required of plaintiff. Such bond shall be in an amount which, in the opinion of the court, shall adequately compensate defendant in the event plaintiff fails to prosecute his suit to effect, and pay all damages and costs as shall be adjudged against him for wrongfully suing out the writ of garnishment. The court shall further find in its order the amount of bond required of defendant to replevy, which, unless defendant exercises his option as provided under Rule 664, shall be the amount of plaintiff's claim, one year's accrual of interest if allowed by law on the claim, and the estimated costs of court. The order may direct the issuance of several writs at the same time, or in succession, to be sent to different counties.

RULE 658a. BOND FOR GARNISHMENT

No writ of garnishment shall issue before final judgment until the party applying therefor has filed with the officer authorized to issue such writ a bond payable to the defendant in the amount fixed by the court's order, with sufficient surety or sureties as provided by statute, conditioned that the plaintiff will prosecute his suit to effect and pay to the extent of the penal amount of the bond all damages and costs as may be adjudged against him for wrongfully suing out such writ of garnishment.

After notice to the opposite party, either before or after the issuance of the writ, the defendant or plaintiff may file a motion to increase or reduce the amount of such bond, or to question the sufficiency of the sureties. Upon hearing, the court shall enter its order with respect to such bond and the sufficiency of the sureties.

Should it be determined from the garnishee's answer if such is not controverted that the garnishee is indebted to the defendant, or has in his hands effects belonging to the defendant, in an amount or value less than the amount of the debt claimed by the plaintiff, then after notice to the defendant the court in which such garnishment is pending upon hearing may reduce the required amount of such bond to double the sum of the garnishee's indebtedness to the defendant plus the value of the effects in his hands belonging to the defendant.

RULE 659. CASE DOCKETED

When the foregoing requirements of these rules have been complied with, the judge, or clerk, or justice of the peace, as the case may be, shall docket the case in the name of the plaintiff as plaintiff and of the garnishee as defendant; and shall immediately issue a writ of garnishment directed to the garnishee, commanding him to appear before the court out of which the same is issued at or before 10 o'clock a.m. of the Monday next following the expiration of twenty days from the date the writ was served, if the writ is issued out of the district or county court; or the Monday next after the expiration of ten days from the date the writ was served, if the writ is issued out of the justice court. The writ shall command the garnishee to answer under oath upon such return date what, if anything, he is indebted to the defendant, and was when the writ was served, and what effects, if any, of the defendant he has in his possession, and had when such writ was served, and what other persons, if any, within his knowledge, are indebted to the defendant or have effects belonging to him in their possession.

[RULE 660. Repealed effective December 31, 1947]

RULE 661. FORM OF WRIT

The following form of writ may be used:

"The State of Texas.

"To E.F., Garnishee, greeting:

"Whereas, in the _____ Court of _____ County (if a justice court, state also the number of the precinct), in a certain cause wherein A.B. is plaintiff and C.D. is defendant, the plaintiff, claiming an indebtedness against the said C.D. of _____ dollars, besides interest and costs of suit, has applied for a writ of garnishment against you, E.F.; therefore you are hereby commanded to be and appear before said court at _____ in said county (if the writ is issued from the county or district court, here proceed: at 10 o'clock a.m. on the Monday next following the expiration of twenty days from the date of service hereof.' If the writ is issued from a justice of the peace court, here proceed: at or before 10 o'clock a.m. on the Monday next after the expiration of ten days from the date of service hereof.' In either event, proceed as follows:) then and there to answer upon oath what, if anything, you are indebted to the said C.D., and were when this writ was served upon you, and what effects, if any, of the said C.D. you have in your possession, and had when this writ was served, and what other persons, if any, within your knowledge, are indebted to the said C.D. or have effects belonging to him in their possession. You are further commanded NOT to pay to defendant any debt or to deliver to him any effects, pending further order of this court. Herein fail not, but make due answer as the law directs."

RULE 662. DELIVERY OF WRIT

The writ of garnishment shall be dated and tested as other writs, and may be delivered to the sheriff or constable by the officer who issued it, or he may deliver it to the plaintiff, his agent or attorney, for that purpose.

RULE 663. EXECUTION AND RETURN OF WRIT

The sheriff or constable receiving the writ of garnishment shall immediately proceed to execute the same by delivering a copy thereof to the garnishee, and shall make return thereof as of other citations.

RULE 663a. SERVICE OF WRIT ON DEFENDANT

The defendant shall be served in any manner prescribed for service of citation or as provided in Rule 21a with a copy of the writ of garnishment, the application, accompanying affidavits and orders of the court as soon as practicable following the service of the writ. There shall be prominently displayed on the face of the copy of the writ served on the defendant, in ten-point type and in a manner calculated to advise a reasonably attentive person of its contents, the following:

"To _____ , Defendant:

"You are hereby notified that certain properties alleged to be owned by you have been garnished. If you claim any rights in such property, you are advised:

"YOU HAVE A RIGHT TO REGAIN POSSESSION OF THE PROPERTY BY FILING A REPLEVY BOND. YOU HAVE A RIGHT TO SEEK TO REGAIN POSSESSION OF THE PROPERTY BY FILING WITH THE COURT A MOTION TO DISSOLVE THIS WRIT."

RULE 664. DEFENDANT MAY REPLEVY

At any time before judgment, should the garnished property not have been previously claimed or sold, the defendant may replevy the same, or any part thereof, or the proceeds from the sale of the property if it has been sold under order of the court, by giving bond with sufficient surety or sureties as provided by statute, to be approved by the officer who levied the writ, payable to plaintiff, in the amount fixed by the court's order, or, at the defendant's option, for the value of the property or indebtedness sought to be replevied (to be estimated by the officer), plus one year's interest thereon at the legal rate from the date of the bond, conditioned that the defendant, garnishee, shall satisfy, to the extent of the penal amount of the bond, any judgment which may be rendered against him in such action.

On reasonable notice to the opposing party (which may be less than three days) either party shall have the right to prompt judicial review of the amount of bond required, denial of bond, sufficiency of sureties, and estimated value of the property, by the court which authorized issuance of the writ. The court's determination may be made upon the basis of affidavits, if uncontroverted, setting forth such facts as would be admissible in evidence; otherwise, the parties shall submit evidence. The court shall forthwith enter its order either approving or modifying the requirements of the officer or of the court's prior order, and such order of the court shall supersede and control with respect to such matters.

On reasonable notice to the opposing party (which may be less than three days) the defendant shall have the right to move the court for a substitution of property, of equal value as that garnished, for the property garnished. Provided that there has been located sufficient property of the defendant's to satisfy the order of garnishment, the court may authorize substitution of one or more items of defendant's property for all or for part of the property garnished. The court shall first make findings as to the value of the property to be substituted. If property is substituted, the property released from garnishment shall be delivered to defendant, if such property is personal property, and all liens upon such property from the original order of garnishment or modification thereof shall be terminated. Garnishment of substituted property shall be deemed to have existed from date of garnishment on the original property garnished, and no property on which liens have become affixed since the date of garnishment of the original property may be substituted.

RULE 664a. DISSOLUTION OR MODIFICATION OF WRIT OF GARNISHMENT

A defendant whose property or account has been garnished or any intervening party who claims an interest in such property or account, may by sworn written motion, seek to vacate, dissolve or modify the writ of garnishment, and the order directing its issuance, for any grounds or cause, extrinsic or intrinsic. Such motion shall admit or deny each finding of the order directing the issuance of the writ except where the movant is unable to admit or deny the finding, in which case movant shall set forth the reasons why he cannot admit or deny. Unless the parties agree to an extension of time, the motion shall be heard promptly, after reasonable notice to the plaintiff (which may be less than three days), and the issue shall be determined not later than ten days after the motion is filed. The filing of the motion shall stay any further proceedings under the writ, except for any orders concerning the care, preservation or sale of any perishable property, until a hearing is had, and the issue is determined. The writ shall be dissolved unless, at such hearing, the plaintiff shall prove the grounds relied upon for its issuance, but the court may modify its previous order granting the writ and the writ issued pursuant thereto. The movant shall, however, have the burden to prove that the reasonable value of the property garnished exceeds the amount necessary to secure the debt, interest for one year, and probable costs. He shall also have the burden to prove facts to justify substitution of property.

The court's determination may be made upon the basis of affidavits, if uncontroverted, setting forth such facts as would be admissible in evidence; otherwise, the parties shall submit evidence. The court may make all such orders including orders concerning the care, preservation or disposition of the property (or the proceeds therefrom if the same has been sold), as justice may require. If the movant has given a replevy bond, an order to vacate or dissolve the writ shall vacate the replevy bond and discharge the sureties thereon, and if the court modifies its order or the writ issued pursuant thereto, it shall make such further orders with respect to the bond as may be consistent with its modification.

RULE 665. ANSWER TO WRIT

The answer of the garnishee shall be under oath, in writing and signed by him, and shall make true answers to the several matters inquired of in the writ of garnishment.

RULE 666. GARNISHEE DISCHARGED

If it appears from the answer of the garnishee that he is not indebted to the defendant, and was not so indebted when the writ of garnishment was served upon him, and that he has not in his possession any effects of the defendant and had not when the writ was served, and if he has either denied that any other persons within his knowledge are indebted to the defendant or have in their possession effects belonging to the defendant, or else has named such persons, should the answer of the garnishee not be controverted as hereinafter provided, the court shall enter judgment discharging the garnishee.

RULE 667. JUDGMENT BY DEFAULT

If the garnishee fails to file an answer to the writ of garnishment at or before the time directed in the writ, it shall be lawful for the court, at any time after judgment shall have been rendered against the defendant, and on or after appearance day, to render judgment by default, as in other civil cases, against such garnishee for the full amount of such judgment against the defendant together with all interest and costs that may have accrued in the main case and also in the garnishment proceedings. The answer of the garnishee may be filed as in any other civil case at any time before such default judgment is rendered.

RULE 668. JUDGMENT WHEN GARNISHEE IS INDEBTED

Should it appear from the answer of the garnishee or should it be otherwise made to appear and be found by the court that the garnishee is indebted to the defendant in any amount, or was so indebted when the writ of garnishment was served, the court shall render judgment for the plaintiff against the garnishee for the amount so admitted or found to be due to the defendant from the garnishee, unless such amount is in excess of the amount of the plaintiff's judgment against the defendant with interest and costs, in which case, judgment shall be rendered against the garnishee for the full amount of the judgment already rendered against the defendant, together with interest and costs of the suit in the original case and also in the garnishment proceedings. If the garnishee fail or refuse to pay such judgment rendered against him, execution shall issue thereon in the same manner and under the same conditions as is or may be provided for the issuance of execution in other cases.

RULE 669. JUDGMENT FOR EFFECTS

Should it appear from the garnishee's answer, or otherwise, that the garnishee has in his possession, or had when the writ was served, any effects of the defendant liable to execution, including any certificates of stock in any corporation or joint stock company, the court shall render a decree ordering sale of such effects under execution in satisfaction of plaintiff's judgment and directing the garnishee to deliver them, or so much thereof as shall be necessary to satisfy plaintiff's judgment, to the proper officer for that purpose.

RULE 670. REFUSAL TO DELIVER EFFECTS

Should the garnishee adjudged to have effects of the defendant in his possession, as provided in the preceding rule, fail or refuse to deliver them to the sheriff or constable on such demand, the officer shall immediately make return of such failure or refusal, whereupon on motion of the plaintiff, the garnishee shall be cited to show cause upon a date to be fixed by the court why he should not be attached for contempt of court for such failure or refusal. If the garnishee fails to show some good and sufficient excuse for such failure or refusal, he shall be fined for such contempt and imprisoned until he shall deliver such effects.

[RULE 671. Repealed effective December 31, 1947]

RULE 672. SALE OF EFFECTS

The sale so ordered shall be conducted in all respects as other sales of personal property under execution; and the officer making such sale shall execute a transfer of such effects or interest to the purchaser, with a brief recital of the judgment of the court under which the same was sold.

RULE 673. MAY TRAVERSE ANSWER

If the plaintiff should not be satisfied with the answer of any garnishee, he may controvert the same by his affidavit stating that he has good reason to believe, and does believe, that the answer of the garnishee is incorrect, stating in what particular he believes the same to be incorrect. The defendant may also, in like manner, controvert the answer of the garnishee.

RULE 674. TRIAL OF ISSUE

If the garnishee whose answer is controverted, is a resident of the county in which the proceeding is pending, an issue shall be formed under the direction of the court and tried as in other cases.

RULE 675. DOCKET AND NOTICE

The clerk of the court or the justice of the peace, on receiving certified copies filed in the county of the garnishee's residence under the provisions of the statutes, shall docket the case in the name of the plaintiff as plaintiff, and of the garnishee as defendant, and issue a notice to the garnishee, stating that his answer has been so controverted, and that such issue will stand for trial on the docket of such court. Such notice shall be directed to the garnishee, be dated and tested as other process from such court, and served by delivering a copy thereof to the garnishee. It shall be returnable, if issued from the district or county court, at ten o'clock a.m. of the Monday next after the expiration of twenty days from the date of its service; and if issued from the justice court, to the next term of such court convening after the expiration of twenty days after the service of such notice.

RULE 676. ISSUE TRIED IN OTHER CASES

Upon the return of such notice served, an issue shall be formed under the direction of the court and tried as in other cases.

RULE 677. COSTS

Where the garnishee is discharged upon his answer, the costs of the proceeding, including a reasonable compensation to the garnishee, shall be taxed against the plaintiff; where the answer of the garnishee has not been controverted and the garnishee is held thereon, such costs shall be taxed against the defendant and included in the execution provided for in this section; where the answer is contested, the costs shall abide the issue of such contest.

RULE 678. GARNISHEE DISCHARGED ON PROOF

It shall be a sufficient answer to any claim of the defendant against the garnishee founded on an indebtedness of such garnishee, or on the possession by him of any effects, for the garnishee to show that such indebtedness has been paid, or such effects, including any certificates of stock in any incorporated or joint stock company, have been delivered to any sheriff or constable as provided for in Rule 669.

RULE 679. AMENDMENT

Clerical errors in the affidavit, bond, or writ of garnishment or the officer's return thereof, may upon application in writing to the judge or justice of the court in which the suit is filed, and after notice to the opponent, be amended in such manner and on such terms as the judge or justice shall authorize by an order entered in the minutes of the court (or noted on the docket of the justice of the peace), provided such amendment appears to the judge or justice to be in furtherance of justice.

SECTION 5. INJUNCTIONS

RULE 680. TEMPORARY RESTRAINING ORDER

No temporary restraining order shall be granted without notice to the adverse party unless it clearly appears from specific facts shown by affidavit or by the verified complaint that immediate and irreparable injury, loss, or damage will result to the applicant before notice can be served and a hearing had thereon. Every temporary restraining order granted without notice shall be endorsed with the date and hour of issuance; shall be filed forthwith in the clerk's office and entered of record; shall define the injury and state why it is irreparable and why the order was granted without notice; and shall expire by its terms within such time after signing, not to exceed fourteen days, as the court fixes, unless within the time so fixed the order, for good cause shown, is extended for a like period or unless the party against whom the order is directed consents that it may be extended for a longer period. The reasons for the extension shall be entered of record. No more than one extension may be granted unless subsequent extensions are unopposed. In case a temporary restraining order is granted without notice, the application for a temporary injunction shall be set down for hearing at the earliest possible date and takes precedence of all matters except older matters of the same character; and when the application comes on for hearing the party who obtained the temporary restraining order shall proceed with the application for a temporary injunction and, if he does not do so, the court shall dissolve the temporary restraining order. On two days' notice to the party who obtained the temporary restraining order without notice or on such shorter notice to that party as the court may prescribe, the adverse party may appear and move its dissolution or modification and in that event the court shall proceed to hear and determine such motion as expeditiously as the ends of justice require.

Every restraining order shall include an order setting a certain date for hearing on the temporary or permanent injunction sought.

RULE 681. TEMPORARY INJUNCTIONS: NOTICE

No temporary injunction shall be issued without notice to the adverse party.

RULE 682. SWORN PETITION

No writ of injunction shall be granted unless the applicant therefor shall present his petition to the judge verified by his affidavit and containing a plain and intelligible statement of the grounds for such relief.

RULE 683. FORM AND SCOPE OF INJUNCTION OR RESTRAINING ORDER

Every order granting an injunction and every restraining order shall set forth the reasons for its issuance; shall be specific in terms; shall describe in reasonable detail and not by reference to the complaint or other document, the act or acts sought to be restrained; and is binding only upon the parties to the action, their officers, agents, servants, employees, and attorneys, and upon those persons in active concert or participation with them who receive actual notice of the order by personal service or otherwise.

Every order granting a temporary injunction shall include an order setting the cause for trial on the merits with respect to the ultimate relief sought. The appeal of a temporary injunction shall constitute no cause for delay of the trial.

RULE 684. APPLICANT'S BOND

In the order granting any temporary restraining order or temporary injunction, the court shall fix the amount of security to be given by the applicant. Before the issuance of the temporary restraining order or temporary injunction the applicant shall execute and file with the clerk a bond to the adverse party, with two or more good and sufficient sureties, to be approved by the clerk, in the sum fixed by the judge, conditioned that the applicant will abide the decision which may be made in the cause, and that he will pay all sums of money and costs that may be adjudged against him if the restraining order or temporary injunction shall be dissolved in whole or in part.

Where the temporary restraining order or temporary injunction is against the State, a municipality, a State agency, or a subdivision of the State in its governmental capacity, and is such that the State, municipality, State agency, or subdivision of the State in its governmental capacity, has no pecuniary interest in the suit and no monetary damages can be shown, the bond shall be allowed in the sum fixed by the judge, and the liability of the applicant shall be for its face amount if the restraining order or temporary injunction shall be dissolved in whole or in part. The discretion of the trial court in fixing the amount of the bond shall be subject to review. Provided that under equitable circumstances and for good cause shown by affidavit or otherwise the court rendering judgment on the bond may allow recovery for less than its full face amount, the action of the court to be subject to review.

RULE 685. FILING AND DOCKETING

Upon the grant of a temporary restraining order or an order fixing a time for hearing upon an application for a temporary injunction, the party to whom the same is granted shall file his petition therefor, together with the order of the judge, with the clerk of the proper court; and, if such orders do not pertain to a pending suit in said court, the cause shall be entered on the docket of the court in its regular order in the name of the party applying for the writ as plaintiff and of the opposite party as defendant.

RULE 686. CITATION

Upon the filing of such petition and order not pertaining to a suit pending in the court, the clerk of such court shall issue a citation to the defendant as in other civil cases, which shall be served and returned in like manner as ordinary citations issued from said court; provided, however, that when a temporary restraining order is issued and is accompanied with a true copy of plaintiff's petition, it shall not be necessary for the citation in the original suit to be accompanied with a copy of plaintiff's petition, nor contain a statement of the nature of plaintiff's demand, but it shall be sufficient for said citation to refer to plaintiff's claim as set forth in a true copy of plaintiff's petition which accompanies the temporary restraining order; and provided further that the court may have a hearing upon an application for a temporary restraining order or temporary injunction at such time and upon such reasonable notice given in such manner as the court may direct.

RULE 687. REQUISITES OF WRIT

The writ of injunction shall be sufficient if it contains substantially the following requisites:

(a) Its style shall be, "The State of Texas."

(b) It shall be directed to the person or persons enjoined.

(c) It must state the names of the parties to the proceedings, plaintiff and defendant, and the nature of the plaintiff's application, with the action of the judge thereon.

(d) It must command the person or persons to whom it is directed to desist and refrain from the commission or continuance of the act enjoined, or to obey and execute such order as the judge has seen proper to make.

(e) If it is a temporary restraining order, it shall state the day and time set for hearing, which shall not exceed fourteen days from the date of the court's order granting such temporary restraining order; but if it is a temporary injunction, issued after notice, it shall be made returnable at or before ten o'clock a.m. of the Monday next after the expiration of twenty days from the date of service thereof, as in the case of ordinary citations.

(f) It shall be dated and signed by the clerk officially and attested with the seal of his office and the date of its issuance must be indorsed thereon.

RULE 688. CLERK TO ISSUE WRIT

When the petition, order of the judge and bond have been filed, the clerk shall issue the temporary restraining order or temporary injunction, as the case may be, in conformity with the terms of the order, and deliver the same to the sheriff or any constable of the county of the residence of the person enjoined, or to the applicant, as the latter shall direct. If several persons are enjoined, residing in different counties, the clerk shall issue such additional copies of the writ as shall be requested by the applicant. The clerk must retain a copy of the temporary restraining order or temporary injunction in the court's file.

RULE 689. SERVICE AND RETURN

The officer receiving a writ of injunction shall indorse thereon the date of its receipt by him, and shall forthwith execute the same by delivering to the party enjoined a true copy thereof. The officer must complete and file a return in accordance with Rule 107.

RULE 690. THE ANSWER

The defendant to an injunction proceeding may answer as in other civil actions; but no injunction shall be dissolved before final hearing because of the denial of the material allegations of the plaintiff's petition, unless the answer denying the same is verified by the oath of the defendant.

RULE 691. BOND ON DISSOLUTION

Upon the dissolution of an injunction restraining the collection of money, by an interlocutory order of the court or judge, made in term time or vacation, if the petition be continued over for trial, the court or judge shall require of the defendant in such injunction proceedings a bond, with two or more good and sufficient sureties, to be approved by the clerk of the court, payable to the complainant in double the amount of the sum enjoined, and conditioned to refund to the complainant the amount of money, interest and costs which may be collected of him in the suit or proceeding enjoined if such injunction is made perpetual on final hearing. If such injunction is so perpetuated, the court, on motion of the complainant, may enter judgment against the principal and sureties in such bond for such amount as may be shown to have been collected from such defendant.

RULE 692. DISOBEDIENCE

Disobedience of an injunction may be punished by the court or judge, in term time or in vacation, as a contempt. In case of such disobedience, the complainant, his agent or attorney, may file in the court in which such injunction is pending or with the judge in vacation, his affidavit stating what person is guilty of such disobedience and describing the acts constituting the same; and thereupon the court or judge shall cause to be issued an attachment for such person, directed to the sheriff or any constable of any county, and requiring such officer to arrest the person therein named if found within his county and have him before the court or judge at the time and place named in such writ; or said court or judge may issue a show cause order, directing and requiring such person to appear on such date as may be designated and show cause why he should not be adjudged in contempt of court. On return of such attachment or show cause order, the judge shall proceed to hear proof; and if satisfied that such person has disobeyed the injunction, either directly or indirectly, may commit such person to jail without bail until he purges himself of such contempt, in such manner and form as the court or judge may direct.

RULE 693. PRINCIPLES OF EQUITY APPLICABLE

The principles, practice and procedure governing courts of equity shall govern proceedings in injunctions when the same are not in conflict with these rules or the provisions of the statutes.

RULE 693a. BOND IN DIVORCE CASE

In a divorce case the court in its discretion may dispense with the necessity of a bond in connection with an ancillary injunction in behalf of one spouse against the other.

SECTION 6. MANDAMUS

RULE 694. NO MANDAMUS WITHOUT NOTICE

No mandamus shall be granted by the district of county court on ex parte hearing, and any peremptory mandamus granted without notice shall be abated on motion.

SECTION 7. RECEIVERS

RULE 695. NO RECEIVER OF IMMOVABLE PROPERTY APPOINTED WITHOUT NOTICE

Except where otherwise provided by statute, no receiver shall be appointed without notice to take charge of property which is fixed and immovable. When an application for appointment of a receiver to take possession of property of this type is filed, the judge or court shall set the same down for hearing and notice of such hearing shall be given to the adverse party by serving notice thereof not less than three days prior to such hearing. If the order finds that the defendant is a nonresident or that his whereabouts is unknown, the notice may be served by affixing the same in a conspicuous manner and place upon the property or if that is impracticable it may be served in such other manner as the court or judge may require.

RULE 695a. BOND, AND BOND IN DIVORCE CASES

No receiver shall be appointed with authority to take charge of property until the party applying therefor has filed with the clerk of the court a good and sufficient bond, to be approved by such clerk, payable to the defendant in the amount fixed by the court, conditioned for the payment of all damages and costs in such suit, in case it should be decided that such receiver was wrongfully appointed to take charge of such property. The amount of such bond shall be fixed at a sum sufficient to cover all such probable damages and costs. In a divorce case the court or judge, as a matter of discretion, may dispense with the necessity of a bond.

SECTION 8. SEQUESTRATION

RULE 696. APPLICATION FOR WRIT OF SEQUESTRATION AND ORDER

Either at the commencement of a suit or at any time during its progress the plaintiff may file an application for a writ of sequestration. The application shall be supported by affidavits of the plaintiff, his agent, his attorney, or other persons having knowledge of relevant facts. The application shall comply with all statutory requirements and shall state the grounds for issuing the writ, including the description of the property to be sequestered with such certainty that it may be identified and distinguished from property of a like kind, giving the value of each article of the property and the county in which it is located, and the specific facts relied upon by the plaintiff to warrant the required findings by the court. The writ shall not be quashed because two or more grounds are stated conjunctively or disjunctively. The application and any affidavits shall be made on personal knowledge and shall set forth such facts as would be admissible in evidence; provided that facts may be stated based upon information and belief if the grounds of such belief are specifically stated.

No writ shall issue except upon written order of the court after a hearing, which may be ex parte. The court, in its order granting the application, shall make specific findings of facts to support the statutory grounds found to exist, and shall describe the property to be sequestered with such certainty that it may be identified and distinguished from property of a like kind, giving the value of each article of the property and the county in which it is located. Such order shall further specify the amount of bond required of plaintiff which shall be in an amount which, in the opinion of the court, shall adequately compensate defendant in the event plaintiff fails to prosecute his suit to effect and pay all damages and costs as shall be adjudged against him for wrongfully suing out the writ of sequestration including the elements of damages stated in Sections 62.044 and 62.045, Civil Practice and Remedies Code. The court shall further find in its order the amount of bond required of defendant to replevy, which shall be in an amount equivalent to the value of the property sequestered or to the amount of plaintiff's claim and one year's accrual of interest if allowed by law on the claim, whichever is the lesser amount, and the estimated costs of court. The order may direct the issuance of several writs at the same time, or in succession, to be sent to different counties.

RULE 697. PETITION

If the suit be in the district or county court, no writ of sequestration shall issue, unless a petition shall have been first filed therein, as in other suits in said courts.

RULE 698. BOND FOR SEQUESTRATION

No writ of sequestration shall issue until the party applying therefor has filed with the officer authorized to issue such writ a bond payable to the defendant in the amount fixed by the court's order, with sufficient surety or sureties as provided by statute to be approved by such officer, conditioned that the plaintiff will prosecute his suit to effect and pay to the extent of the penal amount of the bond all damages and costs as may be adjudged against him for wrongfully suing out such writ of sequestration, and plaintiff may further condition the bond pursuant to the provisions of Rule 708, in which case he shall not be required to give additional bond to replevy unless so ordered by the court.

After notice to the opposite party, either before or after the issuance of the writ, the defendant or plaintiff may file a motion to increase or reduce the amount of such bond, or to question the sufficiency of the sureties thereon, in the court in which such suit is pending. Upon hearing, the court shall enter its order with respect to such bond and sufficiency of the sureties as justice may require.

RULE 699. REQUISITES OF WRIT

The writ of sequestration shall be directed "To the Sheriff or any Constable within the State of Texas" (not naming a specific county) and shall command him to take into his possession the property, describing the same as it is described in the application or affidavits, if to be found in his county, and to keep the same subject to further orders of the court, unless the same is replevied. There shall be prominently displayed on the face of the writ, in ten -point type and in a manner calculated to advise a reasonably attentive person of its contents, the following:

> "YOU HAVE A RIGHT TO REGAIN POSSESSION OF THE PROPERTY BY FILING A REPLEVY BOND. YOU HAVE A RIGHT TO SEEK TO REGAIN POSSESSION OF THE PROPERTY BY FILING WITH THE COURT A MOTION TO DISSOLVE THIS WRIT."

RULE 700. AMENDMENT

Clerical errors in the affidavit, bond, or writ of sequestration or the officer's return thereof may upon application in writing to the judge of the court in which the suit is filed and after notice to the opponent, be amended in such manner and on such terms as the judge shall authorize by an order entered in the minutes of the court, provided the amendment does not change or add to the grounds of such sequestration as stated in the affidavit, and provided such amendment appears to the judge to be in furtherance of justice.

RULE 700a. SERVICE OF WRIT ON DEFENDANT

The defendant shall be served in any manner provided for service of citation or as provided in Rule 21a, with a copy of the writ of sequestration, the application, accompanying affidavits, and orders of the court as soon as practicable following the levy of the writ. There shall also be prominently displayed on the face of the copy of the writ served on defendant, in ten-point type and in a manner calculated to advise a reasonably attentive person of its contents, the following:

> "To _____, Defendant:

> "You are hereby notified that certain properties alleged to be claimed by you have been sequestered. If you claim any rights in such property, you are advised:

"YOU HAVE A RIGHT TO REGAIN POSSESSION OF THE PROPERTY BY FILING A REPLEVY BOND. YOU HAVE A RIGHT TO SEEK TO REGAIN POSSESSION OF THE PROPERTY BY FILING WITH THE COURT A MOTION TO DISSOLVE THIS WRIT."

RULE 701. DEFENDANT MAY REPLEVY

At any time before judgment, should the sequestered property not have been previously claimed, replevied, or sold, the defendant may replevy the same, or any part thereof, or the proceeds from the sale of the property if it has been sold under order of the court, by giving bond, with sufficient surety or sureties as provided by statute, to be approved by the officer who levied the writ, payable to plaintiff in the amount fixed by the court's order, conditioned as provided in Rule 702 or Rule 703.

On reasonable notice to the opposing party (which may be less than three days) either party shall have the right to prompt judicial review of the amount of bond required, denial of bond, sufficiency of sureties, and estimated value of the property, by the court which authorized issuance of the writ. The court's determination may be made upon the basis of affidavits, if uncontroverted, setting forth such facts as would be admissible in evidence; otherwise, the parties shall submit evidence. The court shall forthwith enter its order either approving or modifying the requirements of the officer or of the court's prior order, and such order of the court shall supersede and control with respect to such matters.

RULE 702. BOND FOR PERSONAL PROPERTY

If the property to be replevied be personal property, the condition of the bond shall be that the defendant will not remove the same out of the county, or that he will not waste, ill-treat, injure, destroy, or dispose of the same, according to the plaintiff's affidavit, and that he will have such property, in the same condition as when it is replevied, together with the value of the fruits, hire or revenue thereof, forthcoming to abide the decision of the court, or that he will pay the value thereof, or the difference between its value at the time of replevy and the time of judgment and of the fruits, hire or revenue of the same in case he shall be condemned to do so.

RULE 703. BOND FOR REAL ESTATE

If the property be real estate, the condition of such bond shall be that the defendant will not injure the property, and that he will pay the value of the rents of the same in case he shall be condemned so to do.

RULE 704. RETURN OF BOND AND ENTRY OF JUDGMENT

The bond provided for in the three preceding rules shall be returned with the writ to the court from whence the writ issued. In case the suit is decided against the defendant, final judgment shall be rendered against all the obligors in such bond, jointly and severally, for the value of the property replevied as of the date of the execution of the replevy bond, and the value of the fruits, hire, revenue, or rent thereof, as the case may be.

RULE 705. DEFENDANT MAY RETURN SEQUESTERED PROPERTY

Within ten days after final judgment for personal property the defendant may deliver to the plaintiff, or to the officer who levied the sequestration or to his successor in office the personal property in question, and such officer shall deliver same to plaintiff upon his demand therefor; or such defendant shall deliver such property to the officer demanding same under execution issued therefor upon a judgment for the title or possession of the same; and such officer shall receipt the defendant for such property; provided, however, that such delivery to the plaintiff or to such officer shall be without prejudice to any rights of the plaintiff under the replevy bond given by the defendant. Where a mortgage or other lien of any kind is foreclosed upon personal property sequestered and replevied, the defendant shall deliver such property to the officer calling for same under order of sale issued upon a judgment foreclosing such mortgage or other lien, either in the county of defendant's residence or in the county where sequestered, as demanded by such officer; provided, however, that such delivery by the defendant shall be without prejudice to any rights of the plaintiff under the replevy bond given by the defendant.

RULE 706. DISPOSITION OF THE PROPERTY BY OFFICER

When the property is tendered back by the defendant to the officer who sequestered the same or to the officer calling for same under an order of sale, such officer shall receive said property and hold or dispose of the same as ordered by the court; provided, however, that such return to and receipt of same by the officer and any sale or disposition of said property by the officer under order or judgment of the court shall not affect or limit any rights of the plaintiff under the bond provided for in Rule 702.

RULE 707. EXECUTION

If the property be not returned and received, as provided in the two preceding rules, execution shall issue upon said judgment for the amount due thereon, as in other cases.

RULE 708. PLAINTIFF MAY REPLEVY

When the defendant fails to replevy the property within ten days after the levy of the writ and service of notice on defendant, the officer having the property in possession shall at any time thereafter and before final judgment, deliver the same to the plaintiff upon his giving bond payable to defendant in a sum of money not less than the amount fixed by the court's order, with sufficient surety or sureties as provided by statute to be approved by such officer. If the property to be replevied be personal property, the condition of the bond shall be that he will have such property, in the same condition as when it is replevied, together with the value of the fruits, hire or revenue thereof, forthcoming to abide the decision of the court, or that he will pay the value thereof, or the difference between its value at the time of replevy and the time of judgment (regardless of the cause of such difference in value, and of the fruits, hire or revenue of the same in case he shall be condemned to do so). If the property be real estate, the condition of such bond shall be that the plaintiff will not injure the property, and that he will pay the value of the rents of the same in case he shall be condemned to do so.

On reasonable notice to the opposing party (which may be less than three days) either party shall have the right to prompt judicial review of the amount of bond required, denial of bond, sufficiency of sureties, and estimated value of the property, by the court which authorized issuance of the writ. The court's determination may be made upon the basis of affidavits, if uncontroverted, setting forth such facts as would be admissible in evidence; otherwise, the parties shall submit evidence. The court shall forthwith enter its order either approving or modifying the requirements of the officer or of the court's prior order, and such order of the court shall supersede and control with respect to such matters.

RULE 709. WHEN BOND FORFEITED

The bond provided for in the preceding rule shall be returned by the officer to the court issuing the writ immediately after he has approved same, and in case the suit is decided against the plaintiff, final judgment shall be entered against all the obligors in such bond, jointly and severally for the value of the property replevied as of the date of the execution of the replevy bond, and the value of the fruits, hire, revenue or rent thereof as the case may be. The same rules which govern the discharge or enforcement of a judgment against the obligors in the defendant's replevy bond shall be applicable to and govern in case of a judgment against the obligors in the plaintiff's replevy bond.

RULE 710. SALE OF PERISHABLE GOODS

If after the expiration of ten days from the levy of a writ of sequestration the defendant has failed to replevy the same, if the plaintiff or defendant shall make affidavit in writing that the property levied upon, or any portion thereof, is likely to be wasted or destroyed or greatly depreciated in value by keeping, and if the officer having possession of such property shall certify to the truth of such affidavit, it shall be the duty of the judge or justice of the peace to whose court the writ is returnable, upon the presentation of such affidavit and certificate, either in term time or vacation, to order the sale of said property or so much thereof as is likely to be so wasted, destroyed or depreciated in value by keeping, but either party may replevy the property at any time before such sale.

RULE 711. ORDER OF SALE FOR

The judge or justice granting the order provided for in the preceding rule shall issue an order directed to the officer having such property in possession, commending such officer to sell such property in the same manner as under execution.

RULE 712. RETURN OF ORDER

The officer making such sale shall, within five days thereafter, return the order of sale to the court from whence the same issued, with his proceedings thereon, and shall, at the time of making such return, pay over to the clerk or justice of the peace the proceeds of such sale.

RULE 712a. DISSOLUTION OR MODIFICATION OF WRIT OF SEQUESTRATION

A defendant whose property has been sequestered or any intervening party who claims an interest in such property, may by sworn written motion, seek to vacate, dissolve, or modify the writ and the order directing its issuance, for any grounds or cause, extrinsic or intrinsic, including a motion to reduce the amount of property sequestered when the total amount described and authorized by such order exceeds the amount necessary to secure the plaintiff's claim, one year's interest if allowed by law on the claim, and costs. Such motion shall admit or deny each finding of the order directing the issuance of the writ except where the movant is unable to admit or deny the finding, in which case movant shall set forth the reasons why he cannot admit or deny. Unless the parties agree to an extension of time, the motion shall be heard promptly, after reasonable notice to the plaintiff (which may be less than three days), and the issue shall be determined not later than ten days after the motion is filed. The filing of the motion shall stay any further proceedings under the writ, except for any orders concerning the care, preservation, or sale of any perishable property, until a hearing is had, and the issue is determined. The writ shall be dissolved unless, at such hearing, the plaintiff shall prove the grounds relied upon for its issuance, but the court may modify its previous order granting the writ and the writ issued pursuant thereto. The movant shall, however, have the burden to prove that the reasonable value of the property sequestered exceeds the amount necessary to secure the debt, interest for one year, and probable costs.

The court's determination may be made upon the basis of affidavits, if uncontroverted, setting forth such facts as would be admissible in evidence; otherwise, the parties shall submit evidence. The court may make all such orders, including orders concerning the care, preservation, or disposition of the property (or the proceeds therefrom if the same has been sold) as justice may require. If the movant has given a replevy bond, an order to vacate or dissolve the writ shall vacate the replevy bond and discharge the sureties thereon, and if the court modifies its order or the writ issued pursuant thereto, it shall make such further orders with respect to the bond as may be consistent with its modification.

RULE 713. SALE ON DEBT NOT DUE

If the suit in which the sequestration issued be for a debt or demand not yet due, and the property sequestered be likely to be wasted, destroyed or greatly depreciated in value by keeping, the judge or justice of the peace shall, under the regulations hereinbefore provided, order the same to be sold, giving credit on such sale until such debt or demand shall become due.

RULE 714. PURCHASER'S BOND

In the case of a sale as provided for in the preceding rule, the purchaser of the property shall execute his bond, with two or more good and sufficient sureties, to be approved by the officer making the sale, and payable to such officer, in a sum not less than double the amount of the purchase money, conditioned that such purchaser shall pay such purchase money at the expiration of the time given.

RULE 715. RETURN OF BOND

The bond provided for in the preceding rule shall be returned by the officer taking the same to the clerk or justice of the peace from whose court the order of sale issued, with such order, and shall be filed among the papers in the cause.

RULE 716. RECOVERY ON BOND

In case the purchaser does not pay the purchase money at the expiration of the time given, judgment shall be rendered against all the obligors in such bond for the amount of such purchase money, interest thereon and all costs incurred in the enforcement and collection of the same; and execution shall issue thereon in the name of the plaintiff in the suit, as in other cases, and the money when collected shall be paid to the clerk or justice of the peace to abide the final decision of the cause.

SECTION 9. TRIAL OF RIGHT OF PROPERTY

RULE 717. CLAIMANT MUST MAKE AFFIDAVIT

Whenever a distress warrant, writ of execution, sequestration, attachment, or other like writ is levied upon personal property, and such property, or any part thereof, shall be claimed by any claimant who is not a party to such writ, such claimant may make application that such claim is made in good faith, and file such application with the court in which such suit is pending. Such application may be supported by affidavits of the claimant, his agent, his attorney, or other persons having knowledge of relevant facts. The application shall comply with all statutory requirements and shall state the grounds for such claim and the specific facts relied upon by the claimant to warrant the required findings by the court.

The claim shall not be quashed because two or more grounds are stated conjunctively or disjunctively. The application and any affidavits shall be made on personal knowledge and shall set forth such facts as would be admissible in evidence; provided that facts may be stated based upon information and belief if the grounds of such belief are specifically stated.

No property shall be delivered to the claimant except on written order of the court after a hearing pursuant to Rule 718. The court in its order granting the application shall make specific findings of facts to support the statutory grounds found to exist and shall specify the amount of the bond required of the claimant.

RULE 718. PROPERTY DELIVERED TO CLAIMANT

Any claimant who claims an interest in property on which a writ has been levied may, by sworn written motion, seek to obtain possession of such property. Such motion shall admit or deny each finding of the order directing the issuance of the writ except where the claimant is unable to admit or deny the finding, in which case claimant shall set forth the reasons why he cannot admit or deny. Such motion shall also contain the reasons why the claimant has superior right or title to the property claimed as against the plaintiff in the writ. Unless the parties agree to an extension of time, the motion shall be heard promptly, after reasonable notice to the plaintiff (which may be less than three days), and the issue shall be determined not later than 10 days after the motion is filed. The filing of the motion shall stay any further proceedings under the writ, except for any orders concerning the care, preservation, or sale of any perishable property, until a hearing is had, and the issue is determined. The claimant shall have the burden to show superior right or title to the property claimed as against the plaintiff and defendant in the writ.

The court's determination may be made upon the basis of affidavits, if uncontroverted, setting forth such facts as would be admissible in evidence, but additional evidence, if tendered by either party shall be received and considered. The court may make all such orders, including orders concerning the care, preservation, or disposition of the property, or the proceeds therefrom if the same has been sold, as justice may require, and if the court modifies its order or the writ issued pursuant thereto, it shall make such further orders with respect to the bond as may be consistent with its modification.

RULE 719. BOND

No property shall be put in the custody of the claimant until the claimant has filed with the officer who made the levy, a bond in an amount fixed by the court's order equal to double the value of the property so claimed, payable to the plaintiff in the writ, with sufficient surety or sureties as provided by statute to be approved by such officer, conditioned that the claimant will return the same to the officer making the levy, or his successor, in as good condition as he received it, and shall also pay the reasonable value of the use, hire, increase and fruits thereof from the date of said bond, or, in case he fails so to return said property and pay for the use of the same, that he shall pay the plaintiff the value of said property, with legal interest thereon from the date of the bond, and shall also pay all damages and costs that may be awarded against him for wrongfully suing out such claim.

The plaintiff or claimant may file a motion to increase or reduce the amount of such bond, or to question the sufficiency of the sureties thereon, in the court in which such suit is pending. Upon hearing, the court shall enter its order with respect to such bond and sufficiency of the sureties.

RULE 720. RETURN OF BOND

Whenever any person shall claim property and shall duly make the application and give the bond, if the writ under which the levy was made was issued by a justice of the peace or a court of the county where such levy was made, the officer receiving such application and bond shall endorse on the writ that such claim has been made and application and bond given, and by whom; and shall also endorse on such bond the value of the property as assessed by himself, and shall forthwith return such bond with a copy of the writ to the proper court having jurisdiction to try such claim.

RULE 721. OUT-COUNTY LEVY

Whenever any person shall claim property and shall make the application and give the bond as provided for herein, if the writ under which such levy was made was issued by a justice of the peace or a court of another county than that in which such levy was made, then the officer receiving such bond shall endorse on such bond the value of the property as assessed by himself, and shall forthwith return such bond with a copy of the writ, to the property court having jurisdiction to try such claim.

RULE 722. RETURN OF ORIGINAL WRIT

The officer taking such bond shall also endorse on the original writ, if in his possession, that such claim has been made and application and bond given, stating by whom, the names of the surety or sureties, and to what justice or court the bond has been returned; and he shall forthwith return such original writ to the tribunal from which it issued.

RULE 723. DOCKETING CAUSE

Whenever any bond for the trial of the right of property shall be returned, the clerk of the court, or such justice of the peace, shall docket the same in the original writ proceeding in the name of the plaintiff in the writ as the plaintiff, and the claimant of the property as intervening claimant.

RULE 724. ISSUE MADE UP

After the claim proceedings have been docketed, and on the hearing day set by the court, then the court, or the justice of the peace, as the case may be, shall enter an order directing the making and joinder of issues by the parties. Such issues shall be in writing and signed by each party or his attorney. The plaintiff shall make a brief statement of the authority and right by which he seeks to subject the property levied on to the process, and it shall be sufficient for the claimant and other parties to make brief statements of the nature of their claims thereto.

RULE 725. JUDGMENT BY DEFAULT

If the plaintiff appears and the claimant fails to appear or neglects or refuses to join issue under the direction of the court or justice within the time prescribed for pleading, the plaintiff shall have judgment by default.

RULE 726. JUDGMENT OF NON-SUIT

If the plaintiff does not appear, he shall be non-suited.

RULE 727. PROCEEDINGS

The proceedings and practice on the trial shall be as nearly as may be the same as in other cases before such court or justice.

RULE 728. BURDEN OF PROOF

If the property was taken from the possession of the claimant pursuant to the original writ, the burden of proof shall be on the plaintiff in the writ. If it was taken from the possession of the defendant in such writ, or any other person than the claimant, the burden of proof shall be on the claimant.

RULE 729. COPY OF WRIT EVIDENCE

In all trials of the right of property, under the provisions of this section in any county other than that in which the writ issued under which the levy was made, the copy of the writ herein required to be returned by the officer making the levy shall be received in evidence in like manner as the original could be.

RULE 730. FAILURE TO ESTABLISH TITLE

Where any claimant has obtained possession of property, and shall ultimately fail to establish his right thereto, judgment may be rendered against him and his sureties for the value of the property, with legal interest thereon from the date of such bond. Such judgment shall be rendered in favor of the plaintiff or defendant in the writ, or of the several plaintiffs or defendants, if more than one, and shall fix the amount of the claim of each.

RULE 731. EXECUTION SHALL ISSUE

If such judgment should not be satisfied by a return of the property, then after the expiration of ten days from the date of the judgment, execution shall issue thereon in the name of the plaintiff or defendant for the amount of the claim, or of all the plaintiffs or defendants for the sum of their several claims, provided the amount of such judgment shall inure to the benefit of any person who shall show superior right or title to the property claimed as against the claimant; but if such judgment be for a less amount than the sum of the several plaintiffs' or defendants' claims, then the respective rights and priorities of the several plaintiffs or defendants shall be fixed and adjusted in the judgment.

RULE 732. RETURN OF PROPERTY BY CLAIMANT

If, within ten days from the rendition of said judgment, the claimant shall return such property in as good condition as he received it, and pay for the use of the same together with the damages and costs, such delivery and payment shall operate as a satisfaction of such judgment.

RULE 733. CLAIM IS A RELEASE OF DAMAGES

A claim made to the property, under the provisions of this section, shall operate as a release of all damages by the claimant against the officer who levied upon said property.

RULE 734. LEVY ON OTHER PROPERTY

Proceedings for the trial of right of property under these rules shall in no case prevent the plaintiff in the writ from having a levy made upon any other property of the defendant.

PART VII - RULES RELATING TO SPECIAL PROCEEDINGS

SECTION I. PROCEDURES RELATED TO FORECLOSURES OF CERTAIN LIENS

RULE 735. FORECLOSURES REQUIRING A COURT ORDER

735.1. Liens Affected

Rule 736 provides the procedure for obtaining a court order, when required, to allow foreclosure of a lien containing a power of sale in the security instrument, dedicatory instrument, or declaration creating the lien, including a lien securing any of the following:

(a) a home equity loan, reverse mortgage, or home equity line of credit under article XVI, sections 50(a)(6), 50(k), and 50(t) of the Texas Constitution;

(b) a tax lien transfer or property tax loan under sections 32.06 and 32.065 of the Tax Code; or

(c) a property owners' association assessment under section 209.0092 of the Property Code.

735.2. Other Statutory and Contractual Foreclosure Provisions Unaltered

A Rule 736 order does not alter any foreclosure requirement or duty imposed under applicable law or the terms of the loan agreement, contract, or lien sought to be foreclosed. The only issue to be determined in a Rule 736 proceeding is whether a party may obtain an order under Rule 736 to proceed with foreclosure under applicable law and the terms of the loan agreement, contract, or lien sought to be foreclosed.

735.3. Judicial Foreclosure Unaffected

A Rule 736 order is not a substitute for a judgment for judicial foreclosure, but any loan agreement, contract, or lien that may be foreclosed using Rule 736 procedures may also be foreclosed by judgment in an action for judicial foreclosure.

RULE 736. EXPEDITED ORDER PROCEEDING

736.1. Application

(a) **Where Filed**. An application for an expedited order allowing the foreclosure of a lien listed in Rule 735 to proceed must be filed in a county where all or part of the real property encumbered by the loan agreement, contract, or lien sought to be foreclosed is located or in a probate court with jurisdiction over proceedings involving the property.

(b) **Style**. An application must be styled "In re: Order for Foreclosure Concerning [state: property's mailing address] under Tex. R. Civ. P. 736."

(c) **When Filed**. An application may not be filed until the opportunity to cure has expired under applicable law and the loan agreement, contract, or lien sought to be foreclosed.

(d) **Contents**. The application must:

(1) Identify by name and last known address each of the following parties:

(A) "Petitioner" - any person legally authorized to prosecute the foreclosure;

(B) "Respondent" - according to the records of the holder or servicer of the loan agreement, contract, or lien sought to be foreclosed;

(i) for a home equity loan, reverse mortgage, or home equity line of credit, each person obligated to pay the loan agreement, contract, or lien sought to be foreclosed and each mortgagor, if any, of the loan agreement, contract, or lien sought to be foreclosed;

(ii) for a tax lien transfer or property tax loan, each person obligated to pay the loan agreement, contract, or lien sought to be foreclosed, each mortgagor, if any, of the loan agreement, contract, or lien sought to be foreclosed, each owner of the property, and the holder of any recorded preexisting first lien secured by the property;

(iii) for a property owners' association assessment, each person obligated to pay the loan agreement, contract, or lien sought to be foreclosed who has a current ownership interest in the property.

(2) Identify the property encumbered by the loan agreement, contract, or lien sought to be foreclosed by its commonly known street address and legal description.

(3) Describe or state:

(A) the type of lien listed in Rule 735 sought to be foreclosed and its constitutional or statutory reference;

(B) the authority of the party seeking foreclosure, whether as the servicer, beneficiary, lender, investor, property owners' association, or other person with authority to prosecute the foreclosure;

(C) each person obligated to pay the loan agreement, contract, or lien sought to be foreclosed;

(D) each mortgagor, if any, of the loan agreement, contract, or lien sought to be foreclosed who is not a maker or assumer of the underlying debt;

(E) as of a date that is not more than sixty days prior to the date the application is filed:

(i) if the default is monetary, the number of unpaid scheduled payments,

(ii) if the default is monetary, the amount required to cure the default,

(iii) if the default is non-monetary, the facts creating the default, and

(iv) if applicable, the total amount required to pay off the loan agreement, contract or lien;

(F) that the requisite notice or notices to cure the default has or have been mailed to each person as required under applicable law and the loan agreement, contract, or lien sought to be foreclosed and that the opportunity to cure has expired; and

(G) that before the application was filed, any other action required under applicable law and the loan agreement, contract, or lien sought to be foreclosed was performed.

(4) For a tax lien transfer or property tax loan, state all allegations required to be contained in the application in accordance with section 32.06(c-1)(1) of the Tax Code.

(5) Conspicuously state:

(A) that legal action is not being sought against the occupant of the property unless the occupant is also names as a respondent in the application; and

(B) that if the petitioner obtains a court order, the petitioner will proceed with a foreclosure of the property in accordance with applicable law and the terms of the loan agreement, contract, or lien sought to be foreclosed.

(6) Include an affidavit of material facts in accordance with Rule 166a(f) signed by the petitioner or the servicer describing the basis for foreclosure and, depending on the type of lien sought to be foreclosed, attach a legible copy of:

(A) the note, original recorded lien, or pertinent part of a property owners' association declaration or dedicatory instrument establishing the lien, and current assignment of the lien, if assigned;

(B) each notice required to be mailed to any person under applicable law and the loan agreement, contract, or lien sought to be foreclosed before the application was filed and proof of mailing of each notice; and

(C) for a tax lien transfer or property tax loan:

(i) the property owner's sworn document required under section 32.06(-1) of the Tax Code; and

(ii) the taxing authority's certified statement attesting to the transfer of the lien, required under section 32.06(b) of the Tax Code.

736.2. Costs

All filing, citation, mailing, service, and other court costs and fees are costs of court and must be paid by petitioner at the time of filing an application with the clerk of the court.

736.3. Citation

(a) **Issuance.**

(1) When the application is filed, the clerk must issue a separate citation for each respondent named in the application and one additional citation for the occupant of the property sought to be foreclosed.

(2) Each citation that is directed to a respondent must state that any response to the application is due the first Monday after the expiration of 38 days from the date the citation was placed in the custody of the U.S. Postal Service in accordance with the clerk's standard mailing procedures and state the date that the citation was placed in the custody of the U.S. Postal Service by the clerk.

(b) **Service and Return.**

(1) The clerk of the court must serve each citation, with a copy of the application attached, by both first class mail and certified mail. A citation directed to a respondent must be mailed to the respondent's last known address that is stated in the application. A citation directed to the occupant of the property sought to be foreclosed must be mailed to Occupant of [state: property's mailing address] at the address of the property sought to be foreclosed that is stated in the application.

(2) Concurrently with service, the clerk must complete a return of service in accordance with Rule 107, except that the return of service need not contain a return receipt. For a citation mailed by the clerk in accordance with (b)(1), the date of service is the date and time the citation was placed in the custody of the U.S. Postal Service in a properly addressed, postage prepaid envelope in accordance with the clerk's standard mailing procedures.

(3) The clerk must only charge one fee per respondent or occupant served under this rule.

736.4. Discovery

No discovery is permitted in a Rule 736 proceeding.

736.5. Response

(a) **Generally.** A respondent may file a response contesting the application.

(b) **Due Date.** Any response to the application is due the first Monday after the expiration of 38 days from the date the citation was placed in the custody of the U.S. Postal Service in accordance with the clerk's standard mailing procedures, as stated on the citation.

(c) **Form.** A response must be signed in accordance with Rule 57 and may be in the form of a general denial under Rule 92, except that a respondent must affirmatively plead:

(1) why the respondent believes a respondent did not sign a loan agreement document, if applicable, that is specifically identified by the respondent;

(2) why the respondent is not obligated for payment of the lien;

(3) why the number of months of alleged default or the reinstatement or pay off amounts are materially incorrect;

(4) why any document attached to the application is not a true and correct copy of the original; or

(5) proof of payment in accordance with Rule 95.

(d) **Other Claims**. A response may not state an independent claim for relief. The court must, without a hearing, strike and dismiss any counterclaim, cross claim, third party claim, intervention, or cause of action filed by any person in a Rule 736 proceeding.

736.6. Hearing Required When Response Filed

The court must not conduct a hearing under this rule unless a response is filed. If a response is filed, the court must hold a hearing after reasonable notice to the parties. The hearing on the application must not be held earlier than 20 days or later than 30 days after a request for a hearing is made by any party. At the hearing, the petitioner has the burden to prove by affidavits on file or evidence presented the grounds for granting the order sought in the application.

736.7. Default When No Response Filed

(a) If no response to the application is filed by the due date, the petitioner may file a motion and proposed order to obtain a default order. For the purposes of obtaining a default order, all facts alleged in the application and supported by the affidavit of material facts constitute prima facie evidence of the truth of the matters alleged.

(b) The court must grant the application by default order no later than 30 days after a motion is filed under (a) if the application complies with the requirements of Rule 736.1 and was properly served in accordance with Rule 736.3. The petitioner need not appear in court to obtain a default order.

(c) The return of service must be on file with the clerk of the court for at least 10 days before the court may grant the application by default.

736.8. Order

(a) The court must issue an order granting the application if the petitioner establishes the basis for the foreclosure. Otherwise, the court must deny the application.

(b) An order granting the application must describe:

(1) the material facts establishing the basis for foreclosure;

(2) the property to be foreclosed by commonly known mailing address and legal description;

(3) the name and last known address of each respondent subject to the order; and

(4) the recording or indexing information of each lien to be foreclosed.

(c) An order granting or denying the application is not subject to a motion for rehearing, new trial, bill of review, or appeal. Any challenge to a Rule 736 order must be made in a suit filed in a separate, independent, original proceeding in a court of competent jurisdiction.

736.9. Effect of the Order

An order is without prejudice and has no res judicata, collateral estoppel, estoppel by judgment, or other effect in any other judicial proceeding. After an order is obtained, a person may proceed with the foreclosure process under applicable law and the terms of the lien sought to be foreclosed.

736.10. Bankruptcy

If a respondent provides proof to the clerk of the court that respondent filed bankruptcy before an order is signed, the proceeding under this rule must be abated so long as the automatic stay is effective.

736.11. Automatic Stay and Dismissal if Independent Suit Filed

(a) A proceeding or order under this rule is automatically stayed if a respondent files a separate, original proceeding in a court of competent jurisdiction that puts in issue any matter related to the origination, servicing, or enforcement of the loan agreement, contract, or lien sought to be foreclosed prior to 5:00 p.m. on the Monday before the scheduled foreclosure sale.

(b) Respondent must give prompt notice of the filing of the suit to petitioner or petitioner's attorney and the foreclosure trustee or substitute trustee by any reasonable means necessary to stop the scheduled foreclosure sale.

(c) Within ten days of filing suit, the respondent must file a motion and proposed order to dismiss or vacate with the clerk of the court in which the application was filed giving notice that respondent has filed an original proceeding contesting the right to foreclose in a court of competent jurisdiction. If no order has been signed, the court must dismiss a pending proceeding. If an order has been signed, the court must vacate the Rule 736 order.

(d) If the automatic stay under this rule is in effect, any foreclosure sale of the property is void. Within 10 business days of notice that the foreclosure sale was void, the trustee or substitute trustee must return to the buyer of the foreclosed property the purchase price paid by the buyer.

(e) The court may enforce the Rule 736 process under chapters 9 and 10 of the Civil Practices and Remedies Code.

736.12. Attachment of Order to Trustee's Deed

A conformed copy of the order must be attached to the trustee or substitute trustee's foreclosure deed.

736.13. Promulgated Forms

The Supreme Court of Texas may promulgate forms that conform to this rule.

Comment to 2011 change

Rules 735 and 736 have been rewritten and expanded to cover property owners' associations' assessment liens, in accordance with amendments to chapter 209 of the Property Code. Rule 735.1 makes the expedited procedures of Rule 736 available only when the lienholder has a power of sale but a court order is nevertheless required by law to foreclose the lien. Rule 735.2 makes clear that Rule 736 is procedural only and does not affect other contractual or legal rights or duties. Any lien which can be foreclosed under Rule 736 may also be foreclosed in an action for judicial foreclosure, as Rule 735.3 states, but no lienholder is required to obtain both a Rule 736 order and a judgment for judicial foreclosure. The requirement of conspicuousness in Rule 736.1(d)(5) has reference to section 1.201(b)(10) of the Business and Commerce Code.

[Rules 737-755 Repealed effective August 31, 2013]

SECTION 4. PARTITION OF REAL ESTATE

RULE 756. PETITION

The plaintiff's petition shall state:

(a) The names and residence, if known, of each of the other joint owners, or joint claimants, of such property.

(b) The share or interest which the plaintiff and the other joint owners, or joint claimants, of same own or claim so far as known to the plaintiff.

(c) The land sought to be partitioned shall be so described as that the same may be distinguished from any other and the estimated value thereof stated.

RULE 757. CITATION AND SERVICE

Upon the filing of a petition for partition, the clerk shall issue citation for each of the joint owners, or joint claimants, named therein, as in other cases, and such citations shall be served in the manner and for the time provided for the service of citations in other cases.

RULE 758. WHERE DEFENDANT IS UNKNOWN OR RESIDENCE IS UNKNOWN

If the plaintiff, his agent or attorney, at the commencement of any suit, or during the progress thereof, for the partition of land, shall make affidavit that an undivided portion of the land described in plaintiff's petition in said suit is owned by some person unknown to affiant, or that the place of residence of any known party owning an interest in land sought to be partitioned is unknown to affiant, the Clerk of the Court shall issue citation for publication, conforming to the requirements of Rules 114 and 115, and served in accordance with the directions of Rule 116. In case of unknown residence or party, the affidavit shall include a statement that after due diligence plaintiff and the affiant have been unable to ascertain the name or locate the residence of such party, as the case may be, and in such case it shall be the duty of the court trying the action to inquire into the sufficiency of the diligence so stated before granting any judgment.

RULE 759. JUDGMENT WHERE DEFENDANT CITED BY PUBLICATION

When the defendant has been duly cited by publication in accordance with the preceding rule, and no appearance is entered within the time prescribed for pleadings, the court shall appoint an attorney to defend in behalf of such owner or owners, and proceed as in other causes where service is made by publication. It shall be the special duty of the court in all cases to see that its decree protects the rights of the unknown parties thereto. The judge of the court shall fix the fee of the attorney so appointed, which shall be entered and collected as costs against said unknown owner or owners.

RULE 760. COURT SHALL DETERMINE, WHAT

Upon the hearing of the cause, the court shall determine the share or interest of each of the joint owners or claimants in the real estate sought to be divided, and all questions of law or equity affecting the title to such land which may arise.

RULE 761. APPOINTMENT OF COMMISSIONERS

The court shall determine before entering the decree of partition whether the property, or any part thereof, is susceptible of partition; and, if the court determines that the whole, or any part of such property is susceptible of partition, then the court for that part of such property held to be susceptible of partition shall enter a decree directing the partition of such real estate, describing the same, to be made in accordance with the respective shares or interests of each of such parties entitled thereto, specify in such decree the share or interest of each party, and shall appoint three or more competent and disinterested persons as commissioners to make such partition in accordance with such decree and the law, a majority of which commissioners may act.

RULE 762. WRIT OF PARTITION

The clerk shall issue a writ a partition, directed to the sheriff or any constable of the county, commanding such sheriff or constable to notify each of the commissioners of their appointment as such, and shall accompany such writ with a certified copy of the decree of the court directing the partition.

RULE 763. SERVICE OF WRIT OF PARTITION

The writ of partition shall be served by reading the same to each of the persons named therein as commissioners, and by delivering to any one of them the accompanying certified copy of the decree of the court.

RULE 764. MAY APPOINT SURVEYOR

The court may, should it be deemed necessary, appoint a surveyor to assist the commissioners in making the partition, in which case the writ of partition shall name such surveyor, and shall be served upon him by reading the same to him.

RULE 765. RETURN OF WRIT

A writ of partition, unless otherwise directed by the court, shall be made returnable twenty days from date of service on the commissioner last served; and the officer serving it shall endorse thereon the time and manner of such service.

RULE 766. SHALL PROCEED TO PARTITION

The commissioners, or a majority of them, shall proceed to partition the real estate described in the decree of the court, in accordance with the directions contained in such decree and with the provisions of law and these rules.

RULE 767. MAY CAUSE SURVEY

If the commissioners deem it necessary, they may cause to be surveyed the real estate to be partitioned into several tracts or parcels.

RULE 768. SHALL DIVIDE REAL ESTATE

The commissioners shall divide the real estate to be partitioned into as many shares as there are persons entitled thereto, as determined by the court, each share to contain one or more tracts or parcels, as the commissioners may think proper, having due regard in the division to the situation, quantity and advantages of each share, so that the shares may be equal in value, as nearly as may be, in proportion to the respective interests of the parties entitled. The commissioners shall then proceed by lot to set apart to each of the parties entitled one of said shares, determined by the decrees of the court.

RULE 769. REPORT OF COMMISSIONERS

When the commissioners have completed the partition, they shall report the same in writing and under oath to the court, which report shall show:

(a) The property divided, describing the same.

(b) The several tracts or parcels into which the same was divided by them, describing each particularly.

(c) The number of shares and the land which constitutes each share, and the estimated value of each share.

(d) The allotment of each share.

(e) The report shall be accompanied by such field notes and maps as may be necessary to make the same intelligible.

The clerk shall immediately mail written notice of the filing of the report to all parties.

RULE 770. PROPERTY INCAPABLE OF DIVISION

Should the court be of the opinion that a fair and equitable division of the real estate, or any part thereof, cannot be made, it shall order a sale of so much as is incapable of partition, which sale shall be for cash, or upon such other terms as the court may direct, and shall be made as under execution or by private or public sale through a receiver, if the court so order, and the proceeds thereof shall be returned into court and be partitioned among the persons entitled thereto, according to their respective interests.

RULE 771. OBJECTIONS TO REPORT

Either party to the suit may file objections to any report of the commissioners in partition within thirty days of the date the report is filed, and in such case a trial of the issues thereon shall be had as in other cases. If the report be found to be erroneous in any material respect, or unequal and unjust, the same shall be rejected, and other commissioners shall be appointed by the Court, and the same proceedings had as in the first instance.

SECTION 5. PARTITION OF PERSONAL PROPERTY

RULE 772. PROCEDURE

An action seeking partition of personal property as authorized by Section 23.001, Texas Property Code, shall be commenced in the same manner as other civil suits, and the several owners or claimants of such property shall be cited as in other cases.

RULE 773. VALUE ASCERTAINED

The separate value of each article of such personal property, and the allotment in kind to which each owner is entitled, shall be ascertained by the court, with or without a jury.

RULE 774. DECREE OF COURT EXECUTED

When partition in kind of personal property is ordered by the judgment of the court, a writ shall be issued in accordance with such judgment, commanding the sheriff or constable of the county where the property may be to put the parties forthwith in possession of the property allotted to each respectively.

RULE 775. PROPERTY SOLD

When personal property will not admit of a fair and equitable partition, the court shall ascertain the proportion to which each owner thereof is entitled, and order the property to be sold, and execution shall be issued to the sheriff or any constable of the county where the property may be describing such property and commanding such officer to sell the same as in other cases of execution, and pay over the proceeds of sale to the parties entitled thereto, in the proportion ascertained by the judgment of the court.

SECTION 6. PARTITION: MISCELLANEOUS PROVISIONS

RULE 776. CONSTRUCTION

No provision of the statutes or rules relating to partition shall affect the mode of proceeding prescribed by law for the partition of estates of decedents among the heirs and legatees, nor preclude partition in any other manner authorized by the rules of equity, which rules shall govern in proceedings for partition in all respects not provided for by law or these rules.

RULE 777. PLEADING AND PRACTICE

The same rules of pleading, practice and evidence which govern in other civil actions shall govern in suits for partition, when not in conflict with any provisions of the law or these rules relating to partition.

RULE 778. COSTS

The court shall adjudge the costs in a partition suit to be paid by each party to whom a share has been allotted in proportion to the value of such share.

SECTION 7. QUO WARRANTO

RULE 779. JOINDER OF PARTIES

When it appears to the court or judge that the several rights of divers parties to the same office or franchise may properly be determined on one information, the court or judge may give leave to join all such persons in the same information in order to try their respective rights to such office or franchise.

RULE 780. CITATION TO ISSUE

When such information is filed, the clerk shall issue citation as in civil actions, commanding the defendant to appear and answer the relator in an information in the nature of a quo warranto.

RULE 781. PROCEEDING AS IN CIVIL CASES

Every person or corporation who shall be cited as hereinbefore provided shall be entitled to all the rights in the trial and investigation of the matters alleged against him, as in other cases of trial of civil cases in this State. Either party may prosecute an appeal or writ of error from any judgment rendered, as in other civil cases, subject, however, to the provisions of Rule 42, Texas Rules of Appellate Procedure, and the appellate court shall give preference to such case, and hear and determine the same as early as practicable.

RULE 782. REMEDY CUMULATIVE

The remedy and mode of procedure hereby prescribed shall be construed to be cumulative of any now existing.

Section 8. Trespass to Try Title

RULE 783. REQUISITES OF PETITION

The petition shall state:

(a) The real names of the plaintiff and defendant and their residences, if known.

(b) A description of the premises by metes and bounds, or with sufficient certainty to identify the same, so that from such description possession thereof may be delivered, and state the county or counties in which the same are situated.

(c) The interest which the plaintiff claims in the premises, whether it be a fee simple or other estate; and, if he claims an undivided interest, the petition shall state the same and the amount thereof.

(d) That the plaintiff was in possession of the premises or entitled to such possession.

(e) That the defendant afterward unlawfully entered upon and dispossessed him of such premises, stating the date, and withholds from him the possession thereof.

(f) If rents and profits or damages are claimed, such facts as show the plaintiff to be entitled thereto and the amount thereof.

(g) It shall conclude with a prayer for the relief sought.

RULE 784. THE POSSESSOR SHALL BE DEFENDANT

The defendant in the action shall be the person in possession if the premises are occupied, or some person claiming title thereto in case they are unoccupied.

RULE 785. MAY JOIN AS DEFENDANTS, WHEN

The plaintiff may join as a defendant with the person in possession, any other person who, as landlord, remainderman, reversioner or otherwise, may claim title to the premises, or any part thereof, adversely to the plaintiff.

RULE 786. WARRANTOR, ETC., MAY BE MADE A PARTY

When a party is sued for lands, the real owner or warrantor may make himself, or may be made, a party defendant in the suit, and shall be entitled to make such defense as if he had been the original defendant in the action.

RULE 787. LANDLORD MAY BECOME DEFENDANT

When such action shall be commenced against a tenant in possession, the landlord may enter himself as the defendant, or he may be made a party on motion of such tenant; and he shall be entitled to make the same defense as if the suit had been originally commenced against him.

RULE 788. MAY FILE PLEA OF "NOT GUILTY" ONLY

The defendant in such action may file only the plea of "not guilty," which shall state in substance that he is not guilty of the injury complained of in the petition filed by the plaintiff against him, except that if he claims an allowance for improvements, he shall state the facts entitling him to the same.

RULE 789. PROOF UNDER SUCH PLEA

Under such plea of "not guilty" the defendant may give in evidence any lawful defense to the action except the defense of limitations, which shall be specially pleaded.

RULE 790. ANSWER TAKEN AS ADMITTING POSSESSION

Such plea or any other answer to the merits shall be an admission by the defendant, for the purpose of that action, that he was in possession of the premises sued for, or that he claimed title thereto at the time of commencing the action, unless he states distinctly in his answer the extent of his possession or claim, in which case it shall be an admission to such extent only.

RULE 791. MAY DEMAND ABSTRACT OF TITLE

After answer filed, either party may, by notice in writing, duly served on the opposite party or his attorney of record, not less than ten days before the trial of the cause, demand an abstract in writing of the claim or title to the premises in question upon which he relies.

RULE 792. TIME TO FILE ABSTRACT

Such abstract of title shall be filed with the papers of the cause that within thirty days after the service of the notice, or within such further time that the court on good cause shown may grant; and in default thereof, the court may, after notice and hearing prior to the beginning of trial, order that no written instruments which are evidence of the claim or title of such opposite party be given on trial.

RULE 793. ABSTRACT SHALL STATE, WHAT

The abstract mentioned in the two preceding rules shall state:

(a) The nature of each document or written instrument intended to be used as evidence and its date; or

(b) If a contract or conveyance, its date, the parties thereto and the date of the proof of acknowledgment, and before what officer the same was made; and

(c) Where recorded, stating the book and page of the record.

(d) If not recorded in the county when the trial is had, copies of such instrument, with the names of the subscribing witnesses, shall be included. If such unrecorded instrument be lost or destroyed it shall be sufficient to state the nature of such instrument and its loss or destruction.

RULE 794. AMENDED ABSTRACT

The court may allow either party to file an amended abstract of title, under the same rules, which authorize the amendment of pleadings so far as they are applicable; but in all cases the documentary evidence of title shall at the trial be confined to the matters contained in the abstract of title.

RULE 795. RULES IN OTHER CASES OBSERVED

The trial shall be conducted according to the rules of pleading, practice and evidence in other cases in the district court and conformable to the principles of trial by ejectment, except as otherwise provided by these rules.

RULE 796. SURVEYOR APPOINTED, ETC.

The judge of the court may, either in term time or in vacation, at his own discretion, or on motion of either party to the action appoint a surveyor, who shall survey the premises in controversy pursuant to the order of the court, and report his action under oath to such court. If said report be not rejected for good cause shown, the same shall be admitted as evidence on the trial.

RULE 797. SURVEY UNNECESSARY, WHEN

Where there is no dispute as to the lines or boundaries of the land in controversy, or where the defendant admits that he is in possession of the lands or tenements included in the plaintiff's claim, or title, an order of survey shall be unnecessary.

RULE 798. COMMON SOURCE OF TITLE

It shall not be necessary for the plaintiff to deraign title beyond a common source. Proof of a common source may be made by the plaintiff by certified copies of the deeds showing a chain of title to the defendant emanating from and under such common source. Before any such certified copies shall be read in evidence, they shall be filed with the papers of the suit three days before the trial, and the adverse party served with notice of such filing as in other cases. Such certified copies shall not be evidence of title in the defendant unless offered in evidence by him. The plaintiff may make any legal objection to such certified copies, or the originals thereof, when introduced by the defendant.

RULE 799. JUDGMENT BY DEFAULT

If the defendant, who has been personally served with citation according to law or these rules fails to appear and answer by himself or attorney within the time prescribed by law or these rules for other actions in the district court, then judgment by default may be entered against him and in favor of the plaintiff for the title to the premises, or the possession thereof, or for both, according to the petition, and for all costs, without any proof of title by the plaintiff.

RULE 800. PROOF EX PARTE

If the defendant has been cited only by publication, and fails to appear and answer by himself, or by attorney of his own selection, or if any defendant, having answered, fails to appear by himself or attorney when the case is called for trial on its merits, the plaintiff shall make such proof as will entitle him prima facie to recover, whereupon the proper judgment shall be entered.

RULE 801. WHEN DEFENDANT CLAIMS PART ONLY

Where the defendant claims part of the premises only, the answer shall be equivalent to a disclaimer of the balance.

RULE 802. WHEN PLAINTIFF PROVES PART

Where the defendant claims the whole premises, and the plaintiff shows himself entitled to recover part, the plaintiff shall recover such part and costs.

RULE 803. MAY RECOVER A PART

When there are two or more plaintiffs or defendants any one or more of the plaintiffs may recover against one or more of the defendants the premises, or any part thereof, or any interest therein, or damages, according to the rights of the parties.

RULE 804. THE JUDGMENT

Upon the finding of the jury, or of the court where the case is tried by the court, in favor of the plaintiff for the whole or any part of the premises in controversy, the judgment shall be that the plaintiff recover of the defendant the title or possession, or both, as the case may be, of such premises, describing them, and where he recovers the possession, that he have his writ of possession.

RULE 805. DAMAGES

Where it is alleged and proved that one of the parties is in possession of the premises, the court or jury, if they find for the adverse party, shall assess the damages for the use and occupation of the premises. If special injury to the property be alleged and proved, the damages for such injury shall also be assessed, and the proper judgment shall be entered therefor, on which execution may issue.

RULE 806. CLAIM FOR IMPROVEMENTS

When the defendant or person in possession has claimed an allowance for improvements in accordance with Sections 22.021 - 22.024, Texas Property Code, the claim for use and occupation and damages mentioned in the preceding rule shall be considered and acted on in connection with such claim by the defendant or person in possession.

RULE 807. JUDGMENT WHEN CLAIM FOR IMPROVEMENTS IS MADE

When a claim for improvements is successfully made under Sections 22.021 -22.024, Texas Property Code, the judgment shall recite the estimated value of the premises without the improvements, and shall also include the conditions, stipulations and directions contained in Sections 22.021 - 22.024, Texas Property Code so far as applicable to the case before the court.

RULE 808. THESE RULES SHALL NOT GOVERN, WHEN

Nothing in Sections 22.001 - 22.045, Texas Property Code, shall be so construed as to alter, impair or take away the rights of parties, as arising under the laws in force before the introduction of the common law, but the same shall be decided by the principles of the law under which the same accrued, or by which the same were regulated or in any manner affected.

RULE 809. THESE RULES SHALL NOT GOVERN, WHEN

Nothing in these rules relating to trespass to try title shall be so construed as to alter, impair or take away the rights of parties, as arising under the laws in force before the introduction of the common law, but the same shall be decided by the principles of the law under which the same accrued, or by which the same were regulated or in any manner affected.

SECTION 9. SUITS AGAINST NON-RESIDENTS

RULE 810. REQUISITES OF PLEADINGS

The petition in actions authorized by Section 17.003, Civil Practice and Remedies Code, shall state the real names of the plaintiff and defendant, and shall describe the property involved with sufficient certainty to identify the same, the interest which the plaintiff claims, and such proceedings shall be had in such action as may be necessary to fully settle and determine the question of right or title in and to said property between the parties to said suit, and to decree the title or right of the party entitled thereto; and the court may issue the appropriate order to carry such decree, judgment or order into effect; and whenever such petition has been duly filed and citation thereon has been duly served by publication as required by Rules 114 -116, the plaintiff may, at any time prior to entering the decree by leave of court first had and obtained, file amended and supplemental pleadings that do not subject additional property to said suit without the necessity of reciting the defendants so cited as aforesaid.

RULE 811. SERVICE BY PUBLICATION IN ACTIONS UNDER SECTION 17.003, CIVIL PRACTICE AND REMEDIES CODE

In actions authorized by Section 17.003, Civil Practice and Remedies Code, service on the defendant or defendants may be made by publication as is provided by Rules 114 -116 or by service of notice of the character and in the manner provided by Rule 108.

RULE 812. NO JUDGMENT BY DEFAULT

No judgment by default shall be taken in such case when service has been had by publication, but in such case the facts entitling the plaintiff to judgment shall be exhibited to the court on the trial; and a statement of facts shall be filed as provided by law and these rules in suits against nonresidents of this State served by publication, where no appearance has been made by them.

RULE 813. SUIT TO EXTINGUISH LIEN

If said suit shall be for the extinguishment of a lien or claim for money on said property that may be held by the defendant, the amount thereof, with interest, shall be ascertained by the court; and the same deposited in the registry of the court, subject to the drawn by the parties entitled thereto; but in such case no decree shall be entered until said sum is deposited; which fact shall be noted in said decree.

PART VIII - CLOSING RULES

RULE 814. EFFECTIVE DATE

These rules shall take effect on September 1st, 1941. They shall govern all proceedings in actions brought after they take effect, and also all further proceedings in actions then pending, except to the extent that in the opinion of the court their application in a particular action pending when the rules take effect would not be feasible or would work injustice, in which event the former procedure shall apply. All things properly done under any previously existing rule or statutes prior to the taking effect of these rules shall be treated as valid. Where citation or other process is issued and served in compliance with existing rules or laws prior to the taking effect of these rules, the party upon whom such citation or other process has been served shall have the time provided for under such previously existing rules or laws in which to comply therewith.

RULE 815. SUBSTANTIVE RIGHTS UNAFFECTED

These rules shall not be construed to enlarge or diminish any substantive rights or obligations of any parties to any civil action.

RULE 816. JURISDICTION AND VENUE UNAFFECTED

These rules shall not be construed to extend or limit the jurisdiction of the courts of the State of Texas nor the venue of actions therein.

[RULE 817. Renumbered as Rule 3a effective April 1, 1984]

RULE 818. REFERENCE TO FORMER STATUTES

Wherever any statute or rule refers to any practice or procedure in any law, laws, statute or statutes, or to a title, chapter, section, or article of the statutes, or contains any reference of any such nature, and the matter referred to has been supplanted in whole or in part by these rules, every such reference shall be deemed to be to the pertinent part or parts of these rules.

RULE 819. PROCEDURE CONTINUED

All procedure prescribed by statutes of the State of Texas not specifically listed in the accompanying enumeration of repealed articles shall, insofar as the same is not inconsistent with the provisions of these rules, continue in accordance with the provisions of such statutes as rules of court. In case of inconsistency between the provisions of these rules and any statutory procedure not specifically listed as repealed, these rules shall apply.

RULE 820. WORKERS' COMPENSATION LAW

All portions of the Workers' Compensation Law, Articles 8306--8309-1, Revised Civil Statutes, and amendments thereto, which relate to matters of practice and procedure are hereby adopted and retained in force and effect as rules of court.

RULE 821. PRIOR COURT RULES REPEALED

These rules shall supersede all Court Rules heretofore promulgated for any court; and all of said prior Court Rules are hereby repealed; provided, however, any rules or procedure heretofore adopted by a particular county or district court or by any Court of Appeals which were not of general application but were solely to regulate procedure in the particular court promulgating such rules are to remain in force and effect insofar as they are not inconsistent with these rules.

RULE 822. TITLE

These rules may be known and cited as the Texas Rules of Civil Procedure.

www.ingramcontent.com/pod-product-compliance
Lightning Source LLC
Chambersburg PA
CBHW061418210326
41598CB00035B/6260